CATULLUS' BEDSPREAD

The Life of Rome's Most Erotic Poet

DAISY DUNN

WILLIAM
COLLINS

William Collins
An imprint of HarperCollins*Publishers*
1 London Bridge Street
London SE1 9GF
WilliamCollinsBooks.com

First published in Great Britain by William Collins in 2016
This William Collins paperback edition published in 2017

A catalogue record for this book is available from the British Library

ISBN 978-0-00-755432-4

Set in Centaur and Trajan by Birdy Book Design

Maps by John Gilkes

Printed and bound in Great Britain by Clays Ltd, St Ives plc

For my parents and my sister, Alice

This bedspread,

Embroidered with the shapes of men

Who lived long ago, unveils the virtues of heroes

Through the miracle of art

CONTENTS

MAPS

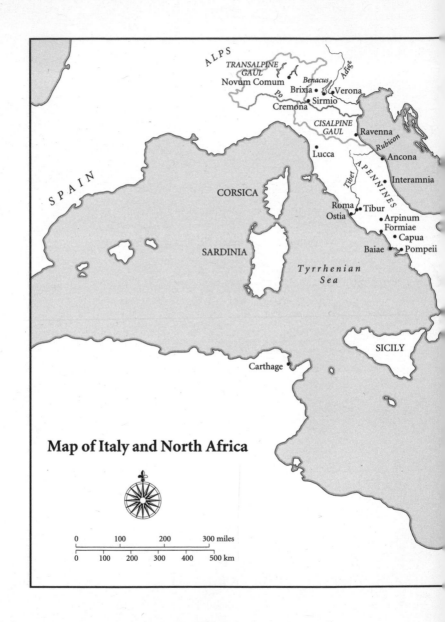

ALPS

TRANSALPINE
GAUL
Novum Comum
Benacus
Brixia • •Verona
Sirmio
Cremona

Po

Adige

CISALPINE
GAUL
Ravenna

Rubicon

Lucca
Ancona

APENNINES

Tiber
Interamnia

Roma •Tibur
Ostia
• Arpinum
Formiae
• Capua
Baiae •• Pompeii

SPAIN

CORSICA

SARDINIA

Tyrrhenian
Sea

SICILY

Carthage
•

Map of Italy and North Africa

0	100	200	300 miles

0	100	200	300	400	500 km

Map of Greece and the East

0   100   200   300 miles
0   100   200   300   400   500 km

Ionian Sea

MACEDONIA

THRACE

Propontis

Hellespont

Thessalonica •

THESSALY
Mt Pelion
Iolcus •
Pharsalus •

Mt Ida
Rhoeteum
Troy

Aegean Sea

LESBOS

Mitylene •

Smyrna •

• Sardis

• Ephesus

GREECE

DELOS
NAXOS

MELOS

RHODES

Mt Ida

CRETE

Amastris •

• Nicomedia
• Nicaea

BITHYNIA &

ASIA

MEDITERRANEAN

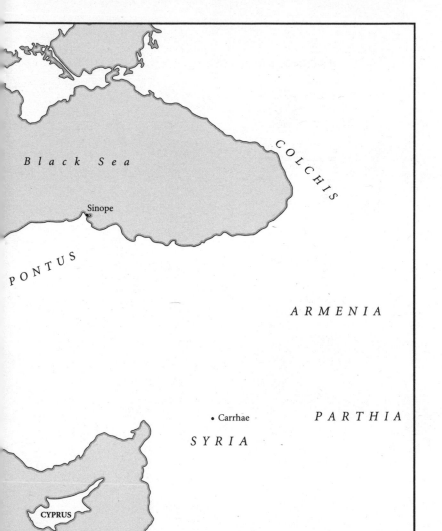

Black Sea

COLCHIS

Sinope

PONTUS

ARMENIA

• Carrhae

PARTHIA

SYRIA

CYPRUS

SEA

Author's Note

The Political System in Rome

Politicians in Rome followed an established ladder of power. At the top sat two chief magistrates, known as consuls. Male citizens of Rome (aged seventeen and above) elected the two consuls each year, and the Senate guided them, while also managing the civic purse and foreign relations. The first consuls had been plucked from the richest families; the first senators' descendants were the patricians, or aristocrats, of Catullus' Rome.

Before a man could even think about becoming a consul, he needed to gain some experience. As he approached the age of thirty, a budding patrician politician would strive first to be elected as a *quaestor*, whose tedious responsibilities involved supervising the treasury. At the end of the year, funds permitting, quaestors became life members of the Senate, and the more appealing prospect of running for the senior magistracies, *aedile*, *praetor*, then consul, suddenly became feasible. Beyond the consulship, men could become censors, who routinely examined the membership of the Senate.

The Senatorial magistrates

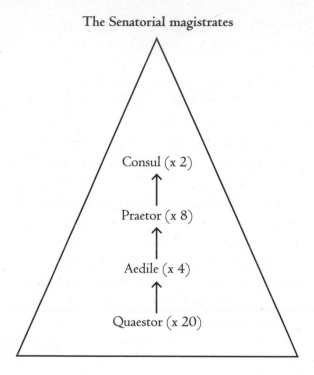

Before they could run for the senior magistracies, plebeian candidates, by contrast, could achieve the tribunate. Every year Catullus spent in Rome he would see ten tribunes of the people elected from the plebeian class, scurry off to their own assemblies to consider legislation, and veto measures, and each other, at will.

While the four aediles (two plebeian, two patrician) took charge of public works and entertainment, the eight praetors were as though deputies to the consuls, and oversaw legal matters, such as trials and disputes arising in the provinces. Few could wait until the end of the year, when they had the chance to proceed to a command overseas. The two consuls tended to progress to more senior foreign commands at the end of their year, too.

Men did not belong to political parties: they could change their allegiances at will. Some politicians aligned themselves with the *optimates* ('best men') who championed the Senate's authority and sought to work with it; others with the *populares*, who sought a more liberal, reforming approach to policy by appealing to the tribunes to make their voice heard. Populares were often self-interested men who, cunningly veiling their personal ambitions, used the tribunes to propose legislation that would buy them the favour of the common man. The excessive ambition of individual tribunes would contribute to the fall of the Republic, a catastrophe that began less than a decade after Catullus died. A miserable period of civil war and dictatorship would take hold, at the end of which the Romans would bow their heads again to a sole ruler: the future Emperor Augustus.

TIMELINE

753 BC: Rome is founded

509 BC: Overthrow of Rome's last king

218 BC: Hannibal the Carthaginian invades Italy

204 BC: Cybele, the Great Mother, is carried to Rome

133 BC: Tiberius Gracchus becomes tribune

91–89 BC: The Social War (Italian allies demand Roman citizenship); Verona becomes a Roman colony

88 BC: Sulla becomes consul. Beginning of the wars with Mithridates, King of Pontus

80s BC: Civil war between Sulla and Marius

c.82 BC: Birth of **Gaius Valerius Catullus**

81 BC: Sulla is proclaimed dictator

78 BC: Death of Sulla

70s BC: Ongoing conflict between Rome and Mithridates

73 BC: Spartacus leads a slave revolt

71 BC: Crassus defeats Spartacus, Pompey pursues the stragglers

70 BC: Consulship of Pompey and Crassus

67 BC: Pompey vanquishes pirates at sea

66 BC: Pompey succeeds the general Lucullus in spearheading the wars against Mithridates

63: Suicide of Mithridates. Cicero becomes consul. Conspiracy of Catiline

62: Clodius infiltrates the Bona Dea festival

*c.*61 BC: Catullus moves to Rome

61 BC: Trial of Clodius. Caesar governorship in Further Spain. Pompey, now returned from the East, receives his third triumph

60 BC: Metellus Celer and Lucius Afranius become consuls. Caesar returns from Spain

59 BC: Caesar, now part of a coalition ('The First Triumvirate') with Pompey and Crassus, becomes consul alongside Marcus Calpurnius Bibulus. Death of Metellus Celer

58 BC: Start of Caesar's Gallic War. Clodius is tribune. Cicero goes into exile. Ptolemy XII Auletes is driven from his throne

57 BC: Catullus goes to Bithynia. After a considerable battle for his recall, Cicero returns to Rome

56 BC: Catullus returns from Bithynia and visits Lake Garda. Trial of Caelius Rufus. The triumvirs hold summits to repair their coalition

55 BC: Pompey and Crassus become consuls again. Opening of the Theatre of Pompey. Caesar's first invasion of Britain

54 BC: Cato becomes praetor. Crassus leaves for Syria. Caesar's second invasion of Britain. Death of Pompey's wife (Caesar's daughter) Julia

53 BC: The Battle of Carrhae and death of Crassus

*c.*53 BC: Death of **Gaius Valerius Catullus**

52 BC: Death of Clodius

49 BC: Caesar crosses the Rubicon, sparking civil war

48 BC: Death of Pompey

44 BC: Death of Caesar

PROLOGUE

GAIUS VALERIUS CATULLUS had endured a difficult night in Rome: 'Undone by passion I tossed and turned all over the bed.' He had spent the evening drinking wine and composing poetry, and was far too stimulated to rest. He longed only to taste daylight and swap stanzas once more with his friend and fellow poet, a small man named Calvus. Poetry remains the insomniac's gift.

Catullus was as familiar with what it was like to have another warm 'his chilly limbs in the bed you left behind', as he was with the bedchamber that bore the remnants of lust:

> Steeped in flowers and the oil of Syrian olive,
>
> Knackered and tattered, pillows everywhere,
>
> Creaking and shaking,
>
> The trembling bedstead shattered
>
> (Poem 6)

He also knew what it was like to obsess over a bedspread. Even when he didn't have the stirrings of passion and unfinished lines circling his mind, the poet was seldom at rest. Born in Verona around 82 BC, Catullus moved to Rome, and travelled the south border of the Black Sea, where men waded with fine fishing nets and built boats shaped like beans. He made his way to Rome's countryside, and to his family's second home on a peninsula of Lake Garda. The hundreds of poems he wrote across the course of his short life were as varied as the landscapes he wandered.[1]

Catullus was Rome's first lyric poet. He was also a conflicted man. At any one time he could hate and love, curse and censure, consider himself rich but call himself poor. While lending themselves perfectly to poetry, such extremes of emotion at times made his life unbearable. He wrote not only of the feelings that plagued his own mind, but of the way he felt about others, not least Julius Caesar, a man his father called a friend: in one particularly scabrous poem he described the politician and future dictator as little more than 'a shameless, grasping gambler'.

One may ask why a collection of Latin poems from over two thousand years ago matters so much today. Catullus' book is the earliest surviving poetry collection of its kind in Latin. Full of emotion, wit, and lurid insight into some of the key Roman personalities, it provides a rare and highly personal portrait of a life during one of the most critical moments in world history.

Catullus lived in some of the most uncertain and turbulent times Rome had ever known: the late Republic, before the emperors came to rule. Centuries earlier, kings had governed Rome until, as legend had it, the son of the haughty seventh ruler raped a woman named Lucretia, and her husband and his friend waged a war to destroy the monarchy forever. Its legacy lived on into the Republic, which was founded after the kings on the very principle that no one man should rule Rome again. Every year, the male citizens elected magistrates to govern their city under the guidance of the Senate. The political system was carefully calibrated to prevent power from falling into the hands of any one man, but the balance of power between Senate and individual magistrates had begun to swing increasingly in the magistrates' favour, and they knew it.

So Catullus found himself surrounded by towering politicians: Pompey the Great, Marcus Licinius Crassus, Julius Caesar, who vied desperately for power over Rome and her empire, which was larger than it had ever been, and growing larger still. By the time Catullus was born, the Romans had made provinces of North Africa, Sicily, Sardinia, and Corsica; Spain, which they divided into two provinces, Nearer and Further; Transalpine Gaul, stretching across the south of France and north-east into Switzerland; Cisalpine Gaul, which encompassed northern Italy, including Catullus' Verona; Macedonia; Asia (western Turkey), and extended their global rule through numerous allied states.

Ever inquisitive, Catullus cast his eye across this tremendous world map as well as the more insular world of Roman politics. One moment he would find himself recounting adventures at sea in breathless syllables; the next, describing a private dinner with friends; the next, weeping that his lover did not feel things as intensely as he.

Perhaps it is because our ideas about ancient poetry are so coloured by the awe-inspiring epics of Homer and their lofty themes of humanity that many of Catullus' poems seem so surprising and immediate. While some of his poems are highly learned and erudite, others are mischievous, goatish, direct. With characteristic boldness, he requests a woman he loves to:

Give me a thousand kisses, then a hundred

Then another thousand, then a second hundred.

Then – don't stop – another thousand, then a hundred . . .

(Poem 5)

In Latin these lines begin so abruptly – *da, dein, deinde* – it is as if we hear them with Catullus' quickening heartbeat. I was seventeen when I first discovered them, and they made Catullus feel more alive to me than any other poet I knew. I have read them hundreds of times since, and they still have the same effect.

One of the reasons Catullus' poems are still so readable I think is that they show that the people of his world were not always so very different from us. The characters he encounters and describes in the streets and bawdy inns of Italy call to mind the stock cast of a Roman comedy – or even a scene in late-night Soho – teeming with heartbroken lovers, drunken cavorting youths, old men pining for women a fraction of their age, money-grabbing brothel-keepers, mercenary *meretrices* (prostitutes), slaves who know too much.

Catullus' immense skill as a poet lay in his ability to combine many literary genres in the Latin tongue, not just elements of comedy, but the clarity of Sappho, the celebrated female poet, the compact and erudite style of Hellenistic poets, and the wit of lewd graffiti in Rome, with themes as various as love, the writer's life, and the myth of Jason and the Argonauts. The Roman province of Macedonia incorporated much of mainland Greece, and in Catullus' day Greek culture had well and truly permeated Rome's own.

While never enslaved to his Greek predecessors, when he

wanted to be particularly learned, Catullus adapted their poetic ideas to convey them with new feeling. He forged new Latin words and was partial to diminutives (*miselle passer* – poor little sparrow; *scortillum* – little tart). He feverishly combined elegantly phrased sentiment with colloquialism and obscenity, unnerving the more serious Romans who believed that a jibe at one man's sexual inadequacy was what high-spirited youths scribbled on walls and brandished in tense moments, not what educated writers preserved in fine papyrus scrolls. His work would therefore prove unsettling for some of the older generation, as well as important public figures such as Cicero, the great orator, who had rather conservative tastes.

Such readers in Rome were used to epic and chronicles and meandering excursus on the history that made Rome august. They had the patience to work through manual-like offerings on farming, if not to write them. Prior to Catullus, a cluster of poets, including the little-known Laevius and Valerius Aedituus, had tried to capture the liveliness of the Greek poets in Latin, but their attempts would not generally prove as successful as his; their names are obscure today as a result of the poor survival of their work. Catullus did not shirk sobriety, but framed it unexpectedly and with a finesse of the kind that many of his literary predecessors lacked.

The apparent simplicity of Catullus' poetry often masks far greater, deeper sentiment and subtlety of thought. He helped to shape the genre of Latin love elegy by writing a sustained series of poems to a lover. Ovid, Virgil, Horace, Propertius, Tibullus: all were influenced by his work. So Ovid, in a book of love elegies, confessed that he had a wandering eye and could not help but feel attracted to many different women: 'I hate what I am but, though

I long to, can't fail to be what I hate.'[2] It is a striking line, but partly because it is a response to one of Catullus' most remarkable poems which begins: 'I hate and I love' (Poem 85). The Latin love-poet Propertius, who was about thirty years younger than Catullus, pledged that his poetry would make the beauty of his mistress Cynthia most famous of all, '*pace* Catullus'.[3] Catullus remained a monumental figure of reference for the poets who sprang up over the decades following his death.

In his pithy observations of day-to-day life and bitter polemic against his enemies, Catullus also pre-empted the great satirists of the Roman Empire, particularly the writers Martial and Juvenal. He called his poetry *nugae* ('ramblings', or 'sweet nothings') partly out of false modesty, but with the understanding that the word also meant 'mimes'.[4] Many of his poems offer vignettes, at once silent and resounding with the colourful characters he observed.

There are secrets and allusions in Catullus' Latin which take some teasing out, but once found, throw Catullus' poetry in a more dazzling light than one could ever have imagined. As soon as I realised this, I decided that I wanted to know Catullus, to read his work with the emotion with which it was written, to get as close as I could to this man who lived more than two thousand years ago. And so I began to write this book, which I hope will inspire others to discover, or rediscover, his exquisite poems.

There are very few surviving sources for Catullus' life. Practically everything that can be known about him must be extracted from his book of poetry. This may resemble a series of jumbled diary entries, describing episodes from his life, but Catullus wrote it for public consumption, and not necessarily as a faithful account. He addressed love poems to a certain 'Lesbia', for example, a woman he gave life to through his verse. Lesbia was a pseudonym for Clodia Metelli, the eldest sister of a wealthy and influential politician in Rome.[5]

Of the 117 poems which survive in his collection, none bears a title. They are traditionally numbered according to the order in which they appeared in the earliest manuscripts, which is neither chronological nor entirely thematic, but hardly random either. Like a good music album, there is style in the progression and un-expected swing of one story to another, back and forth in time. It might have been a poet who established the poems' order.

Catullus was much more than a love-poet. His poems to Lesbia form only a fraction of his book. The longest and most accom-plished poem that survives, Poem 64, makes no explicit mention of her at all, focusing instead on a luxurious bedspread. I like to call it Catullus' 'Bedspread Poem' because it contains as its centre-piece a long, digressive passage on the myths that adorned the wedding bedspread of one of Jason's Argonauts. In it, Catullus set the themes of love and war against the backdrop of the myth of the Ages, a sequence of five eras against which writers of ancient Greece and Rome mapped their semi-mythical history.[6]

The first of these eras was the Golden Age, an idyllic, Garden of Eden-like time when there was no work, no war, no sickness, no travel; the earth gave freely and amply of its own accord, and gods and men lived harmoniously. There followed an inferior Silver Age, which Jupiter, king of the gods, destroyed since its people were criminals who no longer offered sacrifice to the gods. A Bronze Age came about, dominated by warfare and weaponry. Its people destroyed each other. Then followed the Heroic Age, which offered a reprieve from the decline, a time of heroes descended from the gods themselves, warriors who fought in the Trojan War, and Jason and his Argonauts. When they died, an Iron Age arrived. It was the worst of the five eras, an age of anxiety, pain, hard work, and murder. The Iron Age myth was a fitting tribute to the grim realities of late Republican Rome.

The upheavals of the times contributed to the picture of decline that haunts a number of Catullus' writings, particularly the Bedspread Poem. Matters in Rome had come to a head shortly before Catullus was born, when the *optimates*, politicians who championed the Senate's authority, clashed with the *populares*, individuals who sought a more liberal, reforming approach to policy. Decades earlier, the Romans had established the province of Asia near Pontus, a Hellenised kingdom on the south coast of the Black Sea, in what is now Turkey. Not a little perturbed by the fact that the Romans had proceeded to fill the East with grasping tax-farmers, the king of Pontus, a Hellenised Iranian called Mithridates VI Eupator – who, like many ambitious men, liked to think that he was descended from Alexander the Great – embarked upon a land-grabbing mission.

Six years before Catullus' birth, the Romans had begun to wage war against Mithridates. To head the campaign, the Senate elected an optimate, Lucius Cornelius Sulla, whose aristocratic roots, intense eyes, and complexion like a mulberry sprinkled with oatmeal marked him out as a man to be reckoned with.[7] His appointment to so prestigious a role proved enough to incense one of the most prominent populares of the day, a plebeian and darling of Rome's army, Gaius Marius. Though little shy of seventy years old, Marius tried to seize control of the commission himself, but then Sulla marched determinedly on Rome with his forces. He discharged Marius and his men from the city, and hurried off to his war.

Although Catullus makes no explicit mention of such disturbances, his poetry contains echoes of some of the political events which danced upon the periphery of his poetic consciousness. The wars against Mithridates in the East, and conflict between politicians such as Marius and Sulla, cast a terrible shadow over his life. The death toll in these wars was enormous. In seeking victory over Mithridates, the Romans approached the king of Bithynia, a land between Pontus and Asia where hyacinths bowed beneath the breeze. Although they persuaded the Bithynian king to attack Mithridates' territory, they were in no way equipped for the scale of Mithridates' retaliation. Over 80,000 Romans and Italians fell in the ensuing conflicts. Mithridates took hold of a string of cities along the Black Sea coast, and soon practically the whole sweep of Black Sea shoreline from Heracleia in the west to Georgia and Lesser Armenia in the east formed part of his sprawling kingdom.[8]

Shortly before Catullus was born, Sulla returned to Italy. He had made some bold forays in the wars, even sacking Athens, whose people Mithridates had cunningly enticed to his side, but it would be more than twenty years before the struggle was formally concluded.

Back in Rome, a state of emergency was declared as Marius' embittered forces prepared to make war on Sulla's returning army. Sulla was declared dictator in the interest of 'settling the state', but his solution made Italy less settled than ever before. Catullus grew up in a world where the names of Sulla's perceived enemies were added to miserable lists in the Forum, their property snatched, their rights destroyed, their lives, too often, cut short. Sulla doubled the number of senators from 300 to 600, and robbed the tribunes, the plebeian politicians at the bottom of the political ladder, of their function.[9] The fallout was carried across Catullus' native Gaul. Sulla gave up his dictatorship after two turbulent years, but then died, leaving Italy in despair and Rome's business with Mithridates unfinished.

While Catullus was growing up, the three politicians who would come to be most prominent in Rome in his adult life, Julius Caesar, Pompey the Great, and Marcus Licinius Crassus, were steadily emerging out of this fraught scene. Crassus was one of Sulla's former adherents. He came from a respectable family, but had lost several of his relatives and estates to Marius' forces. He had everything to fight for, which might have explained why, when Catullus arrived in Rome, he found him desperate to become the richest man in all of Italy. He was charming, unscrupulous, incredibly well connected, and owed his name to his quelling of a slave revolt spearheaded by a gladiator named Spartacus. No sooner had the Senate appointed him to stem the sudden uprising than Crassus had crucified thousands of Spartacus' men along the Appian Way – the now-blood-drenched road leading from Rome to Naples. Crassus proceeded thence to Rome's top political office, the consulship, in 70 BC.

Elected alongside him that year was the son of a wealthy senator, a tough, rugged soldier; a man who thrived on ambition and conquest. His forehead was deeply furrowed and his face was fleshy, but his gaze was unmistakably determined. His name was Pompey, and thanks to his early successes in battle, he had earned the sobriquet 'Magnus' ('the Great').[10] Crassus knew precisely who he was: Pompey, another of Sulla's subordinates, had fought on his side in the civil wars against Marius, then put down the stragglers from Spartacus' revolt.

Although Catullus wrote about Pompey in a couple of poems, he did not capture him from Crassus' perspective. Crassus could not help but look askance at the man who had won plaudits that he could only dream of. The greatest accolade a Roman could win for victories overseas was a triumph, and Pompey had by now won two. For all his efforts in the slave revolt, Crassus received merely an ovation, the next best thing. Nevertheless, Catullus was looking on as the two men proceeded to their shared consulship, during which they reinstated the powers of the tribunes, which Sulla had so shamefully diminished.

Succeeding Sulla in the wars against Mithridates of Pontus was the splendidly named Lucius Licinius Lucullus, who scored a number of impressive victories, but was dismissed before he could bring the wars to an absolute conclusion.[11] Enter Pompey, still high from his successes under Sulla and against Spartacus. He was singled out to succeed Lucullus in tackling the chief problems that plagued the world to Rome's east. Mithridates was the obvious target, but to confront him, Pompey had first to rid the seas of pirates, who had already hindered Italy's corn supply and kidnapped a number of her citizens, including Julius Caesar.

Caesar was a patrician from one of the older families. Unlike Pompey and Crassus, his seniors by six and fifteen years respectively, Caesar had found himself on the opposing end of Sulla's regime. By marriage, he was the nephew of Gaius Marius, the popular politician against whom Sulla had engaged in civil war. Not only that, but he was married to the daughter of Marius' colleague and successor, Cornelia. Wisely, given his patent allegiance, Caesar lay low during Sulla's dictatorship, and completed part of his military service in Bithynia. He was then kidnapped by pirates, not far from Rhodes. When he was eventually released, he crucified his captors.[12]

Having put the pirates to flight, Pompey skilfully led the Roman army in obliterating Mithridates' forces. It was a difficult war and required great manpower, but Pompey saw the hostile king flee towards Colchis, a region that lay between the Black Sea and Caucasus mountains (in the territory of modern Georgia). Finally, in 63 BC, abandoned by his allies, usurped by his own son, Mithridates settled on suicide.[13]

His kingdom, Pontus, fell to Rome. Catullus subsequently evoked it in his poetry. Pompey conquered a good number of Mithridates' territories, and reduced his former ally, Armenia, to a state of dependency on Rome. Syria was among the places which slipped into Roman control.[14] It happened that in the midst of the wars, the king of Bithynia, Nicomedes IV, had bequeathed by agreement his land to Rome, too. Pompey's eyes sparkled at the possibilities. Intent now on lining the south coast of the Black Sea with Roman provinces, he decided to join Pontus and Bithynia together to form one enormous new province.[15]

In his mid-twenties, Catullus boarded a ship with a cohort of other young men in order to escape Rome for this very place. One needed to be a Roman citizen to join the prestigious cohort he did, which is a strong indication that Catullus' father was a local governor or magistrate in Verona.[16] For while the Veronese remained eager to acquire Roman citizenship, for as long as Catullus lived, their magistrates could secure the honour for themselves and their families. Bithynia lay south of the Black Sea, which Jason and his Argonauts were said to have sailed over on their Heroic Age mission to steal the Golden Fleece. The map of Rome's new provinces, I discovered, overlapped with that which inspired the imagery of Catullus' verse.

In the pages that follow I retrace this journey and the life Catullus described in his poems, from Verona to Rome, from Bithynia to Lake Garda. I have worked from the ancient sources that survive to draw out the story Catullus described in his 'little book' – his *libellus*.

Catullus' Bedspread, then, is my little book about Catullus and his life. It is, as far as possible, a life in the poet's own words: Catullus' journey as told through his *carmina*, his poems or 'songs', which I have translated from the Latin. I see this very much as a joint venture: Catullus provides the poetry; I offer something of the world that informed it. I use extracts from his Bedspread Poem as epigraphs at the beginning of each chapter, in the manner of his poetry book – neither chronologically nor entirely haphazardly. If together he and I can bridge the distance that lies between us, then even the most labyrinthine of his poems should sing.

IN SEARCH OF
CATULLUS

Since my fate and your determined virtue snatch you

Away from me against my will, though my tired eyes are

Not yet drunk with the dear shape of my son,

I shall not send you rejoicing with a happy heart

Or allow you to carry the signs of good fortune,

But first I shall free my heart of countless laments

(Poem 64, lines 218–24)

CATULLUS COULD HEAR his father in the dining room, conversing with Julius Caesar on the peculiarities of the world. He was used by now to travel-weary men arriving at his home, seeking soft cushions, pickled fish, and pork fattened on the acorns of Verona's oak trees. As this one tucked into the feast laid out before him, he talked about the wonders of the Black Sea, savage Gauls, and Britons lining the chalk-white cliffs, remote and terrifying giants.

Catullus, who took more pleasure between the sheets than talking at the table with his father's friends, stepped outside.[1] The rain was pounding the streets which streamed and steamed with sewage. The Adige river was flowing quickly on the lap-like curve that held the town. As a boy, Catullus had often crossed its waters and felt the chill they bore from the Alps. He remembered the evening he first witnessed a locked-out lover, sitting in a door-way here on a lowly street. The youth had been crying, trying in vain to write a poem to voice his lament. For some time, Catullus had stood there, watching. Poor boy, his buttocks aching with the damp cold of the doorstep. Would not the door have more to say than the inconsolable youth? The door belonged to the house of a love-poet called Caecilius. Catullus transcribed its words:

It's not my fault (I hope to impress Caecilius, I am now in

His charge), although they say it is my fault

No one can honestly say I've done anything wrong.

It's true what people tell you – blame the door . . . [*line partly corrupt*]

Whenever some crime is discovered

Everyone shouts at me: 'Door, it's your fault!'

(Poem 67)

The door was not weeping but lamenting, slammed shut and berated with every misfortune that had passed through it. Catullus captured in the pace of its speech all the urgency and forcefulness a man would expect from one whose words had been stifled for most of its lifetime. With its ear for gossip, the door went on to reveal that, before Caecilius was resident in the house, a 'virgin' had moved in and confided in her female slaves. 'Virgin', because it transpired that the scamp had a former father-in-law, who lay with her when she discovered his son's 'little sword dangling more flaccid than a delicate beet'. In Catullus' poem, one image was layered upon another, contorting what was masculine, if small, into an effeminate and unedifying vegetable.

The so-called virgin came from fertile Brixia (Brescia), to Verona's west. 'Brixia beloved mother of my Verona,' Catullus exclaimed, reflecting on the Gauls who had travelled between it and his home.[2] The Gauls and their many tribes were inclined like geese to migrate whenever the desire took them.[3] Lately, Gallic tribes had been flying through Transalpine Gaul, to Verona's north, endangering Rome's control over its provinces. So Caesar rested here, at Catullus' father's home, wearied by the Gallic War he was now waging. It was 55 BC.

Catullus had come back to Verona, where he reflected nostalgically upon his roots. It was a Roman colony now, but remained in his mind a place of Gauls and Etruscans.[4] While the sleeping fields of Brescia evoked his Gallic line, the summers he spent in his family villa on nearby Sirmio (Sirmione), an attractive peninsula on Lake Garda, tended to carry him back into the arms of his ancient ancestors. Whenever its waves shivered in the breeze, he would dream of the Etruscans, the great lords of Italy before the rise of the Romans, and their curious origins in faraway lands.

They had come to Italy to escape a famine that had struck their home in ancient Lydia (near Sart, Turkey). In around 1200 BC, their king had divided the surviving people into two groups, and drawn lots. The more fortunate ones followed his son Tyrrhenus out of Lydia to Smyrna (Izmir), and onwards for distant coasts. In the north and the centre of Italy they scattered, and called themselves 'tyrrhenians' after their prince, or *'tusci'*, 'Etruscans'. Their descendants preferred 'Umbrians' and 'Tuscans'.[5]

Part Gaul, part Etruscan, Catullus never doubted that he had Asiatic blood, however Italian he looked. His hair was light brown, and he styled it like a man who was afraid of losing it. Combed forward, it formed the beginnings of a fashionable fringe, which tickled the deep olive skin of his forehead. He had a round, boyish characterful face, which a well-meaning woman might tell him was sweet or endearing, but then immediately regret saying anything at all. He was, in sum, shapely, especially about the arms. His waist was thick (Catullus being no stranger to the odd hors d'oeuvre) but his nose was delicate, and gently curving brows met at its arch. He had full lips and a sincere smile, but his most distinctive features had to be his eyes. They were large and brown, though the left one drooped slightly beneath a heavy lid, giving the impression that it was half closed. The portrait, discovered at the site of his family home on Sirmio, had no title to identify it as the poet Catullus, only the clues that lay in the painted plaster. The young man looked contemplative and refined as he grasped a scroll in his left hand, while he drew the fingers of his right with pride across its edges, edges he perhaps 'polished off not a moment ago with dry pumice stone' (Poem I). The distinctive lazy eye was meant to make him recognisable, even years later. He wore the toga of the late Republic with tunic, fringed with a narrow purple band.

Dirt tended to splash against this strip of purple, which proclaimed his status – 'equestrian' – to passers-by. They were descended from the cavalry, the equestrians, but less likely by now to be seen on a horse than in a forum, ensuring that they still satisfied the 400,000-*sesterce* wealth qualification that bought them membership of the elite order. Senators wore thicker purple stripes on their togas, and had at least a million *sesterces* each, but Catullus knew that his stripe made him more important than ordinary plebeians, who had no purple at all.

Catullus had put on the adult toga at the age of sixteen and indulged in so much sex, and so much poetry – 'joys which your sweet love encouraged' he once reminded his brother – that he remained forever nostalgic for those happy, carefree days. He never wrote of their mother, as he did of the mothers of friends:[6] she might have died some years before her son enjoyed this 'pleasant spring':

> From the time the pure toga was first put upon me,
>
>> When the bloom of my youth enjoyed its pleasant spring,
>
> I sported hard enough. I was no stranger to the goddess
>
>> Who mixes sweet bitterness with love's woe
>
> (Poem 68)

As he pottered around his old home to the sound of slaves clattering plates – a sign that his father's dinner was coming to an end – Catullus looked back on his youngest days. He remembered his first experiences of love and verse, his life's spring, as well as the moment that presaged the change in season, the moment he decided to leave Verona to pursue a career as a poet in Rome.

✳

In 62 BC a carriage had pulled into Cisalpine Gaul from which there disembarked a man in his early forties – a brother-in-law of Pompey the Great, Metellus Celer. He had recently completed a senior magistracy at Rome, the praetorship, and been intent on achieving the consulship before the decade was out. His appointment to a new post, governor of Cisalpine Gaul, had come about in return for his help in quelling a terrifying conspiracy in Rome.

A disaffected young patrician politician, Catiline, a former ally of the erstwhile dictator Sulla, had planned with his supporters to murder the most senior members of the Roman Senate, ravage the city with fire, and fling open Rome's gates to an army of several thousand that had gathered in the north.[7] Catiline's campaign for the consulship of 63 BC had been unsuccessful. Cicero, who had been elected to one of the two seats, foiled his conspiracy and took charge of a full-scale security operation. Determined to save his beloved Republic from extinction, he rounded up some of the chief conspirators – who included rogue senators – and the Senate agreed to put them to death without trial as enemies of the state. Metellus Celer helped Cicero by blocking the plotters' rampage.

Cicero had hoped to win praise for his swift response. Instead, Metellus Celer's brother, a feisty tribune in Rome, vetoed him from delivering his parting address from his consulship, saying that he should not have had the conspirators executed without trial. Technically, he was right.[8] The incident was still haunting Cicero to this day.

Catullus moved to Rome probably soon after the conspiracy. Whether it was in Verona that he had first met Metellus Celer, or in the great city itself, that moment had proved a turning point.

For little though Catullus could have anticipated it upon their first meeting, Metellus Celer would become something of an obstacle for him. In recent years Catullus had fallen passionately in love with his wife.

THE HOUSE ON THE PALATINE HILL

But the house receded every which way

In regal opulence, and sparkled and glimmered

With gold and silver.

Ivory glinted off thrones, cups dazzled off tables,

The whole household delighted in the lustre of

Royal treasure.

(Poem 64, lines 43–6)

THE DIN OF MEN hammering pieces of leather, and the sighs as youths stretched them into myriad shapes; the expletives of the vendors who pushed past them, elbows first, clutching bottles of perfume to their chests. The coughs of the workers loitering outside the Argiletum; the high-pitched laughter of a drunk man on a stall and cry as he fell and cut his hand. The bark of dogs who gathered for the wound, and mutterings of the old lady passing by. The indelicate tongue of the prostitutes who were circling, doused in new scents, smelling fresh blood. But after twelve days on the road to Rome, frankly, Catullus did not have the energy this afternoon.

He laughed, moved by the earthy scenes of the Subura, where the man recently elected Pontifex Maximus had lived before relocating to the Forum to its west. The up-and-coming politician Julius Caesar had lately secured enough money from somewhere to buy a place in the elections for this prestigious post, which would make him head of Rome's most renowned priestly college. On polling day he had kissed his mother goodbye, and told her that, if he did not return to her as Pontifex Maximus, he would not return at all. When morning passed to afternoon, he appeared again, triumphant.

As Catullus entered the Forum, he passed open-air law courts, inns, market stalls, and temples, including one dedicated to 'Twin Castor and twin of Castor, Pollux' – the gods of travel – whom he thanked dutifully for his safe journey from Verona. The building where Caesar was now based lay in the distance, adjacent to the hallowed residence of the Vestal Virgins, who dedicated their lives to chastity and worship of the goddess of the hearth. The goddess' flame was burning brightly, kept alight by her servants' diligence and the will of the Romans, who would sooner have seen an ill-omened lightning strike fill the sky than her fire be extinguished and with it, they feared, their own hearths and livelihoods.

Success in life, as Catullus well knew, depended upon the support of the gods, who were in constant need of appeasing. The divinities gave curious signs to voice their approval, or otherwise, of men's actions. So fearful were mortals of misconstruing divine messages that they filled roles dedicated to their interpretation. Augurs examined the movements of birds. They divined the mood of the gods from the sounds the birds made and direction of their flight, while haruspices searched the livers of sacrificial animals for meaningful abnormalities.

A raven flew south towards the Palatine Hill, at the far end of the Forum. The hill's large plateau, crosshatched with grey and clay-red masonry, dotted with umbrella pines, housed the very wealthiest Romans. As he drew near it, Catullus was half-minded to join them, but he needed something to eat before he could muster the strength for conversation. Thankfully, the Romans saw little purpose in waiting for evening to fall before retiring to their dining rooms. Darkness rendered even the simplest of walks a fiendish pursuit, during which an unexpected ditch posed almost as much risk as a bandit. The late afternoon was a more sociable hour, and for Catullus, as for the many citizens who began work after dawn, it could not come quickly enough.

Having wolfed down eggs and bread at some miserable inn, he made his way hastily towards the base of the Aventine Hill, where the poor plebeians lived. He passed streets of *insulae*, ramshackle tenement buildings constructed so high that they often fell down, burned down, or were pulled down for obstructing the view of the augurs as they tried to interpret bird flight.[1] Catullus imagined how good life would be with 'no fears – not fires, not grievous building collapses, not criminal activity, not creeping poison, nor any other threat of danger'.

There were men in this city who made a living from those who had lost their modest homes. The ambitious politician Marcus

Licinius Crassus was notorious for it. Determined to recover the riches his family had lost in the civil wars, Crassus had been among the first to benefit from the sale of citizens' property proscribed under Sulla. Not even his success in quelling Spartacus' forces and reaching a consulship checked his appetite for wealth. He noted the dilapidated state of Rome's crowded blocks and developed ravaged sites on the cheap, using slaves with builders' training.[2] Many more apartments could be squashed into the spaces occupied by the older villas, too. The new homeless could do little but accept Crassus' miserly offers.

Catullus' father would never have allowed his son to come to such a place had he not already established contacts for him in the heart of the city. Rome's population exceeded a million, a quarter of whom were slaves. Metellus Celer, former governor of Cisalpine Gaul, had lately returned to Rome and intended to achieve a consulship for 60 BC. Catullus could seek him out, distract him from his campaigning.[3] As his father must have told him a thousand times, being associated with a man like Metellus could do wonders for his status. If Metellus had dined at their house in Verona, then he was obliged to invite his son to dine at his in Rome.

Catullus could not have been thrilled at the prospect. He need only have exchanged a few words with Metellus to know that he was far from the most exciting man in Rome. Even Cicero, who had often praised him for his steadfastness to his beliefs, had to admit that there was something inhuman about him: Metellus was 'not a man but "a seashore and air and utter isolation"'.[4] Many of his forebears had been consuls, and though Metellus was not old, by anyone's standards, he was worthy, bloody-minded and arrogant, falling rather too readily into the category of men Catul-

lus liked to call *senes severiores* – 'our elders . . . dourer than most'
(Poem 5).

Grateful as Catullus had to be for his father's introductions
to the great and the good, he itched to find his own place among
the poets.[5] He would not need to work as hard to sustain conver-
sation with them as he did with the politicians – though Catullus
always stayed well informed, not least because he knew that such
diligence would stand him in good stead for city life. Without
an acute interest in the minutiae of the law courts or small-scale
political intrigues, there was very little to talk about.

This was a perennial problem for those who found themselves
at dinner with men directly involved in Roman politics. The idea
that business and leisure were entirely distinct was written firmly
into the Latin language: *negotium*, the former, was simply the nega-
tive of *otium*, the latter. Leisure was, quite literally, an absence of
business. Clutching for conversation that was both suitable to
bridge that gap and sufficient to last the course of a Roman dinner
– from eggs to apples – proved a headache. There was no fun to
be had with men who thought that 'salt' was merely a condiment.
For Catullus, *sal* sooner suggested the kind of verbal wit no dinner
guest should be without. Just as salt itself was considered funda-
mental to human life for its healing and alimentary qualities, so
'salt' encapsulated the intelligent mind's capacity to lay aside its
troubles, seek pleasure, and deliver it to others through wit.[6] As far
as Catullus was concerned, there was no ingredient more necessary
for a dinner party, and this included its hosts.

Nonetheless, even if he believed that Metellus was merely
paying his father a favour, and had little interest in what he had to
say, these were not grounds for declining his hospitality. A fleeting
glance at his address would have been enough to pique anyone's

curiosity. Metellus Celer might have been short of *sal*, but he was evidently not short of money.

Metellus' house stood on the north-west side of the Palatine Hill, and 'in sight of almost the whole city'.[7] It was close enough to the Forum for the booming of orators and traders to rattle the portico, but high enough up to protect its inhabitants from their germs and diseases. Apart from affording superior views, properties on this higher ground commanded a premium because they promised cleaner air and at least some protection from the commoners' plagues.

It was said that Romulus, one of the twin sons born to the war god Mars and suckled by a she-wolf in Rome's foundation myth, chose the Palatine on which to found his city. Where nomads constructed rounded huts to call home, the Palatine Hill grew from frugal beginnings to host the grand residences of the Roman emperors; 'Palatine' inspired 'palace'.[8] When Catullus arrived in the city there was a tree on its east façade that residents said was proof of Romulus' magnanimity. The young twin had allegedly hurled a spear made from cornel wood the impossible distance of nearly a kilometre from his brother Remus' chosen hill, the Aventine, to the Palatine Hill, and it rooted itself so deeply that no one could retrieve it. It was the sword in the stone, but with roots and soil eager to nurture them: the cornel tree was born.[9] The Romans built a wall around it, and it flourished until Julius Caesar later asked for the structure to be repaired. His men dug too close to the tree's roots, and like so many things under Caesar – as Catullus would have been quick to point out, had he lived long enough to witness his dictatorship – it withered, and died.

As Catullus made his way to the top of the Palatine Hill, he passed countless bundles of shrub and foliage. The air was fragrant with rosemary and mallow, chamomile and sage. Poppies peeped up between the umbrella pines and masonry, as they do today amidst the Forum monuments. It is as though their pollen never died.

Some of the hill's residents took care not to be too ostentatious in what they grew: there were many who still associated beautiful, intricate gardens with wanton eastern decadence. The Persians had been among the first to celebrate the art of horticulture, and Rome's wealthiest residents had been quick to adopt some of the more luxurious features, such as pleasure gardens, ornamental moats and fishponds. It was into these creations that Lucullus, a general whom Pompey had usurped as commander in the battles against Mithridates of Pontus in the East, poured much of his war wealth. The general's extravagance at a time when so many Romans lived in poverty had been his downfall: a Roman praetor persuaded the people that Lucullus had protracted the war through his love of money and power, which precipitated a vote for his recall.[10] At least Lucullus had something to remember it all by: cherry trees now grew in Rome, cultivated from the seeds he had extracted from eastern soils.

Though he could not approve of such flamboyance, it was difficult for Catullus not to smile. Lucullus did things that Romans had never done before. In addition to the grand gardens he arranged in the north of Rome, he had specialist fishponds created near Naples for his own pleasure. One onlooker, bristling in his masculinity, scoffed: these were the deeds of 'Xerxes in a toga'.[11] Like Xerxes, Persia's most notorious king, Lucullus was made a woman of through his addiction to luxury.

If he was to arrive on time for a dinner with Metellus Celer, Catullus needed to stop idling and keep to the main path. Metellus' residence was on the Clivus Victoriae ('Slope of Victory') which led from the Forum along the west side of the Palatine Hill. The road took its name from the temple consecrated to the goddess Victory that perched there. Nearby stood an enormous further temple, dedicated to an eastern goddess. As Catullus passed these temples he found his eye drawn more by the glinting gilt roof of the 'holy temple of Greatest Jupiter', which sat on the Capitoline Hill at the opposing end of the Forum (Poem 55). At the top of the sun-baked plateau, he approached a line of sprawling villas. Here was the magnificent portico and property of the late politician Quintus Lutatius Catulus. Beside it, framed by trees and grand marble columns, was the house of Cicero, 'most fluent of the grandsons of Romulus' (Poem 49), who had been collecting villas in and around Rome, and had acquired this one just a year earlier.[12] Nearby was the home of another great orator, Hortensius, and on the other side of Catulus' house with its rambling portico was the home of Metellus Celer.

Inside, Metellus' property was large, and gave the impression of being larger still. Each wall carried a different vista: a distant shore, a garden with brightly coloured birds, a few of them flittering in through the window and perching on its lavish architrave; and trees laden with fruit; and dense foliage, and grand colonnades of columns which seemed to recede hundreds of paces back into nowhere, but could not, because none of it was real:[13] the artists who produced these images were masters of trompe l'oeil. Along the villa's walls were rows and rows of boxy wooden cabinets containing the death masks of magistrates, long-since deceased. When a woman married, she brought the masks of her ancestors with her to her husband's home. To look at these walls, one would think Metellus had a dozen wives.

Metellus glided past the rows of unseeing faces, abandoned his cup upon the table, and greeted his guest. How pleased he was that Catullus had made the journey to Rome safely (and at good speed!) and was settling into his new life with such ease. Catullus was to meet his wife, whom, naturally, Catullus had already caught sight of across the room. She was lavishly adorned with jewels, and laughing in their midst.

Clodia Metelli, née Pulchra, of the illustrious Claudius dynasty, was known throughout Rome. Her acquaintances had only to stroll past the Roman Temple of Bellona, the meeting place for councils of war, for her distinguished lineage to be recalled.[14] Her distant grandfather, Appius Claudius Caecus, had consecrated the building in 296 BC, and her father filled its walls with shields painted with his ancestors' faces, and inscriptions bearing their many achievements.[15] Between service under Sulla, his time as consul in 79 BC, and expeditions in Macedonia, he had barely been around to tell his children of their bloodline before he died in 76 BC, while still a young man. They had to be grateful for the memory those shields provided of faces they had never known.

Appius Claudius Caecus, Clodia's ancestor, had been a consul twice, and had sought to challenge the power of the Senate by filling it with the sons of freedmen (former slaves).[16] He was also responsible for bold public works, including the first ever aqueduct, built just outside Rome, funded by public money and without senatorial decree. Glorious though it was, like the Appian Way, another of his magnificent creations, it wrung the people dry.[17]

It was from Appius Claudius Caecus, perhaps, that Clodia and several of her five siblings inherited their egalitarian tastes. She, like her brother, Publius Clodius Pulcher, made the statement of changing the spelling of her name 'Claudia' to 'Clodia'. The original spelling 'Claudia' was too upper-crust. 'Clodia' gave the old name a fashionable plebeian twist. It was the kind of gesture that drove young Catullus wild.[18]

Catullus watched her – watched her husband watching her – and almost passed out:

> . . . my tongue freezes, a gentle flame flows down
>
> Under my limbs and my ears ring with their own sound.
>
> Both my eyes are blinded by night.

> (Poem 51)

His inspiration was a poem by Sappho, the poet born on the island of Lesbos in the seventh century BC. Her blood was blue, like Clodia's, but had not spared her a difficult life. Lesbos' aristocratic rulers had been deposed before her birth, and she lived under a series of tyrants, under one of whom she left with her family for exile in Sicily. In spite of her experience, her ties with Lesbos were never broken. She married a man, with whom she had a daughter, Cleïs, but it was the memory of her as Lesbos' native poet who had feelings for women that preserved the association between her and 'lesbian' love.

In her poem Sappho describes a woman whom she desires enjoying the attentions of her male lover. Her tongue is paralysed – a light flame runs under her skin – her vision vanishes – she turns paler than grass. As the girl laughs sweetly in the man's presence, Sappho feels close to death.

Catullus, who found in Sappho's lines the unfussiness and raw honesty that he sought in his own work, adopted her Sapphic stanzas, changing only the odd detail. His senses are lost, her heart is aflutter. Clodia is laughing, and her husband is watching.[19] Metellus is to the left of the frame, but too prominent to be cut out of it.[20] As if to depart from earlier models, Catullus would end his version of Sappho's poem with an original final stanza, to bring the reverie back to earth.

As Clodia stood there before him for the first time, neither youthful nor particularly noteworthy in her physical stature, she was indefinably captivating. If at first she seemed detached and aloof, there was a passion and volatility that lay beneath her round, dark, darkly shadowed eyes – Cicero called them her 'oxen eyes' – that promised that this veil could be lifted.[21] A combination of intensity and introspection lent her a gravitas Catullus had never seen in a woman before. She unleashed in him a longing to accomplish something, even if he did not know what it was.

Catullus had probably only been in Rome for a few months when he heard some shocking news: Clodia's youngest brother was due in court. The Senate had it on good authority that Clodius Pulcher had infiltrated the festival of the Bona Dea – a women-only religious festival, which had been held at Caesar's residence the previous December – dressed in drag.

To uphold the secrecy of the Bona Dea, Caesar had given his wife, his mother, and sister free use of his property as a secure base from which to perform their duties with other female worshippers. The year that Caesar embarked formally upon his political career, 69 BC, had seen him lose his wife, Cornelia, though their daughter, Julia, survived. He was now married to Pompeia – a curious choice considering that she was the granddaughter of his late enemy Sulla, but the union might entice to his populist cause some of Sulla's supporters.

No man yet had been so brazen as to attempt to watch the rites of the Bona Dea, which women conducted in the presence of the Vestal Virgins. Cicero tried to assure his fellow men that this was a solemn religious event, but the secrecy and obscurity that shrouded it naturally made them curious. Some reported hearing loud music emanating through the walls whenever it took place, and tried to imagine what it signified.[22] Others swam in far deeper fantasies of hip-shaking women drunk on wine, their hair loose and tangled by the blow of the pipe; of bouncing bottoms and female voyeurs; of arousal that was clear for all to see, without the need for full exposure. They wagered that these women could endure the frustration for only so long, and that they would feel compelled at any moment to summon men to the celebrations, or failing men, slaves – an ass, even; anything that could satisfy their lust.[23]

Such fantasy had clearly got the better of Clodius, who had long had a taste for high drama. Like his brother-in-law Metellus Celer and so many men of his generation, he had spent his formative years with his eldest brother Appius, a staunch optimate, in the East as part of the war effort against Mithridates. Though placed in the service of Lucullus, the fishpond-loving commander who was married to the youngest of his three sisters until 66 BC, Clodius had incited a mutiny among his troops, and found himself discharged.[24] He had subsequently travelled to Cilicia, Syria, Antioch, and Gaul, before embarking upon a political career at Rome.

Clodius' worldliness had put no check on his appetite for adventure. Aged thirty, he was old enough to know better, but viewed the prospect of disrupting a strangely secretive women's festival as a thrilling game. Evening fell, summoning the beginning of the rites. Like a comic stage actor, Clodius threw on a saffron gown with purple sashes, women's slippers, and entered Caesar's house.[25]

The women had already commenced their secret rites when he arrived. Clodius, who must have known that he was chancing his luck, struck unlucky. A slave girl addressed him, he replied in a suspiciously deep voice, and the game was up. The girl swiftly sounded the alarm and Clodius was ejected. The women were compelled to start their rites anew in order to preserve their sanctity. So much for that.

The Senate ruled that a trial should take place in May 61 BC. Clodius was accused of *incestum*, a crime which in this context described the threat male intrusion had caused to the chastity of the Vestal Virgins.[26] As the date of the trial drew near, the gossips began to speculate on the meaning of Clodius' transgression. Some said he had been driven to his dastardly deed out of lust for Caesar's wife.[27] Caesar meanwhile lodged a divorce from Pompeia, stressing that it was not right that his family should suffer suspicion and accusation.[28] Driven by a desire for recognition and pre-eminence, throughout his life Caesar would do anything to distance himself from scandal.

Lucullus, returned from Pontus, was now summoned as a witness for the prosecution. Having divorced Clodius' youngest sister, he now took the opportunity to pounce. He decided not only to shame Clodius publicly for his mutinous behaviour in the war in the East, but to swear on oath that he had committed incest with his former wife. It was not long before people were applying the incest slur to all three of Clodius' sisters.[29] At that moment,

Catullus could never have imagined that he would one day be fanning the same empty rumour.

Outraged by his juvenile disregard for religious practice, Cicero prepared himself to give evidence against Clodius. Cicero came from a family of wealthy landowners in Arpinum (Arpino), a pretty hill town to the south-east of Rome, which made them worthy enough, but none of them had ever been a senator. Although Cicero was a *novus homo*, a *new man*, he was at heart a traditionalist, who was determined to do all he could to preserve Rome's ancient institutions: the *mos maiorum*, custom of the elders. Clinging to the vain hope that the Republic might flourish again after the disturbances of recent decades, he sought to strengthen the authority of the Senate. He had convinced himself, if not the population in its entirety, that in foiling Catiline's conspiracy a couple of years earlier, he had saved the Republic from ruin. The trial of Clodius presented yet another opportunity to champion sobriety.

Cicero easily destroyed Clodius' alibi, but the young Pulcher, living up to his family name (meaning 'beautiful'), was alluring enough to be able to wield bribes, both pecuniary and sexual, and managed to get himself acquitted.[30] If Cicero needed an excuse to engage in the distasteful incest badinage that Lucullus had set in train, he now had it.

———————

Unscathed though Caesar was by the scandal of Clodius Pulcher, the repercussions were an embarrassment. Reluctant to dwell on the matter, or have others do the same, he had hurried off to Further Spain to take up a year-long governorship, the follow-up to a praetorship in Rome. Of the two provinces Rome owned across the territory, Further Spain – consisting of the coastal region of Baetica (including modern Baelo Claudia), swinging up in an arc to incorporate modern Portugal – was the one furthest away from Italy.

Catullus watched Caesar's departure with a newcomer's eyes. For all his tremendous self-belief and optimism, it was evident that the commander was feeling down on his luck. As he marched he positively jangled with the bags of money Crassus had lent him for the venture.[31] Electioneering had only become more expensive since the days of Sulla, and on proceeding as far as the praetorship, one post down from the coveted consulship, Caesar had accumulated considerable debts. In 65 BC, he had dazzled Rome's crowds with spectacular games – wild beast hunts, plays, and a gladiatorial show.[32] It was in honour of his late father, he said, that an unprecedented 320 pairs of gladiators fought for their entertainment. He would buy a gladiatorial school in Campania.

Increasingly through his life, Catullus would disapprove of squander, of Romans mining the provinces and despoiling the world beyond for their own gain, but it was proving more and more necessary for those who sought power to do so. All Caesar could think about were the spoils he could acquire in Further Spain, as he worked his way towards a triumph. To qualify for this noble accolade, he would need to convince the Senate that he had reduced the province to a peaceful state with little loss to his men. Although Caesar suppressed the rebellion he encountered in the province, there were rumours that he had contributed to the chaos, his eye fixed on glory.[33]

It had not escaped his notice either how quickly Pompey had emerged as a force. In his younger years, Caesar had wept bitterly before a statue of Alexander the Great, in sorrow at how much the commander had achieved by the time he was his age.[34] As much as he courted Pompey's favour and support, Caesar could only feel inadequate when he looked at his precocious achievements. Normally, a man was eligible for a triumph only after fulfilling a praetorship or consulship, but Pompey had celebrated two before achieving either. What was more, he expected to be granted a third.

Pompey had returned from the East to a city in jittery expectancy over his next triumph, a grand finale to his work in the East. Fearful of Pompey's eminence, however, the senators delayed the ratification of his eastern settlement. They would provide no closure to his victories: his veteran soldiers remained in need of land; equestrian tax-farmers and landowners began demanding rebate for the financial losses they had accrued following his restructure of Asia and Bithynia; Crassus took up their cause, but struggled to make much progress.

Now that he was back in Italy, Pompey, like Caesar, and like Lucullus before him, filed for divorce from his wife. Mucia, a sister of Metellus Celer, had already given him children, but he had in mind a politically more lucrative match with a niece of Cato, a particularly staunch optimate senator.[35] Catullus knew that ambition was not the only reason for Pompey's divorce. In a poem, he noted how, during Pompey's first consulship in 70 BC, Mucia had taken a lover. By popular repute Mucia – or Maecilia, as he called her, perhaps to distinguish her from a sister – was sleeping with both Pompey and Caesar.[36] Fifteen years later, Catullus jested that 'the two remain, but a thousand men compete against each' (Poem 113). Pompey was remarkably short-sighted about the repercussions of his divorce. Not only did he fail to obtain the hand of Cato's niece, but he incurred the wrath of Metellus

Celer, who could not take in good grace such an ignoble slight to his sister. In the coming years, Pompey would face considerable opposition from Metellus as he sought to advance in his political career.

Catullus was not interested in panegyric, so it came as no surprise that he wrote nothing to mark the occasion, in September 61 BC, when on his forty-fifth birthday Pompey finally celebrated his third triumph for his achievements against the pirates and King Mithridates of Pontus. Had Catullus chosen to do so, the imagery would have been palpable: crowds packing Rome's streets; placards proclaiming Pompey's conquests – Pontus, Armenia, Cappadocia, Paphlagonia, Media, Colchis, Iberia, Albania, Syria, Cilicia, Mesopotamia, Phoenicia and Palestine, Judaea, Arabia, 'and everything the pirates had on land and sea that had now been overthrown'.[37] Hostages, among them the chief pirates Pompey had scourged from the seas, were paraded among the trophies and pearl crowns.

One particularly large golden statue tottered on its stand. Pompey had chosen to display the statue, rather than the slain body of the king, because the embalmer had done such a bad job.[38] The issue was not the gore, it was more that it would have prompted doubts as to whom Pompey had really vanquished. The youngsters of Rome jostled to catch a glimpse of the statue and, still more pressingly, of Pompey, the man who had succeeded where so many Romans had not. Within four years of being entrusted with the command, he had claimed the final defeat of King Mithridates VI Eupator of Pontus, and reduced him to a glitzy showpiece.

Wearing a cloak he claimed was once owned by Alexander the Great, Pompey made it known that the majority of the prisoners on show would be sent home straight after the occasion.[39] As

Catullus must have realised, this was meant as a great show of clemency towards the defeated. Few displays could have endeared him more to the Roman people, who loved to hate eastern luxury, but could not help but be fascinated by it.

Though Catullus was not seduced by the event, he could not close his eyes to what it signified. The pitiful appearance of so many foreign faces poignantly asserted the authority Rome had regained over Asia, as well as its proud ownership of Bithynia, which stood now larger than ever on the Black Sea coast. It was as though the Romans had regained a shattered crown, and acquired extra jewels in the process. The victory at once made viable the prospect of freely walking on its soil. Catullus' elder brother ventured to Asia, possibly to assist in the war effort or gain grounding for a political career. But Catullus, for his part, had too much to detain him in Rome to contemplate Bithynia just yet.

That blinding, tongue-freezing moment with Clodia Metelli had left its mark. But the wine had been free-flowing that night and put some of his memories to flight. It had been difficult for a Gaul like him to gauge his new limits when he realised that the Romans drank their wine with water, and frowned upon those who did not.[40] The idea of drinking wine, especially a fine Falernian,[41] anything but straight had long struck Catullus as anathema: '. . . water, spoiler of wine . . . off you pop to the dour kind', he sang, after a few (Poem 27).

AN ELEGANT NEW
LITTLE BOOK

Heroes, born in the moment most admired

Beyond measure of all Ages, godly race,

Offspring of a noble mother,

Again and again I beseech you.

I shall commemorate you often in my poem

(Poem 64, lines 23–4)

EVENINGS WERE FOR WRITING POEMS, as much as for drinking wine. Catullus could not explain why, but when he sat down to write he found himself picturing Cornelius Nepos, a historian and poet from Gaul. Inquisitive, not to say obsessive, about the figures who had shaped the world around him, Cornelius had written *On Famous Men* and *Outstanding Generals of Foreign Peoples*, and

---

composed a recondite history of the Greeks and Romans in three volumes, the *Chronica* (sadly now lost).[1] Cornelius also had a weakness for learned and elegant poetry – a fact which did not elude Catullus who decided that if there was anyone worth impressing while also challenging with the directness and erudition of his verse, it was he.

Rather than trouble himself with acquiring a patron – whose persistent requests and inability to be satisfied with fine lines might have proved an inconvenient distraction – Catullus decided to make Cornelius the dedicatee of his poetry collection. Poetry was a painful enough profession as it was, in which days of intense thought seldom resulted in anything other than frustration and a wax tablet stamped under foot. By the end of each day, it was less a case of finding a line he liked than one he could tolerate; and even if Catullus could do that, he would have struggled to satisfy a patron. It was finished articles they wanted, not salvaged syllables. The very notion of writing on demand was a distinctly unpoetic one. No, he would be independent, not an unusual situation for the times, but one for which he needed private means and public prominence.

Catullus possessed the means: his family had acquired riches enough to carry him through, and Rome's foreign conquests had gilded his world in luxuries. The poor reached out to taste them, but like Tantalus forever striving to savour a drink in the Underworld, few ever reached their fruits. While landowners suffered as more and more produce was imported from the new provinces, many an equestrian exulted in the new trade. Catullus, however, was never much interested in the trappings of new money, and was at pains to play down his wealth. 'The wallet of your Catullus is full of cobwebs,' he once told a friend, as if he had slipped his hand into the fold of his toga and found not emptiness, but the deception of emptiness, a web that proved to have fallen short of its purpose through possessing too many holes (Poem 13).[2] It was too easy for a young dandy to complain about a lack of money when his accounts ran dry, or when his father replenished them to an extent he considered pitiful.

As for public prominence, Metellus Celer could introduce him to Cornelius Nepos, in the first instance. Metellus knew the man well enough to tell him a curious tale of how the king of the Suebi, a Germanic tribe, once gave him certain Indians who had come ashore in Gaul following a storm at sea.[3] He said little more on the matter, which put him at risk of sounding like a self-aggrandising fantasist. Whether the story was true or not, Cornelius Nepos believed it enough to repeat it. He was a lofty figure for Catullus to dedicate his self-confessed 'ramblings' to, but the elder poet did recognise their worth: twenty years after Catullus' death, Cornelius would remember him as one of the finest poets of the age.[4]

Catullus pictured the 'elegant new little book' he would give him, a handsome papyrus scroll prepared from strips of sedge plant. A specialist craftsman pressed the strips and laid them out in the sun to fuse together. Then he used a dry pumice stone to polish the edges of the papyrus, which would otherwise prove perilous to the delicate fingertips of the learned.[5] In a gruelling exercise in self-criticism, Catullus would fill the book with his best work, for not even the largest scroll in Rome was big enough to hold all the poems he had ever written.[6] He hoped that his poetry would be just as well polished as his scroll and therefore survive for 'over a hundred years', a *saeculum*, the longest span a Roman supposed a man could live (Poem 1).[7]

Waking from his reverie, he decided to concentrate for the

moment on publishing what he had by word of mouth, and in draft form among friends and more public groups before considering any amendments and overseeing the production of further copies on papyrus. Latin poetry did not rhyme, but could be written in many different metres, to which the ancient ear was well attuned. Catullus was ever promiscuous in his choice. The first fifty-nine poems in his collection as it survives vary in metre (the 'polymetrics'); the last fifty are epigrams, written in the elegiac metre. In between are eight poems, which rely upon a variety of different rhythms and beats.

No sooner had he begun to circulate his first drafts in Rome, than a 'filthy slut' told him he was a 'joke', and promptly made off with several of his wax tablets. He watched her, 'strutting shamefully, laughing nastily as if in a mime with a face like a Gallic puppy's' (Poem 42). Even as she did so, Catullus put the joke back on himself. The Latin for 'puppy' was *catulus*; Catullus was a Gaul. Her facial expression was ugly, but she was mimicking him, like a mime actress. He looked at her and saw his reflection: a Gallic dogface.

The sight antagonised him, as did the slattern's words. Rich men could write leisurely while other men were plying more physically exhausting trades, but it was certainly no 'joke'. When spent wisely, leisure – *otium* – could produce magnificent results. He documented the process earnestly, but with heightened fervour, in a poem to another poet, Licinius:

Yesterday, Licinius, on a lazy day,

We messed around for ages in my writing tablets

Risqué as agreed,

Scribbling short verses, you then me,

Playing now with this metre and now with that,

Swapping them between us over laughter and wine.

(Poem 50)

He went on to describe the sleepless night that followed, worked up as he was in admiration for this man's great wit and the passion they had made in metres and refrains. When their professional lives were so tied up together, it felt only natural for Catullus to feature the man in his lines. The poem was a gift to him – *ocelle* (an affectionate diminutive that literally meant 'little eye') – so that there could be no doubt about the depth of his affection.

Catullus was no stranger to what it meant to feel an intense or passing attraction to another man. All around him, adolescent boys from good families were enjoying sexual liaisons with other boys. Some kept a *concubinus* at home, a man of lower social standing with whom he could while away the years of youth before proceeding to marriage with an eligible girl. Sex between the two boys could be perfunctory, but a *concubinus* could form a lasting emotional attachment to his partner and begrudge the day he left him behind: 'miserable, miserable concubine' (Poem 61). As Romans talked freely about each other's sex lives, an adult man of respectable status could be quite open about the penetration of a male slave or subordinate. To be penetrated himself, and therefore give another man pleasure, was, on the other hand, deeply shameful. There was no word for homosexuality in Catullus' day, but the poet was fond of using language then considered risqué to describe a man who took on the receptive role with another man.

Catullus decided to pursue Licinius – full name Gaius Licinius

Calvus Macer – not as a lover, but as close enough a friend for later poets to recall them often as a pair.[8] On further acquaintance, Catullus discovered that the fellow preferred to go by the name Calvus, an unpretentious two syllables which he hoped would put distance between him and his father's shadow. Poor Calvus had barely to sit down to dinner before someone would ask him if he was related to Gaius Licinius Macer, an influential historian and political adviser: a wunderkind descended from 300 years of political gold. The father had committed suicide upon being indicted for extortion, but people had not forgotten the high esteem in which he had been held. And here was his son, Calvus, trying to make his way in the world, a short man with very little hair – if he lived up to his preferred name which meant 'bald'.[9]

At least he had the example of Julius Caesar to heed. The tall and well-built commander was developing a bald patch as he aged. He tended to remove excess body hair with tweezers, but was so anxious to maintain the semblance of a full mane that he fashioned a comb-over and relished the opportunity to wear a laurel wreath when this honour was bestowed upon him.[10]

Others wrestled with the same problem. Several hundred years later, Synesius of Cyrene, a Neoplatonist who became a bishop, wrote an essay *In Praise of Baldness* (in response to one historian's *In Praise of Hair*). There was no shame in the head being bald, he insisted, provided that the mind was hirsute, or ruffled with ideas. Sheep, after all, were hairy but stupid. Not satisfied with explaining how many of the most intelligent figures in the ancient world had been hairless – most famously of all, Socrates – he proceeded to argue that even the heroes of myth, such as Achilles, shed their hair at an early age. If that did not stop them from achieving eternal recognition, why should it stop anyone else?

Calvus was trying to rise above his appearance and become a respectable lawyer, for which poetry would prove an excellent grounding and distraction. He needed only to look at Cicero, the greatest lawyer of the age, who had spent his younger years composing a poem about a fisherman from Boeotia who ate a herb and turned into a prophetic sea god. The crown of Calvus' poetic achievements, as fortune would have it, would also involve an element of metamorphosis. He wrote about Io, a young girl whom Jupiter, king of the gods, turned into a heifer, and raped: 'Oh unfortunate virgin, you feed on bitter grass.'[11]

Catullus and Calvus struck up a friendship with another poet, Gaius Helvius Cinna, who probably came from Brescia, 'mother' of Catullus' Verona. The proximity of Cisalpine Gaul to Rome and its varied landscapes proved a fertile combination, and Cinna, for one, did not hesitate to proclaim his provincial roots: 'But now a swift chariot pulled by two little horses rushes me through the willow trees of the Cenomani [Gauls].'[12] As a man who rendered even a talented poet a mere 'goose' among 'melodious swans', Cinna had plenty to teach Catullus and Calvus.[13] If only he was not so slow at composition. He was still hard at work on a poem he had begun perhaps five years earlier about an incestuous affair of a princess called Zmyrna.

Into and out of their circle, less salon than fluid coterie, wandered several other poets, including Furius Bibaculus, whom Catullus came to know exceptionally well, and, at their helm, a poet and grammar teacher from Gaul, Publius Valerius Cato. Catullus addressed him in a few lines which made light of their closeness in name and nature, as he described the moment he punished a precocious young boy:[14]

A ridiculous scenario, Cato, hilarious,

Well worth your attention and laughter.

Laugh as much as you love Catullus, Cato!

The scenario is ridiculous and too funny.

Just now I caught my girlfriend's little boy

Wanking; If Dione approves, I took him

With my hard-straining cock.

(Poem 56)

Determined to wind Cato up, Catullus left the identity of the boy he assaulted in his poem unclear; if he were an innocent slave, at worst Catullus would have had to compensate his owner for property damage. In a clever pun, Valerius Catullus sits side by side with Valerius Cato, 'Catullus, Cato!' As Catullus knew, his name was little more than a diminutive that meant 'little Cato'.[15] Joking with his older and wiser namesake, he made it his mission to laugh all the more heartily to make up for the best-known Cato of his day, the optimate politician Cato the Younger, who was famous for never laughing at all.[16] Even Cicero, who was very fond of young Cato, had to confess that he spoke in the Senate 'as if he were in Plato's Republic, not in Romulus' cesspit'.[17]

There was nothing Catullus and his poet circle liked more than picking apart the work of inferior authors. In a similarly jocular tone, Catullus wrote a poem to a friend, Varus, about the poetry of a certain Suffenus:[18] a likeable man, but a terrible poet. Not satisfied with composing ten thousand or more verses on wax tablets, 'this Suffenus' had them copied out on luxurious rolls of papyrus, wound up on new scroll knobs with red tie-thongs, lead-ruled, their edges smoothed. Suffenus the man and Suffenus' poems did not go hand in hand:[19]

> When you read them, that smart and sophisticated
>
> Suffenus suddenly seems like any old goat-milker
>
> Or digger, such is the transformation and discrepancy.
>
> (Poem 22)

As far as Catullus was concerned, good poetry was characterised by *urbanitas*, which was determined less by a poet's background and current surroundings than it was by an aptitude for incisiveness, sophistication and wit. Many a man from the city had failed in that test, and many a provincial flourished. The *urbane* man knew the world, but had experienced it so richly that his observations had become those of an elevated being. He used words such as *lepidus* to mean elegant and *iucundus* to describe something aesthetic and pleasurable to the senses; he spoke as Catullus wrote. Suffenus, whom Catullus described as *urbanus* as a man, aspired to urbanity in packaging his poems the way he did, but his presentation was merely an elaborate attempt to compensate for inadequate, rustic, verse.

Happy though he was to call the poems of Suffenus and other men 'tortures' (Poem 14), and even to contemplate gathering all their 'poison' to give Calvus his comeuppance for making him a present of it, Catullus more than once referred to himself as 'the very worst' poet (Poems 36 and 49). As time would tell, he meant these words sarcastically, but not even sarcasm could disguise his self-knowledge. While he saw these inferior poets as 'unsuited to our times', he was not blind to the fact that his own work was untimely, only in a different sense. A fragment of a draft introduction preserved in his collection classed his poetry as *ineptia* – not just 'ramblings' but 'unsuited' or 'untimely' ramblings: utterings which did not quite fit.

While he frowned upon some other poets' work, not everyone around him approved of his own. Lending them epithets neither of praise nor entirely of criticism, Cicero branded his set *neoteroi*, 'too new', or *poetae novi*, 'new poets'.[20] Ever the stickler for tradition, Cicero saw them as young, subversive, inferior to the great masters who preceded them.

The older elite families had grown up on a diet of epic and historic chronicle, with a smattering of comedy. In the texts of Homer lay praise for the valiant warriors of ancient times, luxurious palaces and perfect islands. The first Roman authors had written in Greek. Others proudly translated the *Odyssey* into Latin, and a man named Ennius then boldly claimed that Homer had entered his soul and inspired him to write. His *Annales*, chronicles of Rome's august history, were precisely the kind of work Catullus despised for their weight and severity. Other Romans savoured them nonetheless, as they did dull agricultural treatises and staid comedies based upon Greek plays. Catullus might have despaired: there was a clutch of poets who had turned their hands in recent decades to translating and adapting Greek poems into Latin, and he was familiar with their efforts.[21] But the civil wars of Sulla and Marius appeared to have resulted in something of a drought of truly elegant literature. Catullus resolved to play the situation to his advantage.

Rebelling against the dry tomes of Ennius and others, seizing the new day after the tragedies of the previous decades, Catullus and his friends relished the corporeal and the earthy: not just a boy indulging himself sexually, but a man airing his buttocks at the baths, or subjecting a crowd to his terrible body odour. Catullus wrote lines that were impish and scatological:

> For your anus is cleaner than a salt-cellar
>
> And doesn't shit ten times a full year
>
> (Poem 23)

His first editors in Renaissance Italy reproduced such fruity poems and commented upon them freely. When it came to disseminating them in England, however, prudishness often got in the way. Some scholars omitted the rude poems or fractions of them from their editions to make them suitable for both schoolchildren and adults to read.[22] Even in the twentieth century, famous scholars, including C. J. Fordyce, have deemed up to a third of Catullus' poems unfit for comment.[23]

Cleverly concealing the fact that he was incredibly *doctus* ('learned') by writing Latin that looked diurnal – mundane – Catullus turned his hand also to composing smart elegiac couplets loaded with sentiment.[24] He had four acquaintances in Verona who were 'double-dating'. When they began to read the poem he wrote about them, they might have thought that he was mocking them:

> Caelius is crazy for Aufillenus, Quintius for Aufillena,
>
>   The flowers of Verona's youth,
>
> The brother one, his sister the other.
>
>   Which is what they call a truly sweet fraternity.

But then he unexpectedly brought the poem round to form a heartfelt tribute to an old friend:

> Whom am I to back of the two? Caelius, you.
>
>   For your friendship alone saw me through the fire
>
> When the mad flames of passion burned me to the marrow.
>
>   May you be happy, Caelius, and a master of love.
>
> (Poem 100)

His poem fell comfortably into two halves, but hinged not merely upon themes of love and friendship, but on the line between life and death. This man's friendship was not to be taken lightly, for it saved Catullus' life.

Charming as such verses were, for people more accustomed to didactics – the kind of poetry that actually taught them something – it was initially difficult to see that Catullus' personal refrains and observations of humdrum life contained lessons of their own. Cicero, in particular, loved grandiloquence. The epics were more his style, not the colloquialisms and newly turned words of Rome's youth. He could not appreciate strings of expletives embedded in otherwise elegant lines, and jilty rhythms, and thousands of diminutives – it was 'little' this, 'little' that – littering self-obsessed and self-obsessing ramblings on love and heartbreak. He got Catullus' references, but not the point of them.

While writing poems like these, Catullus and his friends longed also to capture the sophisticated verve of celebrated Hellenistic poets, men such as Apollonius of Rhodes and Callimachus, whose poetry might imbue their Latin lines with all the learnedness and erudition of the Greek East. Catullus' interest in writing in this poised and intellectual style, as well as in the more colloquial manner favoured by the man in the street, made him a particularly bold and interesting poet.

Callimachus originally came from Cyrene, a Greek foundation on the coast of North Africa (close to modern Shahat in Libya), but now capital of one of Rome's newer provinces, Cyrenaica.[25] He traced his lineage all the way back to its founder, King Battus, and Catullus perpetuated his claims to royal ancestry.

When Callimachus was born, shortly before the third century BC, Alexandria was still a new city. It was at its great Library that he and Apollonius of Rhodes, author of the most famous epic on Jason and the Argonauts, made scholarly erudition fashionable. Quite taken with their cleverness, and with some of the Greek poems they discovered in recent anthologies, Catullus and his friends set about establishing themselves as their Latin heirs. As they did so, they also looked at the work of Meleager, a poet who lived on the island of Cos in the eastern Aegean, who over the last quarter century had gathered together a selection of Greek epigrams spanning the period of history through to the early first century BC. Other poets were producing similar compilations. Catullus was not the first to pick up these works at Rome and respond to them in Latin, but he was among the first to do so successfully.[26]

He perceived early on the ways in which the works of his predecessors could intersect, the Greek with the Latin, the past with the present; Callimachus and his descent from a king who claimed kinship with one of the Argonauts whom Apollonius was celebrating in verse. And there Catullus stood at the far end of their tangled lineage, embracing it as the fount, but just the fount, of the best Roman poetry of all, his own. Apollonius' *Argonautica* would form a starting point for Catullus' Bedspread Poem, a work whose form would be pointedly Callimachean.

People like Cicero ought to have admired the scholarship that Catullus absorbed from these poets. It was said that Callimachus wrote more than 800 papyrus rolls on wide-ranging topics: treatises on the rivers of Europe and the names of fish, collections of tragedies, dramas; a poem about Io, the girl Jupiter turned into a heifer and raped, which must have influenced Calvus as he sat down to write on the same theme; and a poem about Theseus entitled *Hecale*. Catullus was looking particularly at his *Aetia*, a four-book poem on the origins of ancient customs, written in elegiacs, a metre normally reserved for short pieces. It was choppy, but meticulously structured. In its prologue Callimachus explained that his critics despised work that was not written as one continuous long poem on epic themes such as warfare. He disagreed, and argued moreover that sacrificial sheep should be fattened, but verses kept svelte, and that large ideas should be condensed into tiny phrases:

For, when for the first time I put my tablet

On my knees, Lycian Apollo said to me:

'. . . poet, feed the sacrificial animal to be as fat

As possible, but, dear fellow, the Muse to be slender.

And I instruct you as follows, do not tread the path

Which carriages pass over or drive your chariot

Over others' paths or a wide track, but along unworn

Roads, even if you drive a narrower path.'

(Prologue to Callimachus' *Aetia*, Fragment 1.22–8)

Catullus heeded his advice for brevity, ingenuity, variety, and polished erudition. In paying homage to Callimachus he risked treading his path, but determined to move away from translating his poetry and begin adapting merely its precepts to his own particular tongue. That way he would prove himself capable of walking outside the existing tramlines of Latin literature. He echoed Callimachus' criticism of a poet called Antimachus, whose work was notoriously verbose.[27] 'Let the plebs rejoice in puffed-up Antimachus,' Catullus wrote (Poem 95b), while the more concise works of Cinna and Callimachus were to be savoured by those who were learned enough to appreciate the tune of the cicadas over the braying of the ass.[28]

When Catullus later attempted to write in a grand style reminiscent of epic, he would do so in the Callimachean manner of reducing greatness to a small compass, and making every word count. And so Poem 64, his Bedspread Poem, would both feature and become a rich tapestry of allusions to other poets' works and traditions of myth, but woven to a pattern of his own invention. He would choose to use hexameters, a heavier metre than he used for many of his other poems, which gave longer works such as this a grand tone.

Still, Cicero was just too aloof to appreciate his poetry. In another respect, he was too close to him. It was not just the urbanity or 'Greekness' of Catullus' verse that offended him, but the provincial twang that he imposed upon it. Cicero was a new man from Arpinum, to Rome's south; Catullus, though also nouveau riche in the eyes of the patricians, was a Gaul; both were outsiders. To Cicero's ears, the northern tongue was abhorrent.[29] It was normal for a writer to disguise his origins by sticking to standard forms, but Catullus' voice was clearly transposed into some of his poems.

The Gauls tended to keep their mouths open more often than the Romans as they spoke, causing one word to leak into another like a loudly dripping tap. Gaping vowels gave rise to strange inflections and distinctive dialogue, which was exceedingly difficult to lose.[30] And Catullus was not minded to do so. The sheer languidness of the elided vowel lent itself perfectly to love. One of his most famous Latin lines, *Vivamus, mea Lesbia, atque amemus* – 'We should live . . . we should love' (Poem 5) benefited from his dialect. In reading it, no one pronounced the '*ia*' and '*at*' or the '*que*' and '*ame*', but ran them together like this: '*Lesbiatquamemus*'. It sounded like a lover's drawl.

SPARROW

Observe the couch at the heart of the palace,

A fine seat for a goddess,

Finished with ivory from India

And spread with purple tinged with the rose-pink

Dye of the murex fish.

(Poem 64, lines 47–9)

LANGUID SPEECH PROVED particularly helpful when Catullus was writing to woo, and he used it repeatedly in his poetry. He had learned early on that poetry had the potential both to incite and to restrain the act of love. Reading it tended to do the former, writing it the latter; but the outcome depended upon the quality of the verse. Write a good poem, and it might have been enough not to have followed his feelings through to fruition. Write too good a poem, and he risked driving himself mad with desire. It proved a lot harder to write a poem to remedy frustration than to write one for a lover. Amid the difficulties of sourcing solace in poetry, Catullus discovered increasingly that poems intended to satisfy his lust slipped easily into poems that incited him to act on it. In the hands of the person he loved, he always hoped that they might have the same effect.

He decided to put this to the test. Clodia Metelli had been clouding his thoughts, making it impossible for him to think of anything else. Taking in his hands the poem he had written about watching her from under her husband's nose, he made her a copy. He addressed it not to 'Clodia', but to 'Lesbia', establishing there and then an intellectual code for her real name. While 'Lesbia' meant 'woman of Lesbos', where Sappho was born, it also had the same number of syllables as 'Clodia'. Both names provided him with one heavy and two short beats — ‿‿.[1]

Clodia must have been pleased, for she was more than just a muse waiting to be flattered with a Sapphic pseudonym, she was an 'experienced poet of very many plays'.[2] Cicero smirked when he called her that in court one day, hoping he could shift blame away from the man he was defending by characterising her as someone who was capable enough of composing charades to incriminate him. Clodia and his client, as time would tell, had history. But Cicero's prejudice against her ready wit need not have reduced what he said to a fallacy. The poems Catullus composed for Lesbia might well have been touched by subtle reminiscences of what she once wrote, ghosts of Clodia the poet, of whom nothing else survives.

Catullus had no issue with welcoming women poets into his circle, including one Cornificia whose 'distinguished epigrams' were still being read 400 years after she lived.[3] An aristocratic female poet named Sulpicia wrote romantic verses some years later about her relationship with a lover, Cerinthus. She lamented the prospect of spending her birthday without him, and described the fever that coursed her veins. She wrote of her despair when her lover took her for granted, and told him that he would do better to turn his attentions to a whore than take liberties with her affections. While some of her poems survived, bundled together with those of a male poet, Tibullus, other female poets' work did not. Had it not been for her name and marital status, or even for Catullus himself, Clodia Metelli might have erupted with just as much force on the literary scene. But there could never have been room for both Clodia and Lesbia.

Even from the very start, there was a problem. Sappho had won eternal renown for her intellect, but Clodia was already married. She was not about to earn anything more than notoriety as the object of a non-aristocratic, indeed non-Roman, poet's affections. As it was, her illustrious ancestor Appius Claudius had helped to oversee a law against marriage between blue-blood patricians and commoner plebeians. The ruling came under the Twelve Tables legislation, which magistrates drew up in the 450s BC after Greek examples. Though the intermarriage law had since been annulled, the lasting stigma that arose when one married someone who lacked an illustrious family tree was not always lost on their descendants.

Catullus could not even quite decide what it was he liked about Clodia. He tried to define his reasons, but could only do so by comparing her with another woman, Quintia, who was something of a beauty:

Quintia is beautiful by popular repute. To my mind she is

    Pale, tall, poised: these individual qualities I readily concede.

But I deny her total beauty, for there is no charm,

    No grain of salt in so large a frame.

Lesbia is beautiful since her beauty is total,

    And she has stolen every Venus from every woman.

(Poem 86)

He could not deny that Quintia was tall, pale, and had good posture — all features Romans admired in a woman. But there were less tangible things that made her inferior to his beloved. Lesbia could not quite compete with Quintia for height, at least, for he sought to emphasise instead her 'total beauty'. The line in which he described Quintia's lack of 'salt' — or wit — was remarkably balanced so as to emphasise his point. Lesbia was almost aggressively beautiful. The word he used in Latin to describe how she acquired her good qualities was *subripio*, a sudden movement akin to theft. She was *candida*, both pale-skinned and 'shining', as well as beautiful and salty. If Catullus was satisfied that he had finally understood the cause of his attraction, his friend Calvus was left distraught. Quintia just happened to be *his* lover.[4]

While Clodia had total beauty, Catullus had his Gallic dogface with its lazy eye, a physical shortcoming which few in society could have looked upon with much compassion.[5] Catullus' sensitivity was a worthy quality, but hardly strong enough to compensate for his appearance. If he was going to win Clodia's heart, he would need to do so through his poetry. 'A generous girl acts on her word, a chaste one makes no promise,' Catullus once told a girl in Verona (Poem 110). Clodia, he prayed, would now promise.

She needed more persuading than he did to go beyond mere flirtation. A woman's adultery, unlike a man's, was theoretically punishable with death. As Cato's ancestor put it: 'If you should discover your wife committing adultery, you may with impunity kill her without trial; but if she should discover you committing adultery or having an adulterous act performed upon you, she would not dare to lay a finger on you, nor would that be lawful.'[6] In practice it was exceedingly difficult to enforce such measures. The law did little to deter married women from pursuing extramarital liaisons. So it was that the first emperor of Rome, Augustus, would introduce a new law against adultery in 18 BC.

Still, there was a risk; and Catullus was anxious that Clodia should take it. He employed every bit of wit and charm he could. He might only have been writing love poems, but he believed that he was fighting 'great and glorious battles' for her (Poem 37). Catullus the valiant hero-in-arms sat down to compose a poem about her pet sparrow.

He decided he would capture the movement of the sparrow by using one of his favourite poetic metres, hendecasyllables, the origins of which lay in ancient song. The playful, eleven-syllable lines were as suited to flirtation as they were to invective. In hendecasyllables his poem would skip along lightly, like a tiny sparrow on its feet. Sappho had had the goddess of love ride a sparrow chariot in one of her poems.[7] Meleager, the Greek epigrammatist, sought release from his heartache through a grasshopper's song.[8] Catullus sought to go several bases further.

In Verona, sparrows fluttered in and out of human life like rain. They targeted diners distracted by laughter and wine and fearlessly stole bread from their simple linen napkins. They skimmed the waters beneath Verona's grand bridge, the Ponte Pietra, in balletic display, and hopped here and there across the parched soils of Sirmio, unable to keep pace with the scurrying lizards. The 'Cisalpine' genus, *Passer italiae*, a cross between the common and Spanish sparrows, is delicate and tame.

Inspired by the landscapes of home as much as by his poetic forebears, Catullus pictured his darling Lesbia playing with her 'sparrow', which nipped at her fingertips, providing her with some consolation from the 'intolerable burning' he liked to imagine she was feeling:

Sparrow, apple of my girl's eye,

Often she plays with you, holds you in her lap,

Gives you a fingertip when you want it

And urges you to take passionate bites

Whenever she wishes, gleaming in desire for me,

To play with something for pleasure.

And I believe it provides a small release from her

Frustration, as then the intolerable burning fades.

I wish that I could play with you as she does

And lighten the ponderous cares of my mind . . .

I would be as grateful as they say the quick-stepped

Atalanta was for the little golden apple

That loosed the chastity belt that bound her long.

(Poem 2)

Catullus used the short beats in the hendecasyllables to illustrate Lesbia's movement as much as that of her sparrow. One can almost hear her as she 'plays', *ludere*, and moves her 'finger' *digitum*:

Often she plays with you

— — —◡◡ —

Quicum ludere, quem

Gives you a fingertip

— — —◡◡ —

Cui primum digitum

Like many fantasies, Catullus' was inconsistent. Lesbia was seductive enough to play expertly with her sparrow, yet as virginal as Atalanta, a girl from the world of myth, who was to marry the man who defeated her in a footrace after she stooped to pick up golden apples. Pre-empting Shakespeare's Romeo, who wished that he was Juliet's bird, Catullus longed that he would be the one to play with Lesbia's sparrow in her stead.[9]

His persistence, like any lover's, hovered over the indeterminate line between nuisance and flattery. And with time it did what persistence will — drift imperceptibly to where there lies the promise of consummation. Fortunately, he did not have to wait too long before that delicious day arrived. Metellus Celer had just succeeded in being elected to the consulship of 60 BC, alongside Lucius Afranius (a man accused of being better at dancing than politics). The husband's back would now be turned on his domestic life, as he focused on affairs in the public arena.[10]

*

While Catullus was busy picturing Lesbia's sparrow, Pompey was battling the Senate's opposition to the ratification of his eastern campaigns. Its members were fearful that between the lines of his settlement lay the extension of personal powers, and with good reason.[11] Pompey was trying to pass an agrarian law that would grant land to Rome's poor citizens, not just his veterans, and win votes in the process. Lucullus, Clodia's former brother-in-law, led the optimates in blocking Pompey.[12] He was supported by Metellus Celer, who was still smarting from his sister's divorce. As Pompey's tribune put forward the proposals, Metellus Celer contested each point so bitterly that the Senate had him hauled off to jail. Not willing to let this stop him, Metellus haughtily asked for the debate to reconvene outside his cell. Exasperated, Pompey bade his tribune release his opponent. The settlement remained unresolved.

On the other side, Metellus had Clodia's brother to deal with. Still exalting in his freedom after the Bona Dea trial, and fresh from serving as a quaestor in Sicily, Clodius was now plotting to be elected as a tribune: a curious ambition, considering that his patrician birth and status put him above the post. To the man in the street, he must have seemed crazy. But Clodius was no fool. As a tribune, he could strengthen his ties with the plebeians, and also propose legislation to punish Cicero for opposing him in court. Cicero was now convinced that Clodius had a vendetta against him and wanted to destroy him. Since only plebeians were eligible to become tribunes, however, Clodius needed first to be demoted in class.

Clodia was happy to do what she could for her brother. She was acquainted with Cicero, but better acquainted with Cicero's loyal pen friend, Atticus, to whom she passed messages and reported

Clodius' plans, as if to antagonise Cicero further.[13] Cicero could see that Clodia was doing her very best to help her brother succeed, even petitioning her husband on his behalf.[14]

Taking the bait, Cicero set about taunting Clodius over his ambitions for the lowly tribunate. Clodius asked him whether he had ever been in the practice of providing a place for Sicilians at gladiatorial shows.[15]

'No,' replied Cicero.

'Well, I shall initiate the practice as their new patron,' said Clodius; 'only, since my sister occupies so much of the consul's position, she gives me but a single foot.'

'Don't moan about one of your sister's feet when you're allowed to lift them both!' Cicero croaked. He knew that incest jokes were crass, but when Clodia was so meddlesome, so unworthy of her husband, he felt that they were justified. Time and again he called her 'ox-eyes', a sobriquet that emphasised her tempestuousness more than her beauty. In Homer's great epics, it was Zeus' feisty wife Hera whose eyes were 'ox-like'.

Although Clodia seemed to be making headway on behalf of her brother and his quest for plebeian status, for all her arguments she soon found there was nothing she could do to prevent Metellus from blocking the measure in a 'most distinguished opposition'.[16] Her brother and her husband were at loggerheads, and for the moment, there was no way to resolve the stalemate.

Whether it was this that drove her into Catullus' arms – if she was not already there – or the simple fact that the intensity of her husband's new position as consul provided the opportunity for temptation, there were practicalities to be addressed before an affair could become fully fledged. It could not be conducted under Metellus' own roof on the Palatine Hill, for it would be impossible to elude the eyes of so many neighbours, visitors, and slaves. Catullus was also keen to keep any prospective activity away from his own door. A woman was entitled to dine with men, own property, and move fairly freely through the city, but her movements were hampered by her male 'guardian' – ordinarily her husband. So Ovid later complained of his mistress Corinna, 'whom her husband, whom her guardian, whom the hard door (so many enemies!) were guarding, so she could not be taken by any deception'.[17] Even if she managed it, Clodia might easily have been caught.

Catullus was undeterred. He calmly turned to one of many acquaintances he had made during his first months in Rome, a certain Allius, who had offered him his house to use as he desired. The opportunity arose just as Catullus was 'burning like Etna'. In retrospect, and with marvellous poetic litotes, he later wrote that the girl, for her part, 'was not unwilling' (Poem 8). Not without a flattering dose of hyberbole – litotes' happy inverse – he likened his relief at finding such a spot in which to exercise his passion to a favouring breeze arriving suddenly and assisting sailors 'caught in a black hurricane' (Poem 68).

As Catullus' beloved approached the threshold for the very first time she looked like a 'shining goddess'. Ordinarily, a woman would cross the threshold in this way when she became a man's bride, and then carried in his arms. (Few remembered why: the ancient biographer Plutarch made this number twenty-nine of his *Roman Questions* and proposed that it was perhaps a memory of the forceful manner in which the first Romans had taken the Sabine women, who lived on their borders, to be their wives, or through female shyness, or to illustrate that she was now tied to that household.) In usurping the role of the bride and entering alone, Lesbia sounded an ill note; she faltered on the threshold that was already well worn, just as the Trojan Horse famously faltered as it crossed into the ancient city, an evil gift from the Greeks which heralded the collapse of Troy.[18]

Writing later in life, after his travels to Bithynia, Catullus recalled the myth of Protesilaos, the first Greek soldier to have died at Troy. His fate had already been decided when his passionate bride Laodamia crossed the threshold on their wedding night one year before he left for war. Laodamia had also crossed the marriage threshold incorrectly. Their marriage had taken place without due sacrifice to the gods. Catullus and his lover did not even have a marriage to legitimise their affair.

In retrospect, and with some poetic licence, Catullus made himself look the fool for having missed the warning signs. But love, as he knew, renders one deaf and blind to anything sinister beneath the surface. This was a sentiment that anyone could understand. Looking back on his life from a later vantage point, it was clear that fate had not been in favour of this particular relationship. In the hour itself, by contrast, and in the comfort of their safe house, 'fragrant with Assyrian perfume', nothing could ruddy the vision of his lover undressing and laying aside her breast band.

Clodia was at least thirty-five when the affair began, and, it transpired, a mother. Metella, her daughter by Metellus, would marry a patrician politician named Publius Lentulus Spinther when she came of age. Although she would not care for him, and take at least one other lover, her marriage, and divorce, would ensure that the Clodii Pulchri remained in the public eye.[19]

If Metella's existence showed Catullus anything, it was that

Clodia was not barren. Though past her prime, her age might not prevent her from conceiving children again. They needed to be careful. Most women around her placed greater emphasis on abortion than prevention, but that was only because the available methods of contraception were rather less than foolproof. Stories spread by word of mouth of the efficacy of various suppositories and amulets. A particular kind of spider with a large head was said to contain two parasites, which could be removed, inserted into a deer skin, attached to a woman's body, and used to prohibit pregnancy for a year.[20] Coitus interruptus was sometimes more effective. If a man feared that this would rob him of the peak of his pleasure, there were variations on the theme. He could ejaculate, but at that moment his partner was well advised to hold her breath and draw away a little, so that the semen was not thrust too deeply up inside her. Post-coitus, she should squat down and sneeze a good few times, wipe herself down, and have a cold drink.[21]

If he was feeling generous, Catullus might smear some concoction of herbs or berries on his penis as a means of contraception, but the onus was on his partner to safeguard herself against unwanted pregnancy. Silphium (asafetida), a particularly pungent spice from Callimachus' Cyrene, was a popular contraceptive, which women could ingest. She could also insert wool like a plug, or apply olive oil, honey or white lead to her cervix before sex.[22]

Sometimes these measures seemed to have worked. Catullus apparently never fathered a child with his Lesbia or any other woman. He might yet have done so, but considered the subject too close to his heart to publish on. Like one of Rome's artists decorating bowls and vases and everyday objects with explicit sex-

*Silphium, a pungent spice, is weighed before export from Cyrene
(on the coast of North Africa). Among women, it was a popular contraceptive.
Among sheep it was a sedative; among goats, a sneeze-inducing allergen.*

ual scenes, Catullus enjoyed painting a picture in words of the sex acts he performed, or hoped to perform, on several people. He had been happy to jest with the poet Valerius Cato about buggering the 'little boy' of his girlfriend. Then there was a girl, Ipsitilla, whom he instructed to make ready for 'nine consecutive fucks' at midday (Poem 32). He had eaten and was more than ready for her: 'I poke through my tunic and cloak.'

But there were certain matters he was unwilling to divulge. The poems in which he described his love with Lesbia contain no trace of such crudeness, or its accompanying bravado. They are far less sexually explicit, and infinitely more erotic. At most, Catullus recounted years later how his lover 'gave me secret and wondrous little gifts in the night, taken from the very lap of her own husband' (Poem 68). In the moment itself, he would total the number of kisses he desired, but no more.

He would plead with her like a child, each cry an emotion delivered in time with his bounding heart, '*da mi* . . . *deinde* . . . *dein* . . . *dein* . . . *deinde* . . . *deinde* . . . *dein*' ('give me . . . then . . . then . . . then . . . then . . . then . . . then . . .'):

> We should live, my Lesbia, we should love,
>
> We should value at a penny all
>
> The rumours of our elders – they are dourer than most.
>
> The sun can set and rise again
>
> But once our short light has passed beneath its yardarm
>
> We must sleep a night that never ends.
>
> Give me a thousand kisses, then a hundred
>
> Then another thousand, then a second hundred.
>
> Then – don't stop – another thousand, then a hundred
>
> Then when we have shared many thousands
>
> We shall confound them so no one can know
>
> Or cast an evil eye upon us
>
> When he knows that our kisses are so many.

(Poem 5)

In promising to 'confound' their kisses, *conturbo*, he donned the mask of an accountant, who would sooner have used the word to describe overturned piles of money, or bankruptcy, than flustered kisses. Catullus might as well have rolled naked across the banking tables in the Forum. Piquing his elders' interest in his poetry, he showed them quite lithely that there was no way they could know how many kisses he and his lover exchanged, or what actually took place behind closed doors.

In another poem, he desired enormous kisses, *basiationes*, a neologism which, like the kisses of Poem 5, he surreptitiously rendered half his own already. The standard Latin for 'kisses' was *oscula*, not *basia* (although *basia* gave rise to many European words for affection, including Italian, *un bacio*). The word evoked Catullus' Gallic rather than Roman origins. He longed for many, many such kisses:

As great as the number of grains of Libyan sand

That lie on silphium-bearing Cyrene

Between the oracle of steamy Jupiter

And the holy tomb of old King Battus;

Or as many as the stars, when night is quiet,

That watch the secretive liaisons of men . . .

(Poem 7)

Without saying it, he subtly made it known where their kisses could lead. Though his critics would put it down to another cause, Catullus' decision to write explicitly of little more than their kisses was a clear sign that Lesbia was more than just a persona. She was a woman he loved very much.

THE RUMOURS OF
OUR ELDERS

While their minds are desirous, desperate to obtain something,

They are afraid of swearing nothing,

There is nothing they won't promise.

But as soon as the lust in their desirous mind is sated,

They remember none of their words,

Have no fear of perjury.

(Poem 64, lines 145–48)

ALTHOUGH CATULLUS COULD feel the evil eye of spies upon him, and his lover, he was more thrilled by the intrusion than upset by it. The prospect of unnerving friends and dour elders with the depth of his passion only reaffirmed for him the importance of his affair. He could revel all he liked in his thousands of kisses, but to be certain that the relationship was as extraordinary and seminal as he believed it was he needed witnesses.

Lesbia had become his raison d'être – 'my light, whose living makes life sweet for me' (Poem 68). He kissed her. She bit his lips. He wanted her sexually, but he wanted more besides. Catullus followed 'wherever the girl directed, loved by us as much as no woman again will be loved' (Poem 8). He loved her 'not just as a man loves his girlfriend, but as a father loves his sons and sons-in-law', *diligo* as opposed to *amo* (Poem 72). He did not care that he had never experienced the love a parent has for their child, for he believed he knew what it felt like. Clodia was not just a lover, but nor was she merely someone he had formed, like a child; she was part of him: a woman 'dearer to me than myself', 'far dearer to him than his eyes or anything else that is dearer than eyes' (Poem 82). He described her as 'my own life' (Poem 104). Again and again, Catullus clutched for the word or simile or metaphor, the means of expressing how integral Lesbia was to him, but could never quite find it.

Mingled with the long, limping syllables of his disapproving elders were voices he knew well. Several men were taunting him over his thousands of kisses, branding him 'barely male'. Marcus Furius Bibaculus, a rival poet from an elite family in Cremona in Gaul, and Aurelius, probably also a poet on the fringe of his set, had decided that he was 'soft'.[1] Soft – *mollis* – not because he drenched himself in perfume and over-polished his teeth, but because he dared to express how in thrall he was to a woman.[2] Catullus was partial to cunnilingus as well as rampant kissing, but the least he told them 'About my love of licking . . .', the better.[3] Soft men were sodomites, and men who were penetrated during sex were, by default, 'women'. Catullus could see where this was going.

He found the accusations of effeminacy boring and predictable. He decided that jibes at his masculinity veiled the real problem, which was that his accusers were not intelligent enough to appreciate his subtle references. Only the cultured were aware that Cyrene, whose sands numbered the kisses he desired of Lesbia, was the birthplace of Callimachus, and that Callimachus called himself 'Battiades' ('descendant of Battus') after its fabled founder King Battus. Callimachus admired brevity, elegance, obscure references. Catullus had achieved the same qualities in his kiss poems to Lesbia.

While witnesses were necessary in his poems, to affirm that his love was unparalleled, he did not need the challenges they presented him with in real life. In Rome, the gossipmongers worked to preserve the social *mores*, such as the chastity of wives, and sought to break the careers of men they disliked. Their words spread through common inns and dining rooms and seeped perennially into the speeches of the city's orators.

Cicero relied often on such hearsay to add colour to his orations and defence speeches, the latter being his particular talent. He had defended a poet a few years ago called Archias from the accusation that he was not enrolled as a citizen of Rome. He informed the unwitting jury that whenever Archias travelled in Asia and Greece, his arrival was met with immense excitement. Such was Archias' genius, he argued, that if he had not been a Roman citizen to begin with, he ought to be made one at once. His defence was, in all likelihood, an unqualified success.

It was never going to be long before Lesbia's true identity was exposed. Catullus' poems were to become so well known over the next few years that Lesbia would be 'more famous than Helen [of Troy] herself'.[4] Metellus Celer's political ambitions pushed him more firmly into the limelight, and ever since Lucullus' testimony against Clodius there was a discernible appetite for stories about the sexual peccadilloes of the Clodii Pulchri.

Catullus had his feelings alone to protect him. Although never the likeliest of moralists (which is what made the moralising edge of some of his observations so powerful), he counted himself among those who believed that morality was under threat, and that sexual promiscuity among the elite classes was partly to blame for this. Any one of his friends could point out that his affair with a married noblewoman made him part of the problem, but Catullus was not about to be persuaded. The crowd's scorn, together with the warmth of his lover's face and the weight of her words, showed him only that their relationship was unique in its potency, and therefore sacrosanct:

No faith in any pact was ever as great

As that discovered on my part in my love for you.

(Poem 87)

He also considered himself beyond the reach of the worrying trend he observed in Rome, 'fertile is the seed of adultery'. The precariousness of life during Rome's civil wars had driven many to new beds, while the toll of Sulla's proscriptions and the recent foreign wars had pushed well-born widows into having new relationships with good men who could give them children, to ensure that the elite did not die out entirely.[5] When the Roman historian Livy wrote a detailed history of Rome some thirty years later, he opened his first book with words which would ring true for Catullus:

... Then as discipline gradually slides, let [my reader] pay attention to the falling morals, then how they fall more and more, then begin to precipitate at a speed, until he reaches these times, in which we can endure neither our vices nor their remedies ... In recent times wealth has brought greed, and the unwieldy desires of pleasure have instilled a lust for ruining and losing everything through luxury and licentiousness

(Livy *ab urbe condita* prologue 9; 12)

It was in the same period that the Emperor Augustus, no moral paragon himself, passed his legislation to curb adultery, encourage the birth of legitimate children, and resurrect the importance of religion.

On bad days Catullus was given to believe that times were getting worse. On better days he accepted that humans are simply predisposed to finding their own times inferior to those that came before them. Seneca, one of the great thinkers and tragedians of the next century, would explain that 'vice, luxury, and neglect of good morals' were the fault of men, not the times; 'no era has been free from blame'.[6] Catullus would play with the same idea in his Bedspread Poem, when he would draw upon the Greek myth of the Ages in order to weigh up the modern world relative to the past. According to the myth, the world had declined since the pre-historical Golden Age, in which there had been no place for the kind of luxury that Seneca and Livy abhorred. Luxury was, historians insisted, the disease of developed nations, capable of inciting men to become disillusioned with each other and their leaders, and sparking mob rule.[7]

These thoughts might already have been in the back of Catullus' mind as he made it his mission to counter the objections critics raised to the moral ambiguity of his love poetry. Much though he could flaunt his intellectual superiority over Furius and Aurelius, his contemporaries' taunts went further than he acknowledged. Once they had discovered who it was that lay beneath Lesbia's veil, it was easy for them to form their own conclusions about why Catullus wrote merely of their kisses.

Rumour had it that Clodia was a mere coquette, draped in sensual Coan silk, a teasingly transparent fabric from the island of Cos through which one might see a woman 'almost as though she was naked'.[8] 'Coan' punned on the Latin word 'coitus', which was fitting because the cloth was a favourite among the less virtuous. Irresistible and brazen though Clodia was as she sauntered through the dining room in her diaphanous robes, in the bedroom, a spurned lover claimed that she was submissive and meek. If they heard about this, Catullus' acquaintances would have the perfect explanation for why the poet was so coy about his latest romance.

Catullus should have used this cruelty in his lover's defence. Only whores were expected to move at all during intercourse.[9] Well-born women were meant to lie still and exercise self-restraint. The trouble was, the nature of Catullus' relationship with Clodia was such as to cast her as a high-class courtesan rather than chaste wife.

Such courtesans looked to Greece for their elegance and glamour. Even before the Romans established the province of Macedonia in the second century BC, Hellenistic culture had flooded the city. There were Greek tutors for privileged children, Greek books for the inquisitive, Greek sculpture for the cultured, Greek prostitutes for hungry men – and their female counterparts, who became their copycats. Anyone who refused to believe that Clodia was a mistress of dull frigidity could picture her as one such woman.

Catullus might have decided from the outset of their affair to keep their most intimate moments private, but if he was unwilling to give his peers the details, he did not want them imagining anything less than divine. If it was explicit sex they desired, it was explicit sex they would get – if not quite in the manner they expected it:

I shall fuck you anally and orally

Cock-in-mouth Aurelius and sodomite Furius,

Since you judge me by my short poems

Because they are sexy, not pure enough.

It is only right that a poet is restrained and proper

In himself but there is no need at all for his

Little poems to be so.

What's more they have salt and elegance

Despite being sexy and not pure enough

And even have the power to inspire the urge for sex –

I don't mean in boys, but in those hoary old men

Who struggle to raise their cocks up hard.

And because you read of many thousands of kisses

You think me barely male?

I shall fuck you anally and orally.

(Poem 16)

Catullus had demanded kiss upon kiss from Lesbia, but now had the presumption to call himself 'restrained and proper'. He would go still further, swearing before the gods one day that he was a man of decency: 'For whatever men can say or do to be kind to someone, it has been said and done by you' (Poem 76). His rivals could accuse him of lying, but Catullus was not calling himself chaste. 'Please, do not judge my morals by this book,' the poet Martial later wrote, echoing Catullus' words.[10] In a poem it was difficult to convey that one understood where the line lay between what was acceptable and what was not. A young man could sow his seed and maintain his moral rectitude, provided his affairs did not disrupt the lives of others too much. As far as Furius and Aurelius were concerned, Catullus had already over-stepped those boundaries in his life, and showed evidence for this in his poetry. Catullus knew differently. It was love, and that was not wrong.

Anyone reading his poem might have assumed that Catullus had suffered a gross slight. The rape of freeborn men and women was illegal, but not if the victim had committed adultery with another man's wife. But Catullus was not married. It would take a poet to understand that the slight he had suffered was a literary one. Furius and Aurelius were simply hopeless critics, incapable of recognising good poetry – pithy, inventive, concise poetry.[11] Catullus wrote Poem 16 for them because, whatever the cost, he was going to defend poetry that was elegant, witty, yet potent enough to inspire a sexual surge in even the crustiest old man. Asserting his masculinity once and for all, he bragged that he was going to sully their mouths – the source of their poems and their criticism.

With these fiends he suffered none of the concern for discretion he experienced over Lesbia. He had made the decision early in his life that he would direct harsh poems against his well-born friends, if that is what they deserved, as well as to the man in the street. Many of the Greek poems he read in the impressive poetic anthology of Meleager, some of them older than Alexander the Great, others as recent as the decade of his birth, cast aspersions on certain individuals, but seldom were they freeborn men, and seldom were they threatened with punishment for their unedifying habits.[12]

Breaking away from these earlier literary traditions, Catullus sought to raise 'to the skies' not the heroes, but his friends and rivals, lovers, and the women they paid for love. Time and again he put his hand to composing poetry, often in his beloved hendeca-syllables, sprightly eleven-syllable lines, which made comedy out of undesirability. Long before Martial took to the city's streets to lambast unappealing characters in verse, Catullus lifted his wax tablet and scratched its surface with rude little ditties, full-blown polemics, elegant epigrams – all of them observational pieces on characters he knew or knew of. He combined bitter polemic with humour founded on briefly sketched caricatures.

One evening in Rome, he met with some friends at the home of a certain Flavius. Looking around, he realised that Flavius had taken a new lover. For some reason, he was keeping suspiciously quiet about her:

Flavius, if your lover were not

Inelegant and unrefined you would want to speak –

Would not be able not to speak – about her to Catullus.

No doubt you're in love with some feverish

Little slut and it shames you to confess it.

(Poem 6)

The evidence spoke for itself. Flavius' bedroom was 'steeped in flowers and the oil of Syrian olive', a fragrance made from olive oil and exotic Syrian herbs.[13] His bed and pillows looked worn – 'knackered and tattered', clearly a result of an evening's pounding. Flavius himself looked trim. His love handles had vanished through what had no doubt been a period of very vigorous fucking. If his secret lover was any better than an inelegant – *illepida*, the opposite of Catullus' *lepidus* poetry book – and unrefined slut, Catullus decided, Flavius would be telling him all about her. For all his criticisms of Flavius' new lover, Catullus felt excluded.[14] It did not matter that his comments about Flavius' secrecy were deeply hypocritical. Catullus could justify them, if pressed, by explaining that he kept quiet about the details of his affair with Lesbia, not its existence.

At least Flavius had a girl. There were other men they knew who had no luck with the ladies at all, or anyone for that matter, making them even riper for attack. Vibennius was a thief at the baths. Ironically, given the setting, Vibennius could not keep his 'right hand' clean, such was his sexual appetite. His son was still more objectionable, forever offering his hairy buttocks to passers-by:

The father has the filthier right hand

But the son's anus is the more voracious

(Poem 33)

The baths were the perfect place to satisfy one's postprandial lusts, but by the time a man had grown his first beard, he should never have been offering himself up for the passive role.

Catullus wrote disgustedly of the diseases men and women spread among one other. He was horrified when the 'pure kisses of a pure girl' mixed with the 'filthy spittle' of someone he could not even care to name (Poem 78b). Later in life he would describe how a woman passed on gout which she had caught from a lover. Though his medical knowledge could be rather confused, he knew how quickly certain infections could spread through intimacy: Catullus could well have experienced first-hand the misery of a venereal disease.

Catullus need not have limited himself to one lover at a time: he fell in love easily. Part of him even felt that a little leeway was permissible or, more importantly, was in keeping with the lifestyle he idealised. He was anxious not to resemble the prudish men he abhorred when he could recount that even Juno, queen of the goddesses herself, put up with her husband Jupiter's errant ways:

And although she is not satisfied with Catullus alone,

I shall make the most of the stolen pleasures

Of my modest mistress, few and far between,

So as not to live too much by the prudish precepts of dolts.

Often even Juno, mightiest of the heavenly gods,

Stifled her blazing anger at her husband's indiscretions

And she learnt of very many pleasures

Stolen by All-Wanting Jupiter.

(Poem 68)

Although Clodia was not visiting him as often as he wished – he suspected strongly that she was still sleeping with her husband – Catullus consoled himself with 'the stolen pleasures'. In practice, it proved difficult to abide by such rules for freedom. The fact that he could not have her completely rendered their relationship all the more tempestuous:

Lesbia always speaks badly of me,

In fact she never keeps quiet about me.

I'll be damned if Lesbia does not love me.

How can I tell? Because with me it's just the same.

I curse her continuously,

But I'll be damned if I do not love her.

(Poem 92)

When Clodia wasn't biting Catullus' lips she was biting off his head, and he hers. In his poem, Catullus endeavoured to show how well matched they were: mirror images of one another. Metellus could be a source of contention, but perhaps, after all, he had a mirror image of his own.

Catullus' poetic successors delighted in pointing out that he betrayed his own infidelity by writing of more than one lover in his book. Ovid scoffed that 'not content with her [Lesbia], he shared many love poems, confessing in them his own adultery'.[15] Given the depth of his poetic obsessions and jealous temperament, however, Catullus struggled to divide his attentions, poetic and otherwise. The poems he wrote about other lovers might have provided some precedent, rather than adulterous distraction, for the translation of love into poetry that he perfected with Lesbia.

The series of poems he composed about a young Roman boy named Juventius, for example, have much of the romantic longing, but far less of the familiarity of his Lesbia poems. Juventius was a wealthy aristocratic boy with lovely cheeks and plump lips which Catullus longed to kiss. He yearned to give this 'little flower' not one but 300,000 kisses – even more than he demanded of Lesbia. He would not be sated, he wrote, 'even if the crop of our little kisses were thicker than dry corn' (Poem 48). For 'crop' he used the word *seges* (literally a cereal crop). Transferring the 'crop' metaphorically from the fields to his lips, he rendered his kisses dry and countable. The anxious boy would read his poem and then hear one kiss rubbing against another, *aridis aristis*, like the rustle of dry corn.

Such restrained, dry kisses would be less threatening to the youngster, Catullus hoped. But it was no good. His kisses remained forbidden: 'If someone allowed me to kiss forever your honeyed eyes, Juventius . . .' Even when he finally got close enough to give him just one, he could do little more than *steal* a kiss, to which Juventius responded with utter abhorrence. A single peck was enough to make the boy reach for a bowl of water to cleanse his lips, 'as though it were the filthy saliva of an infected whore' (Poem 99). Poor Catullus bemoaned the tear-rendering impact of the rebuff: 'Never again from this day forward shall I steal kisses.'

Worse still, he suspected that Furius and Aurelius, the same pair that shamed him for composing effeminate love poetry, were eager to acquire what he had failed to capture.

In Catullus' view, Furius Bibaculus and Aurelius were disreputable chancers. Furius was always pleading penury, despite the fact that he lived with his father and stepmother:

> Furius, you have neither slave nor savings
>
> Nor bug nor spider nor fire,
>
> But you do have a father and stepmother
>
> Whose teeth can even grind granite.

(Poem 23)

He had a villa of his own, but faced a mortgage 'fifteen-thousand-two-hundred steep' (Poem 26). Catullus imagined Juventius bestowing the 'wealth of Midas' upon Furius, 'that man, who has neither slave nor savings'. Furius' very name evoked the Latin for theft – '*fur*' – while Aurelius' came from the Latin for 'gold'.[16]

Aurelius too had ample time to chase after other men's darlings, cock in hand. Catullus' voice trembled in time with his bleating syllables, *metuo tuoque pene* ('. . . your penis, that's what I fear'). Brandishing again the vocabulary of rape, Catullus threatened Aurelius with a radish or a horridly barbed mullet up his bottom if he dared even to lay a finger on his darling boy; such was the traditional Greek way of punishing adulterers. In his collection, this poem appeared directly before the scabrous Poem 16 ('I shall fuck you anally and orally'):

For your feet will be bound and your backdoor

Pushed open so radishes and mullets can run you through.

(Poem 15)

Catullus wished that his overbearing badinage would be deterrent enough. He need not have worried. Juventius ran off instead with a visitor from Pisaurum (a dilapidated Umbrian town Catullus had little time for). The man was 'paler than a golden statue' (Poem 81) – golder than *Aurelius* – but Juventius did not mind. Of all men, Catullus could not understand why he chose the one he did.

His aggressive jibes at Furius' and Aurelius' alleged poverty and sexual rivalry succeeded in disguising the fact that the deeper source of contention between them was poetry. Catullus yearned to separate himself from Furius Bibaculus by courting comparison with his work. By describing his heavily mortgaged villa, he drew upon an earlier poem Furius had written about the mortgaged home of Valerius Cato, the grammarian and poet with whom Catullus shared a name.

The more Catullus thought about his rivals, the more he took the view that it was his prerogative to write as he pleased. He was a tireless advocate of his own freedom of speech, even if that meant that he would be the one to suffer its repercussions. In his heart he believed that his poems could be a helping hand to whoever found themselves evoked. In years to come, when Caesar was in Gaul, that belief would prove quite monumental.

Mindful of how quickly rumour spread, Catullus proceeded to turn his gaze to a certain Ravidus, whom he accused of provoking a dispute with him just so that he could become famous. He would be famous, Catullus drily assured him, since he chose to love his lover (which one he did not say). Ravidus' fame would grow less from his love affair than from his being immortalised in Catullus' poetry. For Catullus it was a safe investment. There would be immortality for his rival, albeit of a kind he would resent, and immortality for him. For each and every man and woman who achieved fame through his verse, Catullus knew that he inched nearer to immortality himself.

Furius Bibaculus once lamented the futility of studying literature if one's memory will only fade in old age, but Catullus wrestled more with the prospect of being forgotten by the world itself.[17] In his poetry, he described several threats to man's enduring name, not just a 'spider spinning thin web' across it, but 'thick rust', and 'time, flying over the ages of forgetfulness' (Poem 68). Not content with leaving his legacy in the hands of the virgin muse and his dedicatee, Catullus aimed to cheat death through the permanence of work.

THE POWER OF THREE

Then Peleus is said to have burned in love for Thetis.

Then nymph Thetis did not disparage a wedding to a mortal.

Then father Jupiter himself felt that Peleus ought

To be joined to Thetis in matrimony.

(Poem 64, lines 19–21)

IN THE HOT SUMMER OF 60 BC, when Catullus' affair with Clodia was at its height, Caesar returned from his governorship in Further Spain. Steadily, he approached the *pomerium*, the sacred boundary that demarcated the city of Rome, inside which no burials were allowed to take place for fear of religious corruption or 'pollution'. As soon as a soldier crossed it upon his return from battle, he lost the military authority with which he had been endowed to perform his service. Caesar hovered here.

He did not have long before he had to declare himself a candidate for the consulship of 59 BC, which he was required by law to do inside the city itself. He waited and waited, mindful that should he canter forward across the *pomerium*, his military powers would be forfeited and, with them, his chance to celebrate a triumph for his work in the province. He calmly sent a request to the Senate that, in light of the circumstances and timing, he might be allowed to declare himself a candidate for the election there and then.

The politician Quintus Lutatius Catulus, whose father's portico Catullus had passed on his way up the Palatine Hill, had recently died. Cato was proving himself just as vocal and conservative a senator as he had once been. Ever the stickler for protocol, he spoke at such length in the Senate House that there was no time to hold a vote on Caesar's proposal. He hoped that by talking out the duration of the meeting, filibustering, he could reclaim some power for the house from its ambitious magistrates. More generous senators knew that Caesar ought to have had his way.

He now had little choice. Gritting his teeth in defiance, Caesar decided to forgo his shot at the triumph and cross the boundary line into Rome in time to declare himself a candidate. From where Catullus was standing it would have been difficult to tell who was the more perturbed: Caesar, for being so trampled on, or the dour Cato who smugly believed that he had safeguarded Rome from the most ambitious potential consul it had ever seen. Given the opportunity he had lost, there was all the more reason for Caesar to ensure that he was successful in the election. Metellus Celer and Lucius Afranius would give up their consular seats to whoever had won the most votes. As always, it would be the elite who held the most sway. Voters would be divided into blocs according to their property status, and voting stopped when a majority was reached; the richest placed their vote first.[1]

Catullus, more interested at this stage of his life in people than politics, could not help but notice that Caesar's electoral agent and backer for the elections, Arrius, was quite a character. From humble beginnings he had risen to wealth and prominence simply by being a hanger-on.[2] He was self-important, and vacuously so. There he was, hobnobbing with Caesar, clearly expecting that he would have the chance to achieve a consulship of his own in due course. For as long as he still valued his prospects, he determined to make the right impression. As Catullus observed, Arrius had even altered his voice:

> Chonvenient, Arrius would say, whenever he wanted
>> To say 'convenient', and hambush for 'ambush'
> And then assume that he had spoken magnificently
>> After he had said hambush as much as he could.
> I suppose his mother and his freedman uncle spoke like that,
>> And his maternal grandfather and grandmother too.
>
> (Poem 84)

In earlier times, Romans had sometimes aspirated their vowels, lending them an 'h' for effect. Recently, the aspirate had been enjoying a comeback. The fashionable elite in their faux-plebeian affectations had even taken to aspirating some of their consonants, transforming words such as *cicada*, into *khicada*.[3] Given her preference for the plebeian pronunciation of her name 'Clodia' over the rich vowels of 'Claudia', Catullus could not have been surprised if his lover followed suit. As much as he liked urbanity, there was such a thing as taking it too far. Catullus could not get over quite how excessively Arrius used the aspirate in his speeches, even where there was no place for it. The young man was evidently doing all he could to make his language appealing, but could not get it right. Not only was his family poor, but his try-hard manner of speaking was ludicrous. Catullus' mockery did not help his confidence; it made an even greater fool of him than he felt already.

When it came to Caesar and his drive for the consulship, Catullus was comparatively restrained. He did not fear reprisal, but felt that nonchalance, or even blunt dismissal, would be a better way of deflating the politician's ego. The strategy was typical of him, for he never made his political leanings explicit in his verse. In the coming years he would find occasion to criticise the populist politics of Caesar and others, as well as leading optimates. For the moment, just an acerbic couplet acknowledged Caesar's rise:

I have absolutely no desire to want to please you, Caesar,

Nor to know the smallest thing about you.

(Poem 93)

In Latin, this was particularly forthright. Catullus did not want to know whether Caesar was 'black or white' (tanned or pale-skinned) – an idiom Caesar would have found mildly offensive. Whether Catullus was purposely rebelling against the older generation or had some other plan in mind, nobody could say. His poem merely suggested that Caesar was not yet so powerful that he needed no introduction, but powerful enough to have expected people to desire his favour. Provided Caesar knew that he was not among those sycophants, Catullus was happy.

Among the crowds of Rome, there was some sympathy for Catullus' provocative detachment. If some people suspected that the poet's words were partly a reflection of his uncertainty over political developments, they were probably right. Caesar was manoeuvring in private. In silent studies and libraries lit by dripping oil lamps, he was shaping a triumvirate – a pact for power between three men: himself, Pompey, and Crassus. He had established a working relationship with Crassus, his ruthless money-lender who had slipped him the funds he needed to conduct his governorship in Further Spain. But Crassus expected something back. He had so far failed to satisfy the demands that equestrian businessmen were making for compensation for their lost investments in Asia and Bithynia. Caesar had supported Pompey in the past, and in return for Pompey's help now, could promise to help him satisfy his veteran soldiers, who continued to press upon him for land and rights.

Although Crassus had long resented Pompey for winning triumphs when he had received merely an ovation for putting down Spartacus' revolt, Caesar was able to use his skills of diplomacy to bring them together. Holding out promises to pass Pompey's bills if he gave him his support for the election to the consulship, and to assist Crassus in satisfying the equestrians if he did the same, Caesar acquired the influence he sought.

The Senate tempered their fears over Caesar with the hope that Marcus Calpurnius Bibulus, a son-in-law of Cato, would be capable of holding him in check as he was elected alongside him to the consulship. In an attempt to protect their authority further, the senators ruled that the consuls would receive merely the *silvae callesque*, the 'woods and tracks' of Italy, as their province for the following year, rather than the traditional foreign command.

Soon enough the crowds were speaking of the 'consulship of Julius and Caesar'. Bibulus, a lame duck, found himself powerless to act as Caesar ensured that Crassus' disgruntled equestrians were appeased. Violently usurping the rights normally reserved for the tribunes of the people, and not without considerable opposition from the Senate, Caesar passed his own agrarian laws in order to redistribute the land required for Pompey's veteran soldiers.

Catullus found little poetic inspiration in such agreements. Of all the progress the triumvirs made in the early months of 59 BC, he acknowledged just one. To those who were familiar with his work the choice was hardly surprising: Pompey, who had been single since his divorce from Metellus Celer's flirtatious sister Mucia, now wed Caesar's daughter Julia.

While Catullus dallied with Clodia beneath the bedspread in Allius' house, Julia and Pompey languished in the countryside and spent delicious evenings together by the fire. Catullus was quite taken with their fevered romance. Pompey was by all accounts an enthusiastic lover; women had been known to leave his bed wearing the imprint of his teeth.[4]

Pompey and Caesar, as Catullus wrote in a poem, were now *socer generque*, 'father- and son-in-law' (Poem 29). Aeneas' father, Anchises, would echo Catullus' words when he described Caesar and Pompey to his son in Virgil's great epic.[5] Cicero buried his head in his hands, convinced that the union was evidence of Pompey's plans for a dictatorship. Meanwhile, Caesar, having renounced his scandal-marred marriage to Pompeia, took a new wife: Calpurnia, the daughter of an influential senator.

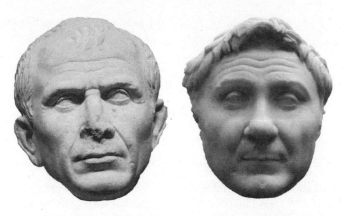

'Father- and son-in-law', Julius Caesar and Pompey the Great.

For now, Catullus had another politician to contend with: Metellus Celer, Clodia's long-suffering husband. The three of them were trapped in a triumvirate of their own. Metellus had just retired from his consulship and would soon be setting out again for Transalpine Gaul to take up a senior command. If Catullus wanted to succeed in persuading Clodia to love him alone, then he needed to use this time to understand what she saw in her husband. Once he knew what Metellus' good qualities were, he might stand a chance of undermining them.

Catullus made little room for the husband in his verse, however. As the other man, Metellus failed to emerge from his poetry as more than a two-dimensional shadow, too imperceptive to realise that his authority and masculinity were under threat. In Poem 83, the three of them stand together in a room. Clodia begins to rail at Catullus, as if his attentions are a nuisance, an embarrassment to her, and as if bitter words would really assuage her of the fact that she is, for all her many protestations, feeling something for him:

> Lesbia says a lot of cruel things to me in front of her husband.
>> The dolt finds considerable happiness in this.
> Mule, do you have no feelings? If she had forgotten me and kept quiet
>> She would be cured. But since she barks and abuses
> Not only does she remember me but – this is far more piercing –
>> She is angry. This is how it is, she burns, and she talks.
>
> (Poem 83)

Possessive, demanding, and determined to make public his lover's allegiance to him over the 'mule' she is married to, Catullus places himself between the married couple, *Lesbia mi praesente viro*: Lesbia, Catullus, Metellus Celer. His poem reads like a lesson in logic, an impassioned speech of an orator who classifies feelings as facts. All that is missing is a witness, and without one, Catullus' testimony is in danger of falling flat. He could raise his arms to the sky, pace the room, and laugh all he liked at the dolt's lack of perceptiveness, but his confidence depended upon his own ignorance. There was no one else there who could confirm how vacant Metellus was, or the real reason he smiled.

It was Catullus who risked being construed as insentient, for believing his rival so easily convinced of their innocence. Anyone who saw this poem would suspect that his lover's husband knew a lot more than he was prepared to let on. Catullus might have misread him, but his reader, anxious for what would happen next, was left hoping desperately that he had not.

Despite the fact that his wife was having an affair with a young poet, Metellus Celer was, according to Cicero, looking in remarkably good health. He had been seen in the Forum, planning his departure for Gaul. He knew it would be a long journey and a difficult posting. Caesar was looking in this direction, too. Disappointed at the prospect of governing the inglorious woods and tracks of Italy when the year came to an end, he saw a law passed by the people granting him an army and five years in which to govern Cisalpine Gaul (an area incorporating Catullus' own Verona) and Illyricum in the Balkans, from where he would be in a strong position to wage a great war against King Burebista of the Dacian people (in Transylvania).

But then, suddenly, some grave news broke in the city. Metellus Celer had been found dead in his house on the Palatine Hill.[6] Nothing could have prepared his fellow senators for this shock. One moment he had been heartily planning his expedition to the north, the next he was lying lifeless in his bed. The unexpectedness of his passing should have numbed even the hardiest of souls, but it did not go unnoticed that his seat in Transalpine Gaul was now empty — and Caesar moved quickly to acquire it.

Perhaps Cicero was being dishonest when he recorded seeing Metellus looking so well hours before his death. He recalled this three years after the event, and in a speech in which he hoped to discredit Metellus' widow. Since no cause of death had been established, he had reached the conclusion that Clodia must have poisoned him. Catullus would never entertain such a ludicrous possibility, nor would anyone without a vendetta against her family.

*

For as long as she had been married, Clodia had been safe to speak to her lover as she pleased. Her marriage was, at its most rudimentary, her escape route whenever Catullus' affections became too intense. She knew that he loved her in excess of 'both my eyes', and that whenever he wrote those words he meant them as more than idle idiom, because the eyes were what separated the living from the dead. *Lumina* were not just 'eyes', windows of the soul, but 'daylight', and when night covered them over, the soul departed. Marriage had allowed Clodia to remain aloof from such intensity, and any other man in her life had been obliged to try to accept this. Now, all that changed.

There were occasions when Catullus found her willing to become more involved with him. He raised his hopes accordingly for something more than a short season of illicit romance. He had once portrayed himself and Lesbia as evenly matched, cursing each other because they were in love. As his anticipation grew, doubts began to seep in about her sincerity and the evenness of their feelings:

> You dangle before me, my love and life, the prospect
>
>> That this love of ours will be cherished and last forever.
>
> Great gods, make it that she can promise truthfully,
>
>> And say it sincerely and from her heart
>
> So that we may live our whole lives
>
>> By this everlasting pact of sanctified love.
>
> (Poem 109)

Looking forwards, to the skies, to the ground, he addressed her, then the gods, and finally themselves as a couple. The prospect of their affair becoming permanent seemed too good to be true. So Catullus tried to trap her with his words. In his poem, he called their relationship a 'pact' – *foedus* – a word which cut rather too close to marriage to have been accurate. For as long as he could not literally have her as a wife, he pledged his commitment to her in absolute terms. He was, in effect now, her 'husband'. For the time it did not matter that a pact between two people required two signatures to be valid. It was possible to live part of a life, if not a whole life, he thought, in the hope that an 'everlasting pact of sanctified love' would one day be verified. He deluded himself into believing that this day was now imminent.

His hope transcended emotional manipulation. Marriage was the cog by which society turned, particularly among the elite, who had seen many a feud buried before now by a lucrative union and merry occasion. A wedding offered at least the semblance of stability, and in turbulent times, this was often as good as it got.

The formality and familiar rhythm of the rites held almost as much appeal as the institution itself for Catullus as a bachelor poet, who found something of that steadiness in the measured procession and choral song, and the steady shower of nuts sprinkled like confetti, and the predictability of the bride's departure from mother's bosom to groom's embrace at the end of the wedding banquet. Marriage was on his mind, and the hymns he now proceeded to compose for it were among the first to have been written in Latin. They embraced a tradition that spanned the distance from Homer's contemporaries via Sappho to Callimachus to the Roman ceremony itself.

He had received a commission to write such a hymn for the wedding of one Lucius Manlius Torquatus, the son of a former consul, whose family had long pledged allegiance to the optimates, and his bride Junia Aurunculeia.[7] Etching his tablet with joyful words, Catullus summoned Hymen, god of marriage, to attend the maiden as she put on her saffron bridal cloak and slippers. She might have been fourteen, or even younger. Catullus gave her some encouragement as her bridesmaids escorted her to the hall of her father's house, and her right hand was placed in the right hand of her husband. The groom was some years older than his bride, and although unlikely to have been a virgin, Catullus sang just as optimistically of his faithfulness as hers. He would not fall into the arms of another woman, but be entwined with her like tree and vine in wedded pleasure. Some marriages were founded on love, and these were the only kind Catullus wished for.

Should Catullus ever marry, his wedding day would run much like theirs.[8] After the joining of hands, families and guests would gather together to perform a sacrifice and enjoy a feast. There would be a wedding cake, which would be offered to Jupiter. Anticipation would mount until the evening star, Hesperus, raised its head and beckoned the *domum deductio*, the procession home.

Traditionally, the bride would struggle in staged resistance (sometimes she had needed little assistance in her acting) as a band of boys removed her from her mother's side to lead her to her new husband's home. By candlelight, the boys would target the groom with nuts and 'Fescennine jesting' – rude jibes to set him on the road to marital sex and mark a departure from the encounters he, like many men from elite households, would have enjoyed with other boys through adolescence. A wedding bed awaited the newlyweds, once the groom had carried his bride over the threshold without faltering. An older woman would turn down the bedspread before the young couple attempted to fulfil their wedding hymn's desire for children to be their heirs and carers when they grew infirm:

Close the doors, virgins,

We have played enough. But

Noble husband and wife,

Live well and devote your youthful

Energies to the deed repeatedly.

(Poem 61)

Catullus hoped that Manlius Torquatus and his bride would have a son who resembled his father in looks and mother in virtue. Telemachus, son of Odysseus and Penelope, was a worthy paradigm against which he could be measured.

As if to make it known to his lover that he understood how far the female experience of marriage differed from the male, Catullus wrote a second hymn. It staged a competition between young maidens and boys. The boys feared that the girls were more diligent in their song rehearsals, and the girls lamented the loss to the virgin sisterhood that evening summoned. No sooner did the girls voice these laments than the boys, in their quarter, balked that a bride's resistance was pure theatre:

For when you come the guard is always vigilant,

At night the thieves hide, and often you turn back on them,

Hesperus, you catch them as your name turns to Dawn.

But the maidens love to carp at you in contrived complaint.

But why, if they carp, do they seek you in the silence of their hearts?

Hymen, o Hymenaee, Hymen come, o Hymenaee.

(Poem 62)

Presenting male and female viewpoints consecutively, boys then girls then boys then girls, Catullus revealed how far they differed. He could not help but empathise more with the female experience. He compared the virgin to a hidden flower in a garden, untouched by flock or plough. A plucked or fallen flower was unattractive, but a flower kissed by sun, rain and breeze was what 'many boys, many girls desire'. In his *Metamorphoses*, Ovid would use almost precisely the same line and expressive word order as Catullus to describe not a girl but a boy, Narcissus.[9] A girl's maidenhood was a third her own, a third her father's, a third her mother's, until, with her dowry, her husband got purchase on it. Although this was a woman's rite, Catullus lived to bear testimony to how far a man could comprehend it. In years to come he would compare his own love to a fallen flower at the edge of a meadow, grazed by a passing plough.

Ever partial to role play, Catullus now fantasised that Lesbia was harbouring hidden desires to wed him over everyone else, Jupiter included.

My lady says that she would rather marry no one

But me, not even if Jupiter himself were to ask her.

She says, 'But what a lady says to a lover in the moment

Ought to be written on the wind and running water'

(Poem 70)

Unfortunately, the first line of his poem, 'My lady says that she would rather marry no one', seemed to convey more truth than the full sentence, carried into the next line, 'But me'. No woman could honestly have desired feckless, vengeful Jupiter as her husband. He made the most libidinous lovers of the Republic look like emaciated ciphers. The very comparison undermined the logistics of a marriage, as it suggested that she was no more likely to marry Catullus than the king of the gods himself. And yet, for a time, none of this mattered.

Catullus knew that pillow talk was rarely any different. The inaccuracy or implausibility of a lover's words rarely diminished their appeal in the moment they were spoken. He took inspiration for these final lines from an elegy by Callimachus, and another included in Meleager's Greek anthology. Callimachus had described a boy who swore that he would never love anyone more than his girl, but fell in love with another boy: 'He swore; but it is true when they say that vows to a lover cannot reach the ears of the immortals.'[10] In Meleager's poem a forsaken lover complains that the man who promised her (or him) that he would love her 'now says that those oaths are carried on water'.[11] In Catullus' version, Lesbia usurps the male role. With some foresight, Catullus renders himself the vulnerable woman. When he composed his Bedspread Poem, he lent a variation of this poem to his heartbroken protagonist, a woman, as she spoke of a man who betrayed her trust. Furius and Aurelius, his rivals, were right. Catullus was not immune from emasculation. But it did not come from writing of kisses.

As for his own relationship, Catullus was fooling himself if he believed that marriage would legitimise the affair, or even be a possibility. He could blame this at first on his lover's grief and the decorum of her mourning. All around them, tears were being shed for Metellus Celer. In the outside world, Pompey was proposing to the Senate that Caesar should be the new governor of Transalpine Gaul, and by January 58 BC, the Senate caved. Caesar added this command to his responsibilities over Cisalpine Gaul and Illyricum, laying the road for his Gallic War – a road that would thread past Catullus' home in Verona. But Catullus could barely bring himself to care. He could not help but think that something else was adrift.

I HATE AND I LOVE

If a marriage to me was not in your heart

Because you feared the savage reprimands of your aged father

You might still have led me to your home

To be a slave to you in a joyous labour,

Washing your white feet with pure water,

Spreading your bed with a purple bedspread.

(Poem 64, lines 158–63)

CATULLUS WAS HANGING torturously from a cross, *excrucior*, weeping at the point of its intersection. On the vertical arm lay hatred, on the horizontal, love. Love and hate were his beginning and his end, his torture. The two lines which scored him through became two lines on his tablet:

I hate and I love, why do I so, perhaps you ask?

I do not know, but I feel it, and I am crucified.

(Poem 85)

In the heat of his conflict, he found it impossible to know why, or even how he could be feeling both emotions at once. Clinging to the memory of love made it last; hate consumed. Neither made it go away. They cut his heart like a cross. The battle was a hopelessly internal one. The 'you' of the first line of the couplet was the wounded poet, facing his reflection, trying to pull himself together. No friend or reader of his poetry could clarify his predicament better than he could on an empty page.

Love and hatred he saw as equal forces, but founded in different time zones. Hatred is forward-looking. The pangs of an injustice formerly felt have lasting impact; some things are impossible to change. Love carries one far more pleasurably backwards into a passion enjoyed when there is no need for questions and it convinces, if momentarily, that it would be easier to start anew from that point, drowning out whatever passed between. Both love and hate require forgetfulness. But memory is what drags the mind through both, one and the other, to and fro, and explains why only time can defeat the torment.

It had come to him as if from nowhere, two thoughts colliding like chariots on a blood-strewn racetrack. His lover had been unfaithful not only to her husband, but to him, and to an extent that he could not tolerate.

*

Not long after Metellus Celer's death, and before the traditional mourning period had expired, another young man had climbed the Palatine Hill. It had been raining, for there were small puddles on the path, into which the dew streams dripped from the grass borders. Delicate tracks left by a discreet predator, feathers, the passing interest of gulls overhead, were otherwise all that remained of the night before. Oblivious to them all, Clodius Pulcher stood in the doorway of the grand villa he now owned there, and let the man in. Smiling charmingly, his visitor enquired whether he might rent from him one of the luxury apartments that adjoined his house. Seeing that one was vacant, and that 10,000 *sesterces* rent money was never to be sniffed at, Clodius nodded in agreement, and welcomed his new neighbour.[1]

The man's name was Caelius Rufus. He was tall, handsome, young – Catullus' age – and Catullus' friend, if the 'Rufus' Catullus described in Poem 77 as his 'friend and ally' was indeed him. He had a clear complexion and sported a fashionable little beard.[2]

Cicero put it on record that Clodia was fond of little beards. Men of old, including her distant ancestor Appius Claudius Caecus, wore long beards, but ever since the first barbers entered Rome from Sicily in about 300 BC, most Romans – but not prisoners or mourners – had tended to be clean-shaven.[3] The beard that Clodia so adored was less in the style of the Greek philosophers and more like face topiary (garden topiary was also new in Rome at the close of the Republic). The young men who wore these beardettes were not harking back to Greece so much as aligning themselves with the *déclassés* who could not afford a regular shave. (In Poem 59 for example, Catullus smirks as he passes a woman snatching dinner from funeral pyres whilst being 'banged by the half-shaven cremator'.)

Like Catullus, Caelius Rufus was equestrian by station. He was born in Interamnia (modern Teramo, north-east of Rome), but had been in Rome long enough to know its ways. He was still a boy when his father, ambitious for him to pursue a political career, sent him to the city to study under Cicero and enjoy a guardianship under Crassus. In recent times he had done Cicero serious discredit by being among those who fell prey to the lure of Catiline and the revolutionaries, but had since redeemed himself by pursuing his own career ambitions. As if this was not enough to raise Catullus' hackles, he was a natural writer, adept at combining shrewd observation with witty anecdote. In his older years, Cicero would depend on him to keep him informed of senatorial decisions in his absence from Rome.[4]

Catullus and Caelius had a lot more in common than age, status, and literary skill. Caelius' father, too, was wealthy and well connected. He had business interests in the Roman provinces – in his case Africa – and these could help him to pay his son's rent on Clodius' property on the Palatine Hill.[5] Caelius had already taken the opportunity to travel there as part of a cohort, and was probably still abroad when Catullus first arrived in Rome.

The Rufus Catullus once defined as his friend and ally had 'crept up on me, ripped like a flame through my guts, and stolen all I had from me' (Poem 77). At some point, maybe when he was completing negotiations over his new home with Clodius, he had become acquainted with Clodia. Caelius Rufus and Clodia walked in the same gardens and shot each other furtive glances in the umbra of the trees. They were together, and they were otiose, and all Catullus could do was picture them from his cross, where he hung on the arms of love and hate, like a prisoner undergoing his death sentence.

As early as the seventh century BC, a Greek lyric poet, Archilochus, had written about hate and love, only for a later poet to modify his sentiments into something Catullus knew well: 'I know how to love the man who loves me, and I know that if someone wrongs me, how to hate him.'[6] Yet for Catullus, love and hatred were not so black and white. For him, it was not a question of loving some people while hating others. He had found himself in a far more vexing situation, a love-hate relationship in which his feelings were directed at one goal, neither an enemy nor a friend, or both an enemy and a friend.

Catullus never paused to consider the possibility that his lover had not intended to be cruel or insensitive, or to lead him on. Nor did he believe that her promises of enduring love were, in fact, accidents of love itself, proof that even more than unmixed wine, love loosens the tongue. What struck him now was that he had been blind. The woman was not so much frightened of marriage, but of a commitment, to him, altogether.

In happier times, her sparrow had bitten him, and become his. Resigning those voracious bites to memory, he pictured it, a *miselle passer* – 'poor little sparrow' – a diminutive that, as so often, conveyed not size but pathos. The sparrow was travelling 'that shadowy path from which they allow no return', or as Lord Byron translated it: 'Now having past the gloomy bourne,/From whence he never can return' (Poem 3). Catullus' verse was overblown, ridiculous, but not even his humour could veil his sadness. He looked at his sparrow, and it was dying.

The disorder of the love poems in Catullus' collection only intensified the picture of Clodia sleeping with both him and Caelius Rufus, on and off. It gave the impression that they were not the only ones, either, but the poems were enveloped by such a thick fog of jealousy and angry resentment, of love and hate, that it made it impossible for a reader to imagine what Clodia's version of events might have been.

He compared the happy past with the sorrowful present. When she spoke of her preference for marrying him over Jupiter, he had loved her as a father does his sons, not as a man does his mistress: *diligo*, as opposed to *amo*. At that time, or so she said, he was the only man she knew intimately. But now, that had changed:

> Now I have got to know you. So even if I burn more deeply
>
> You are still much cheaper and less significant to me.
>
> How can that be, you say? Because such a wound compels a lover
>
> To love more, but to like less.
>
> (Poem 72)

The emergence of other lovers, or the sudden ability to see ones who had been there for some time, might have heightened Catullus' jealous desire, but it simultaneously laid him low in despair. It made him love and hate. Had he been told that, between him and Caelius Rufus, he would suffer the lesser fall, he could never have believed it.

'Cheap' was the perfect word for his new vision of Lesbia, not just because it highlighted her promiscuity, but also because it undermined her wealth. Catullus had apparently been given to believe that the husband was the chief obstacle in this equation for love. As and when he had been taken out of it and the solution still failed to materialise, the discomforting truth became manifest. In a sorrowful moment of self-recognition, he realised that he could never be – could never have been – a serious contender for this patrician woman's hand. His love was, by the one measure that counted in Roman marriage, too cheap.

He knew better than to believe the gossipmongers who continued to circulate rumours of an incestuous relationship between Clodia and Clodius. It was obvious that it had only been since Lucullus tainted her sister's name in court that idlers had characterised all three sisters in the same way. But at this moment of heartbreak, the whispers illustrated a convenient truth. Hurt and desperate, Catullus threw his lot in with the muckrakers and wrote that Lesbia preferred her own brother to him and all his countrymen. With a flourish of four lines, he struck – and unveiled Lesbia's identity:

> Lesbius is handsome Pulcher. How couldn't he be?
>
> Lesbia prefers him to you and all your people, Catullus.
>
> But let the handsome one sell Catullus and his people together
>
> If he can find three kisses from the people he knows.
>
> (Poem 79)

The revelation depended upon a pun on her family name. Cicero often called Clodius Pulcher 'pretty boy' – a play on his name *pulcher*. And so Catullus began 'Lesbius is handsome' – *Lesbius est pulcher*. It could not have been much clearer: 'Lesbius' is 'Pulcher' made 'Lesbia' one of Clodius Pulcher's sisters. The detail that Lesbia would prefer her own brother to him ensured that the reference could not be missed. Lesbia was the tempestuous Clodia with the oxen eyes.

Catullus' first concern was not to expose her, nor to jibe further at her family's alleged incest. His main point came in the third line: 'But let the handsome one sell Catullus and his people together.' For all his family's wealth in Verona and Sirmio, neither Catullus nor all his Gallic countrymen together could compete with one of the oldest families in Rome. Class meant more than money; *et pecunia olet* – money smelled of the hands through which it passed, poor, self-made, or veined with blue blood.

Catullus never acknowledged explicitly that by marrying Metellus Celer, Clodia had coupled with a cousin on her mother's side. He did not consider this incest; no one did. The Caecilii Metelli had risen to prominence many centuries ago through holding the top magistracies and seats in the Senate. Catullus could compare Metellus Celer's family with his own, and upbraid Clodia for what he interpreted as an intense social prejudice. He could fly in fury over the many great beauties of his age who prostituted themselves with despicable men in the name of lucrative marriage contracts, and frown desperately at the faces of the grooms with whom he was expected to exchange kisses in the Roman fashion. But he could hardly substantiate his argument of Clodia's prejudice when she had such plebeian tastes. The simple fact was that it was less painful for him to accept rejection on grounds of his social standing than of his personal attractiveness.

He needed only to look at the brother she was closest to, Clodius, who was doing all he could to sever his ties with the elite entirely. In his quest to attain a tribunate, the lowly seat at the bottom of the political hierarchy, he had married Fulvia, the daughter of a wealthy plebeian family. The union was shrewd: Clodius had purposely married beneath himself, because it was to the plebeian class that he needed to be demoted to run for the seat.

*

The period surrounding Metellus Celer's death had witnessed Clodius' plans gather pace, causing Catullus to rail at him, as well as Clodia, in his revelatory Poem 79. If only by associating her so strikingly with her increasingly prominent brother, he could find the empathy he so desperately desired. Clodius, everyone knew, was perceptive, underhand, and had a way of picking precisely the right moment to strike a deal. He also benefited from a certain amount of luck. He had long grown frustrated by Metellus Celer's haughty refusal to grant him the demotion he needed, and found himself instead promising to support Pompey and Caesar in return for this change of status.

Caesar must have felt ground down by Clodius' persistence, as well as by the aggressive rhetoric Cicero was employing to undermine his consular policies in the Senate. Anxious to silence the garrulous orator, he passed a motion to transfer Clodius to the plebeian class.[7] In a bizarre turn of events, Pompey and Crassus agreed: Clodia's brother was adopted into a commoner family as the 'son' of a twenty-year-old man. Through befriending Caesar and plying him with requests, Clodius had achieved the first stage of his plan.

Catullus might have invoked Clodius to 'sell Catullus and his people together', but if anyone sold out it was Clodius, who thence had little trouble in attaining the second stage of his plan: the tribunate. The triumvirs could only wince as they witnessed him reverse his promises. Since forming their coalition, Caesar, Pompey and Crassus enjoyed less support than they had had as individuals, and Clodius now wasted little time in cutting loose from the group. Caesar and Bibulus handed down their consulships to the new candidates for 58 BC: Lucius Calpurnius Piso Caesoninus, who was the father of Caesar's new wife Calpurnia, and a man named Aulus Gabinius. The aspirate-loving Arrius, who failed to receive the support from the triumvirs he had expected, bellowed that the consulship had been 'stolen from him'.[8]

Making the most of his new authority as a tribune, Clodius suggested in a popular assembly that Caesar had been out of his depth – and his rights – in passing the legislation that he had during his consulship of 59 BC. Two of the fairly senior magistrates of the year, the fiercely optimate Lucius Domitius Ahenobarbus and Gaius Memmius, now questioned the legality of Caesar's acts, but the leading members of the Senate failed to reach agreement.

Clodius understood even better than Caesar the power of the lower classes. With little eye for the long term, Clodius tried to buy them off with the free distribution of corn and by legalising the *collegia* (effectively guilds or unions). Thanks to him, politicians could now employ bands of whomever they pleased to help them win elections. Without a police force in Rome, it would be difficult to handle the consequences – but that was not Clodius' problem.

At the end of his Bedspread Poem, Catullus laments: 'All things speakable and unspeakable, muddled together in evil fury, have turned the just minds of our gods away from us.' To found such observations required little more than a glance at the rival gangs which now lined Rome's passageways. In fact, Clodius' staunch acts had precedent in a previous generation, when, in 133 BC, a tribune named Tiberius Gracchus decided to override a veto supported by the Senate and bring legislation directly to the people,[9] in order to support farmers who had fallen on hard times after overseas service. The fallout resulted in his murder. His brother, Gaius, had scored greater successes ten years later when he introduced subsidised corn and drafted legislation (albeit in-effective in his own day) that rendered it illegal to execute or exile any Roman citizen who had not first been represented in court. Like his brother before him, he paid for his politicking with his life.

Still, as Catullus looked out across the city and reflected on his own sorry predicament, he found no reason to doubt that these were the very worst of times. Clodius seemed to be clinging to Gaius Gracchus' spirit as he set forth a bill that would allow people to outlaw any citizen who put other citizens to death without trial. Even past incidents could be investigated. Clodius' opportunity to punish Cicero for his treatment of the Catilinarian conspirators had finally come.

Privately, secretly, the triumvirs were willing to see Cicero removed from public life. At the very least, the senators would be so horrified and distracted by the event that the triumvirs might pursue a more *popular* policy. Caesar threw Cicero a half-hearted lifeline, saying that he could accompany him to Gaul. But Cicero was too in love with Rome to leave. When Cato, the most obstructive optimate of them all, also left Rome in order to help oversee the annexation of Cyprus, it was clear that the Senate's walls were weakening.

Pompey paused for a moment. In the quietness of his study, alone with his thoughts, he experienced something close to a crisis of conscience. Cicero had written to him in the past, addressing him as a friend. There had been times when Cicero invested in him his hopes for reconciliation between the Senate and its magistrates, to put Rome back on an even keel. There was a knock at Pompey's door. Outside, a group of men, dispatched by Cicero, stood poised to ask Pompey to intervene. Clodius had surrounded the Senate with armed bandits, rendering them powerless to act on Cicero's behalf. Cicero assumed that they had abandoned him, that his wealth and intellect meant nothing, his humble birth, everything. Pompey could not bring himself to converse with the men in his doorway, nor to sit there, as their desperate pleas fell upon his doorstep.[10] He was a son-in-law of Caesar now, and that was where his loyalties lay. He made his way to the other end of his house, and slipped out through the back door.

Cicero, whose name translates as 'chickpea'.

Cicero left for exile in spring 58 BC, and grew his beard long, like a mourner. With so eminent a legal career behind him, he quickly became a symbol of justice. Catullus' reflection that 'everyone put justice to flight from his grasping mind' (Poem 64) would prove to be poignant. As far as many men could see, Cicero, and with him justice, had been cast out.

For many months, Cicero confined himself to Thessalonica (Salonika, Macedonia). Weight fell from his frame. He had left behind a wife, young son, and the daughter he admired most of all, Tullia, 'the image of me in face and speech and mind'.[11] He wrote a tearful letter to his friend Atticus: 'Has anyone ever fallen from so significant a station, with so good a cause, with such ability and talent, resourcefulness, favour, and with such great support of all good men?'[12] Word then reached him that Clodius' legislation had been passed. If he were to come within 3,200 *stadia* (around 600 kilometres) of Italy, he risked punishment by execution. There was nothing left to do. From Thessalonica, he progressed to Dyrrachium (Durrës in Albania), the prostitute-ridden 'market-place of the Adriatic' to wait it out (Poem 36).[13]

That same spring, Caesar left for Gaul. The Celtic Helvetii tribe was trying to move west into Transalpine Gaul, savaging peoples friendly to Rome and potentially endangering the province. Caesar seized the opportunity, marched his men towards the area where Geneva now lies, and blocked the Helvetii's path. No sooner had he engaged them in battle than other tribes were asking for Caesar's help against hostile Germanic tribes. One move was sufficient to secure him a war. As he gazed out across the territories of Gaul on the other side of Rome's province – in what is now the north of France, Belgium, Luxemburg, the near side of Germany – Caesar saw the key to funding his continuing career and achieving the particular glory that accompanied Roman conquest.[14]

Catullus' old rival Furius Bibaculus, who had teased him over the effeminacy of his love poetry, turned his hand to composing some *Annals of the Gallic War* to mark the occasion. It would be some time before Catullus felt impelled to engage poetically with the same theme. He was still young, still unstrung by heartbreak.

While the city's politicians hurtled onwards, Catullus grew ever more introspective. He wrote of feelings, and sought reasons.

Looking down on the armour he lacked, he urged himself to 'be strong'.

Left alone with his imaginings, he sought vengeance through literary release. Overcome increasingly by hatred, he wrote poems in which he cast Lesbia in the guise of a harlot. He made no secret of the fact that his poems hindered reconciliation with the woman they vilified:

Annals of Volusius, shit-smeared sheets,

Release a vow on my girl's behalf.

For she vowed to holy Venus and Cupid

That if I were restored to her

And ceased to circulate torturous iambics

She would give the choicest writings

Of the very worst of poets to slow-footed Vulcan

For burning in the merciless flames.

(Poem 36)

Clodia had vowed to burn 'the choicest writings of the very worst of poets' (meaning Catullus) if he ceased to circulate his 'torturous iambics' about her. She would even welcome him back into her arms. Catullus jested that he would gladly see the 'shit-smeared sheets' of a certain Volusius burned, which he was confident the poet Clodia would be familiar with.

He had lost count of how many people had complained about being ravaged by his poems, but he remained resolute. Catullus simply was not prepared to place limits on his own freedom of speech. His lover's pronouncement on him as 'the very worst of poets' made a more lasting impression than her actual request. The torture of loving and hating in unison, Catullus showed, applied not merely to the heart, but also to the writer's hand and voice. His poems about Lesbia became harsher and more explicit than ever before, and there was nothing she could do about it.

Anyone may shoot off cruel lines in the heat of the moment, but it was difficult for a woman to shake them off once they had been circulated. Clodia would have a difficult time trying to extract herself from the grip of gossip crafted by intelligent men.

There is no saying that Catullus ever did find a solution to the vicious circle of loving and hating that inspired these cruel verses. He would not even be so fortunate to have much in the way of time to release him from its torment. But certain events did alter his perspective on his relationship, and cast it in new light. One message in particular was enough to drive him far from Italy in early 57 BC. His family needed him to come home to Verona at once.

Catullus wore a toga and tunic adorned with the narrow purple band of the equestrians, which is visible in this portrait by the writer's right arm. Candidates running for political office in Rome whitened their wool togas with chalk.

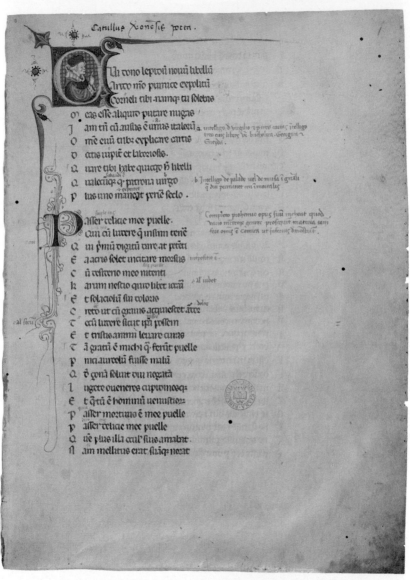

A manuscript of Catullus' poems, discovered just after 1300, disappeared –
but only after copies had been made. This page, showing Poems 1 and 2,
is from manuscript 'O', thought to date from fourteenth-century Verona.

A seafaring scene from the site of Catullus' villa at Sirmio. On his travels, the poet sailed over the Aegean, which was home to the old man Nereus, his wife Doris, and their fifty daughters, the Nereides, among them Thetis. Men lived in hope that the watery nymphs would come to their assistance should they encounter trouble at sea.

Hymen, god of marriage (seated beside the bed), was the handsome, slightly effeminate, son of Apollo and a Muse. Summoned to weddings from at least the fifth century BC, he was an inspiration to the bride, pictured here on the bed, veiled, her saffron wedding cloak ready beside her.

The sale or distribution of bread. Ancient round loaves, like those displayed in this painting, have survived to this day, preserved by being carbonised during the eruption of Vesuvius in AD 79. Examination suggests that ancient bread would be too densely textured for modern tastes.

The work of fullers – the dry-cleaners of ancient Rome – included treading clothes in cleaning agents, such as urine, rinsing them in vats and treating them, sometimes with sulphur.

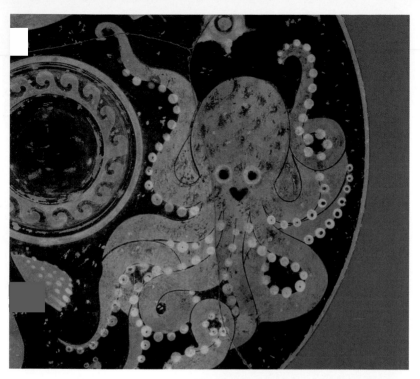

Many a man succumbed to an obsession for seafood – and this obsession could prove an expensive one. Writing in the next century, Pliny the Elder found it ludicrous that 'cooks are being bought for the price of three horses, and fish for the price of three cooks'.

The Athenians celebrated Theseus as their founder king. In his Bedspread Poem, Catullus recounted how the Minotaur demanded the flower of Athens' youth to feast on, until Theseus sought the help of Ariadne, the Minotaur's half-sister, in navigating a labyrinth to kill him.

During the April festival of the Megalensia, eunuch priests of the Great Mother were allowed to wander Rome, begging for money. No male citizen of Rome was allowed to enter her priesthood.

Inspired by Catullus' description of a bedspread adorned with scenes of ancient myth, the Venetian artist Titian painted his *Bacchus and Ariadne*. The snake-enwrapped man at the right of the canvas was based on an ancient sculpture of Laocoön, who warned the Trojans not to trust the Horse.

The punishment of Prometheus, which Catullus alluded to in his Bedspread Poem, was often confused with that of the sinner Tityus during the Renaissance. While Tityus had his liver consumed in the Underworld, Prometheus was generally thought to have suffered the same punishment atop the Caucasus.

Catullus wished that his lover Lesbia (Clodia) would give him as many kisses as there were grains of sand on Cyrene. In this painting of Baiae, Clodia's favourite beach resort, the artist J. M. W. Turner showed not Clodia but the Sibyl of Cumae, who famously asked Apollo to grant her as many years of life as there were grains of dust beside her. She would live long, but age like Baiae.

A magnificent cryptoporticus ran through the monumental villa on Sirmio. It provided its residents with much-needed shade on this sun-soaked peninsula on Lake Garda, or 'Benacus' as the Romans knew it.

VIII

FAREWELL

But first I shall free my heart of countless laments,

And pour soil over my white hair and defile it with ash,

Then hang dyed sails from my bending mast

So that sails dipped in Iberian rust may proclaim

This grief of mine, this blaze in my head.

(Poem 64, lines 223–27)

SOME NEWS INVITES NO REACTION, no breath, no sound. With nothing to see, one opens one's eyes slightly and listens to the blood pumping through the ears as the jaw stiffens. Then a pain shoots through the front of the head, like an explosion before the eyes; the whiteness is so dazzling that one is forced backwards, a step, two steps, intuitively grasping backwards. One still has not breathed, so one does, but the motion pushes the heart still higher, and then the nausea comes. And then the blaze in the head. This was the pain Catullus could not describe when he heard that his brother had died.

His brother had travelled to Asia, years before, perhaps to gain grounding for a political career. And now, somewhere near the plains of ancient Troy, he had perished. A million *stadia* away, on strange soils, lay his remains, his mute remains. He had been stolen from him, and for what? So his family could lament the injustice of his premature death, and the helplessness of being so far away?

In Verona, it was silent. When the rain began to fall, the men and women took cover in storage huts, and watched as steam rose from their roofs. The streets smelled of sulphur, and the dogs were maddened by it.

The river, infected by the sky, seemed to suffer for the down-pour; the drops, continuous now, like the bars that divided beast from spectator, were an impediment to its spate. In the distance, the shadows of cypress trees, weeping like the metamorphosed heroines of some half-forgotten myth, bowed beneath the breeze. Only the stone of the deserted Ponte Pietra gleamed with the whiteness of babies' teeth. It could have been night.

Work had paused on the new building sites. The ground recently cleared for a new forum was fast becoming a mud bath. The holes dug for new gates had once again become soil. Piles of sodden bricks and familiar pinkish stone lay abandoned, a gift for errant bandits.

Catullus pushed past the slaves who had gathered in his door-way, and found his way inside. He did not leave the house for some time. Days would pass as if in darkness, while sleep brought nothing but pain. His skin was mottled with cold, regardless of the hour. He did not, could not, write of how his family fared in this sorrowful household, only of the approaches of friends, who meant well, but were burdensome. Try as he might, he simply could not countenance the comparison they offered between love-loss and loss.

Since the seventh century BC, if not earlier, the Muses had been endowed with the powers to banish grief.[1] When acquaintances suggested to Catullus that he divert his pain to poetry, their words somehow still felt ill-considered, and untimely. He could not see how he could welcome the Muses into his home when he was in so much pain. He was battered by the sleeplessness of bereavement, drained 'by a grief that never ends', an anxiety that summoned him 'away from the versed virgins' (Poem 65).

But then he remembered how fervently his brother had persuaded him to pursue the things he loved; he thought of all the interests which his 'sweet love encouraged' so long as he lived (Poem 68). It was then that he began to listen to his friends, for he perceived that they were thinking of his brother, not him. They made him realise that there was no other way that he could pay his brother homage now but by clinging to these interests with all that remained of his heart. And so Catullus made a vow; and when his friends heard it, they knew that he had seen the light (Poem 65). He would sing always of his brother's death, and with those songs, with those poems, realise his legacy.

This did not stop Catullus from being apologetic about writing. He worried that his ability to do so in such circumstances rendered his distress less convincing. Determined, however, to do as he had resolved, he set about meeting the requests he had received from two of his friends for poems. The first came from 'Hortalus', Quintus Hortensius Hortalus, an orator and senator, who was probably a family friend.[2] Rather than attempt a new composition for him, Catullus decided to return to his roots, and did as he had done thousands of times as a youth. He set his hand to translating a Greek poem into Latin.

He explained to Hortalus, in the poem that formed the cover-letter to the piece, that he was providing him with a translation of a work by Callimachus, so that he had something. It was a close translation, too, to judge by the traces that remain of the end of Callimachus' *Aetia*, from which Catullus sourced his passage. Perhaps Hortalus was bewildered by the theme at first. The poem was written from the viewpoint of a lock of hair that belonged to Queen Berenice II, the wife of Ptolemy III Euergetes of third-century BC Alexandria. But closer inspection yields some subtle comparisons with Catullus' own sorrowful predicament, and a political debate that was now raging at Rome over the status of Egypt's rule.

The Romans had long been in awe of Alexandria. Since the time of Caesar's consulship in 59 BC they had recognised Egypt as their friend and ally. The brother of the current ruler, Ptolemy XII Auletes ('The Flautist'), had been king of Cyprus until a host of Romans, including Cato, reduced it and he committed suicide. In the upheaval, Ptolemy's subjects had driven him from his throne. Desperate, he hastened to Rome to seek help in reclaiming his power. The Alexandrians would send their own embassy to Rome to plead with them not to restore him. The usurped leader would give orders for the violent overthrow of the rival embassy, and the debacle would not be settled until a hefty sum had swapped hands to secure a Roman invasion to restore Ptolemy.[3] By the close of the decade, he would be sharing his throne with his daughter, Cleopatra.

In his poem for Hortalus, Catullus reflected on the distant, more dreamlike history to this episode, which starred the earlier ruler, Ptolemy III and his queen, Berenice. Ptolemy and Berenice were cousins, and together represented a united Alexandria and Cyrene. Catullus must have read the tales of how Berenice had found her husband rather too fond of dice. A slave would be reading him aloud a list of criminals eligible for the death penalty, it was said, and Ptolemy would be gambling away. He would give his summons, but seldom raise his head from his game to do so. When Berenice told her new husband that he should be paying closer attention to his responsibilities, he was delighted, and obeyed her.[4] Soon after their wedding he decided to invade Syria, leaving his bride to pray that he would return safely. If he did so, she pledged, she would dedicate a lock of her hair at a temple of Aphrodite.

Return he did. Catullus described in his poem the subsequent apotheosis of her precious lock as a constellation in the sky. It was Conon, the court astronomer, a man Callimachus described as charting 'how the stars appear', who fixed it in the northern hemisphere, just as Catullus defined it.[5] Astronomers still refer to the tress-shaped constellation as *coma Berenices*, 'hair of Berenice'.[6]

Through the persona of the lock, Catullus drew on the closeness of the newlyweds. While the lock lamented its separation from the queen's head, Berenice mourned separation from her husband.[7] Berenice was said to have assisted in the assassination of a former partner in order to gain power, an act Catullus considered a 'good deed', because the man had committed adultery with her mother. Even though he had cuckolded Metellus, adultery remained, in Catullus' eyes, the worst of crimes.

Catullus might have found little here to alleviate his sorrow, but this was not the only opportunity he had to see how far poetry could assuage his grief. Manlius, the young Roman patrician for whom he had written a wedding hymn, now wrote to him in Verona, requiring a poem. Catullus' prayers for marital bliss for the couple had foundered: Manlius told him in his letter that he endured a 'shipwreck' of a marriage and a loveless bed. The page he entrusted to Catullus' hands was soaked in his tears and anguish.

Catullus made no secret of how troublesome it was to respond to Manlius' request. He fought strongly the compulsion to write, and had a long list of excuses. Just a single crate of manuscripts had followed him from Rome ('that is my home') to Verona, and even if he had more, he believed that no one should have expected anything of him. Though flattered that Manlius considered him a true friend, Catullus felt that this was not the time for him to cheer his spirits. He might have sensed that Manlius could do well enough without him. Though he would die at war before he could achieve his ultimate ambition of becoming a consul, Manlius Torquatus would rise to the praetorship and outlive Catullus.

After all his protestations, however, Catullus' passions wound their way back to Rome and into Manlius' hands. As so often his refusal to write a poem made a poem in itself. It resembled a letter, and Catullus used it to acknowledge, politely, Manlius' lack of tact. Not only had he sought Catullus' sympathy in his letter, he had also decided to bring Catullus up-to-date with events since he had left Rome:

So when you come to write 'It is shameful to be at Verona,

Catullus, when this man, one of the better sort,

Warms his chilly limbs in the bed you left behind',

That, Manlius, is more than shameful, it's pathetic.

(Poem 68)

Catullus did not explain to Manlius, or indeed to Hortalus, how his brother had died, but in letter-poems to both he provided a clue between the lines of his Latin. His brother's body, he wrote, was buried beneath or near the shoreline of Rhoeteum, a promontory just above Troy:

Troia Rhoeteo quem subter litore tellus

ereptum nostris obterit ex oculis . . .

He the land of Troy buried beneath the Rhoetean shore,

Stolen from my eyes . . .

(Poem 65)

Litore, from *litus*, was shore; *tellus* was land. *Litus* could be used to mean shore or territory more widely, but the way Catullus laid it next to *tellus* showed that he sought a contrast between the two. The image poignantly evoked the Homeric picture of soldiers drawing up their ships and waging battle on bloodied Trojan soil. Yet, his insistence on being 'drowned in the waves of fate', and on his household being 'buried' since his brother died (Poem 68), made it seem as though he was intentionally transferring epithets between his brother and himself. Subtly, he was insinuating that his brother had died at sea, that his body had been washed up, and was buried on the shore of Rhoeteum. Manlius had been tactless indeed to describe himself as having endured a 'shipwreck' in his letter.

If only inadvertently, the death of his brother had put Catullus in a new poetic mood. His poem for Manlius (Poem 68) is haunted by the emotional consequences of separation. It is as fractured and fraught with turnings and dead-ends as any of his works to date. He probably wrote it in parts, at different times, as separate poems, which scholars later sewed into one. It was only the first part he addressed to Manlius. The second half contained a retrospective thanksgiving to Allius for providing him with a safe house in Rome to pursue his affair with his mistress, but even in this part he paused to grieve for his brother.[8]

He tells Manlius that his brother's death has stolen all his enthusiasm for love. At the same time, he is desperately seeking to come to terms with what it means to be just one of Lesbia's lovers. He hopes, with one part of his being, that he might yet be reconciled with her.

Here Catullus found at last a kinship between his sorrow for his brother, and his fluctuating feelings for Lesbia: 'our whole household has been buried', he laments, a strong suggestion that neither he nor his brother had yet had children.

He could not conceive of a future for his family now that his brother had died, childless, and now that his lover – former lover – was reluctant to love him alone. He would describe further the similarity between death and painful love in his Bedspread Poem, where a woman, Ariadne, prays that the lover who has forsaken her catches the same grief she suffered when he neglected her.

Catullus now saw little hope that his own father might hold a grandchild and mused on the happiness a new baby could give a more fortunate man:

Not so dear to a grandparent wearied by old age

    Is the child their only daughter feeds, born to her late in life,

An heir found at last for his grandfather's riches,

    His name put on the testament tablets,

Quelling the impious hurrahs of a relative now mocked,

    Putting to flight the vulture from the old man's head.

(Poem 68)

Catullus' father's fears over the inheritance of his properties and wealth could not have been any less pressing, and it was to Catullus' credit that, in these dire times, he recognised this. He could see now that, as the surviving son, he had to assume his elder brother's responsibilities. The loss had aged him, drawn a tragic line between the spring of youth, when he first tasted love, and the uncertainty of his family's future.

In Poem 68 he returned once more to the place his brother's body had been found, not far from Troy – *nefas*, unspeakable Troy – the 'common grave of Asia and Europe'. Catullus reflected on a further tale. The Rhoetean shore was where Ajax, the mighty Greek warrior of Homer's *Iliad*, was said to have been buried, while the first Greek warrior who died in the same war had been Protesilaos.[9] As Ptolemy III had abandoned Berenice (as Lesbia had abandoned Catullus), so Protesilaos had abandoned his new bride, Laodamia, to fight on Troy's battlefields. In his poem to Manlius, it was as if Catullus was insinuating that the moment Lesbia had faltered on the threshold, like Laodamia and the Trojan Horse, she had cursed his brother with the same early death as had met Protesilaos all those generations before.

There was nothing more to be done. In spring 57 BC, turgid with sorrow, red from weeping, Catullus boarded a ship for Bithynia, south of the Black Sea, not far from Rhoeteum. There was only one woman in the world who might have clasped his knees and convinced him to stay, but she did not.

A SEA OF
MACKEREL

Divine Minerva, her keep a citadel

In the city's heights

Streamlined the flying chariot to the breeze

Herself, weaving, joining the pines together

To form a curving keel.

She, the ship, inured the innocent sea

To the flight of ships.

(Poem 64, lines 8–11)

THE OARSMEN HAD MADE THIS TRIP a dozen times but, for all their familiarity with the route, remained reluctant to stray too far from the coastline. It was easy enough to sail down the Po and into the Adriatic. The risk came when their large galley glided past Greece and up through the Aegean towards Asia, where the waters and their hidden rocks could be prey to sudden storms, counter-currents, and the whims of inconstant wind gods.

It was 57 BC, and one of Rome's praetors of the previous year was gleefully en route to his foreign posting. Gaius Memmius, who was to govern in Bithynia, cast his eye over his entourage. There were plenty of strong young Romans here, who, by the looks of them, could not wait to gain the experience they required to ascend the political ladder. There was Cinna, with whom Catullus had whiled away many an evening over poetry and wine. And there was young Catullus, looking wistfully overboard.

Weeks of close confinement with a crew of ambitious men was never going to be easy. The squeal of the sail rope could barely drown out the petty disputes of its handlers. They itched their wrists, crusted with salt, their backs, wet with perspiration, and played over an internal dialogue to dull the moans of the vessel. The one consolation was that Catullus would be safer for the company. For all his emotional experience, he was still unworldly. If business acumen ran through his blood, it was yet to surface with much observable conviction.

In theory, Gaius Memmius would seem to be the perfect mentor for him: he claimed descent from one of the founding members of Rome, and had combined that with a lucrative and strategic marriage to Sulla's daughter, Cornelia Fausta. He had recently fallen foul of Caesar by being among the men who called into question the legality of the acts passed during his consulship in 59 BC.[1] He argued that Caesar should never have received com-mands in Illyricum and Gaul over and above the woods and tracks of Italy which the Senate had originally allotted him.[2] When there had been calls for Lucullus, Clodia's former brother-in-law, to be awarded a triumph for his campaigns against Mithridates, Memmius had been at the head of the opposition. The commander, he argued, had diverted too much property to his own advantage and for dragging out the war so needlessly could never be worthy of a triumph.[3] Though his efforts were ultimately in vain, Memmius had demonstrated his willingness to fight.

Memmius was strong-willed and not afraid to speak his mind – both qualities Catullus admired in a person. He even had proven literary interests. He wrote poetry and patronised it, and in return received a book dedication from the philosopher Lucretius. His name crops up sporadically in his six-volume work on the fundamentals of life, the *De Rerum Natura* ('On the Nature of Things'), inspired by the teachings of Epicurus, the Greek philosopher.

But as Catullus was quick to see, being interested in just about everything did not necessarily make Memmius very good at anything at all. He knew a fraud when he saw one, especially one that had the presumption to consider himself a poet.

Memmius had tried his hand at writing love poetry, and although he was not short of romantic encounters to draw upon, it was obvious that he was more interested in making a name for himself than writing from the heart. According to Ovid, who had the opportunity to read his poetry before it was lost, the verse was crude, in more ways than one.[4] Memmius flexed his oratorical muscle with somewhat more skill, but Cicero, who rightly considered himself an authority in the field, said that his efforts left much to be desired.[5]

Catullus was right to be suspicious. Years after having his name embedded in Lucretius' book of Epicurean philosophy, Memmius contemplated levelling Epicurus' former house and garden in

Athens for a new building project.[6] Cicero, though never the most fervent Epicurean, wrote to Memmius to gauge his intentions over the site, which he knew was supposed to stay in the hands of teachers of the Epicurean school of thought in perpetuity.[7] Whichever way the dispute was eventually resolved, Memmius was clearly a fake who did not care a fig for the philosophy of Lucretius' book.

Catullus had to be grateful that he was not the only true poet in the entourage. Cinna would be good company, especially as there was only room for so many books in the deckhouse. An early draft of Lucretius' *De Rerum Natura* might have been among them.[8] Unlike Catullus, Cinna had travelled to Bithynia at least once before, and therefore knew what treats awaited them on those distant shores. Together, they were more than ready to mine the region for poetic, as well as pecuniary, gain. But first, they had to get there.

The Aegean stretched out before them, peppered with islands. Crete was the largest, but there was no telling this when they glided past its skinny side – the point of the javelin, not the full stretch. On Crete, men said, Jupiter's mother concealed him as an infant so that he might avoid the fate of his brothers and sisters, swallowed whole by their father, the god king Saturn, who feared usurpation by one of his offspring. It was thanks to the secure walls of a cave on Mount Ida here that Jupiter grew up to overthrow his father, and take his seat as the king of the immortals.

The island was home to the ancient kingdom of King Minos, whose wife, it was said, was inspired by divine lust for a bull. She instructed Daedalus, an Athenian master craftsman, to fashion a contraption shaped like a cow, into which she clambered, spread her legs, and had a novel kind of intercourse. The resulting child was the Minotaur. King Minos had him locked up in a complex maze, another piece of ingenious engineering by the great Daedalus. In the story Catullus would furnish in his Bedspread Poem, the Minotaur demanded the flower of Athens' youth to feast on until the Greek hero Theseus arrived and sought the help of Ariadne, the Minotaur's half-sister, in navigating the labyrinth to kill him.

On their ship, Catullus and his crew passed also the island of Naxos, where Theseus was said to have abandoned Ariadne after performing his feat. It was on a beach here, as Catullus would describe, that the wine god Bacchus clapped his lustful eyes upon the young princess for the first time.

Naxos, Melos, Delos: 'Eternal summer gilds them yet, but all, except their sun, is set', as Lord Byron observed in 'The Isles of Greece' for *Childe Harold's Pilgrimage* – and Memmius' crew might have given a similar description. Mithridates had laid waste to many of these isles, leaving their inhabitants in turmoil, and their more fortunate monuments clinging to their foundations. The colours of each charming mass, more islet-like than island, proved nonetheless a welcome reprieve in the midst of the dark velvet sea.

Catullus and his cohort might have changed ships for a smaller vessel once they neared the coast of modern Turkey. Decades later, during Emperor Trajan's rule in the early second century AD, the author Pliny the Younger travelled to Bithynia and tied off at Ephesus before embarking on lighter vessels to complete his journey.[9] On a second boat like his, Catullus could make his way past Lesbos, ancient home of Sappho, and progress up into the Hellespont.

Catullus paused here a while, and looked out from the poop deck towards the oyster-rich city of Lampsacus. In a poem attributed to him, he dedicated the place to Priapus, the fertility god famed for his impressive erection:

I dedicate and consecrate this place to you, Priapus,

Where your own home of Lampsacus lies, and where [*corruption*] Priapus.

For within its own cities the coastal Hellespont,

More oyster-rich than other coasts, worships you above all.

(Fragment I)

Given the erotic associations of the god, Catullus' poem was remarkably restrained and tightly focused. It was as if the novel sight of Lampsacus and its oysters touched him more at that moment than the divinity himself. Catullus was looking enthusiastically across the sea as he travelled through places he had only read about.

His ship swam steadily on into the Propontis (Sea of Marmara), where the waves trussed relentlessly at its sides, and other men's vessels passed like prowling tigers. Starboard was Bithynia. Port was Thrace, where the Romans believed the Bithynians had originated.[10] An ancient king of Thrace, Tereus, it was said, once concealed here his sister-in-law Philomela, raped her, and silenced her by removing her tongue. The woman revealed her tragic ordeal in a tapestry, and her sister, Procne, killed Tereus' son and fed him to his father for dinner. The gods then turned the troubled family into birds. Conquered by Philip II, father of Alexander the Great, Thrace remained a region of varied cultures and ethnic tribes.

As Catullus gazed out across the waters that divided them, he understood why the Thracians and Bithynians shared a passion for shipcraft. Each day, the Thracians trawled their woods and mountains and the Bithynians their forests of oak, beech, plane, and pine for timber. For generations, the men of Bithynia had prided themselves on their ability to load their majestic, beautifully carved vessels with heavy planks for export. Every time a ship passed their coasts, laden with timber – or marble – the townspeople would gaze out admiringly and nod: 'One of ours'.

Centuries ago, Sappho had summoned prayers in a poem for the safe journey of her brother Charaxus as he returned from a trading trip across the sea.[11] Catullus' prayers of the kind had been quite fruitless. The very invention of ships would shortly mark for him, in his poetry, the beginning of man's decline.

For now Bithynia remained full of promise. Following so many weeks of bailing bilge from the ship's filthy decks, that promise was more pregnant than ever as the crew beached their fat-bellied vessel, and began to make their way inland. Great fields brimmed with grain and greenery. The peaks of Mysian Olympus in the distance were still snow-capped, even though it was late spring. Baby crocodiles rolled in the spring at Chalcedon, a town that looked out across the water to Byzantium in the west.[12] Great throngs of people passed by a temple dedicated to the Great Mother, a goddess Catullus would one day write about.[13]

At Nicaea (modern Iznik), Bithynia's second city, Memmius established the group's headquarters. Measuring sixteen *stadia* in circumference, Nicaea was founded on a roughly rectangular plan with four gates and streets constructed on a grid system. So perfect were Nicaea's right angles that someone standing in the middle of the city's gymnasium could easily see every gate.[14] Nearby, the waters of the gentle Ascanian Lake oozed alongside laurels and hyacinths and blossoms. Assuming, for a passing moment, the language of Homer, Catullus described Nicaea's hot plains as 'udder-rich'.

Pompey had worked hard to transform the kingdom into a Roman province, but it still hovered somewhere between the two states. In the shadows of the wheat fields and makeshift enclosures on their borders lay the rust of decades of strife and broken spirits. For centuries kings had viewed the expansive territory and smiled proudly over the crops which looked, to foreign eyes, rich but monotonous. With the kings gone, Bithynia felt desolate. Nowhere was this truer than in Nicomedia, a little north of Nicaea, where the Bithynian royal quarters had been located. There was no one there now to thrash out proposals to the politicians of Rome, as had been their monarchs' wont; only empty halls through which Romans strolled, smiling silently at the scale of their new empire.

Convention dictated that Catullus should approach Nicomedia with solemnity, but that expectation was sufficient in itself to trigger sordid thoughts. As a poet who relished the opportunity to jest at another man's expense, it was difficult for him not to picture Nicomedia as the hallowed spot where Julius Caesar enjoyed his first, exceedingly shameful, sexual encounter.

Many years earlier, Caesar had taken up service in Bithynia under the governor Marcus Minucius Thermus. His particular instruction was to muster a fleet to blockade the port of Mitylene on Lesbos, which was siding with Mithridates in the wars. He did his duty, but dallied so long at the court of the Bithynian king Nicomedes IV that gossip quickly spread that he had become entangled in the royal bedsheets.[15]

Catullus' little poet friend Calvus, he of the bald head, wrote mockingly of 'whatever Bithynia and Caesar's sexual partner ever had', and others of 'the queen's concubine, inside partner of the royal bed'.[16] Seldom one to miss the opportunity to make a lewd reference, Memmius joined in and spread the rumour that Caesar had served as Nicomedes' 'cupbearer' at a debauched dinner party. The handsome boy Ganymede famously served as both cupbearer and beloved of Jupiter. It was far more entertaining to tell these stories than of how valiantly Caesar had performed in Thermus' service. Many would sooner forget the fact that Caesar had been awarded a civic crown of oak leaves for saving the life of another man.[17] The greater his success, the crueller the stories became. Cicero loved every moment of it. To think that the man who claimed descent from the goddess of love chose a foreign king to set him on love's path:

> He was led by attendants to the royal bedchamber, lay down on
>
> a golden couch with a purple bedspread, and the virginity of
>
> the man who was sprung from Venus was taken in Bithynia . . .[18]

It may have been nonsense, but that did not stop Caesar from having to swear on oath that it was not true, and Catullus from adding flame to the rumour whenever he so inclined.

Bithynia, however, was not the place to discuss such things. Memmius and his men had come to help govern it as representatives of Rome. They would smooth out the problems which were endemic to a new province, and ensure that Rome was receiving the full complement of debts owed; Catullus would examine the people's logbooks and correct their mistakes.[19] They had to make decisions about how to run the prisons, deal with the lawless and establish order across the province. Ex-convicts could be put to good use at the baths and in the sewers and on sites of public works, they just needed someone to organise them.[20]

Catullus would also oversee the construction of new sites and the rebuilding of old ones. When in circa III AD Pliny the Younger was sent by the Emperor Trajan to govern Bithynia, he would find a kingdom that had slipped into considerable disorder and disrepair. He wrote constantly to the emperor asking for advice, just as Pompey, who knew the region intimately, was now able to advise Memmius and his men. Pliny would find the main regions of Nicomedia, Nicaea, and Prusa clogged with unfinished projects: new temples, theatres, baths. Some of the sites had been abandoned by builders who lacked the incentive of payment to complete them, while others had sunk into the marshy ground. Bithynia was supposed to be rich in architects and tradesmen. Apparently few understood how to prevent subsidence.[21]

The image of Catullus drawing up columns of taxes and debts, documenting the costs of imports and exports, instructing the tax collectors to tighten their hold on the local land workers who shied away from paying their due, was that of a man considerably matured from the youth who sought only to 'confound', *conturbo* (Poem 5) the kisses he shared with his lover, as though they were loose coins on a banking table. The vocabulary he had subverted for his own ends became in Bithynia his daily reality.

Catullus disapproved of politicians who mined the provinces for their own gain. He was not, however, immune from hypocrisy, and hoped that this year might bring him some tangible profit of his own. Sadly, Memmius was a tough master. It was not long before Catullus realised that any dreams that he and Cinna and the rest of their party had shared of sailing the seas to pocket the rewards of a fresh province were to be dashed by the governor's strict regime. Besides, the ease with which they might have plundered the region advised against it. Many a man in Memmius' position had been convicted of extortion across Rome's provinces, including Calvus' father. There were people at home who could recall how eager Memmius had been to deprive Lucullus of a triumph after he profited from the same region. As much as he revelled in his position as the head of a noble entourage, Memmius was ever aware of how proud Pompey was of his achievements in this part of the world. The last thing the great man wanted was to see the successes he had had in creating this province marred by the behaviour of a subordinate.

It was, however, difficult for the young men in Memmius' cohort to adhere to such strict principles when Roman tax-farmers were pushing the province further into bankruptcy. Catullus must have seen the men who made it their responsibility to raise profits. One of them was Publius Terentius Hispo, a friend of Cicero, for whom the orator sent a letter of recommendation as he made his way to Bithynia from Italy.[22] His job was to collect funds in Bithynia and taxes levied at ports throughout the region.

Catullus managed to break from his duties and wander down to the Black Sea coast and the vast cold waters. There, in the distance, a waif-like man was casting a giant net into the air. It billowed, and touched down perfectly evenly on the sea's surface, like a crane coming in to land. Before long, a thousand mullet, mackerel, and baby tuna were streaming into the flaxen web, 'like battle ranks of the sea'.[23]

The anchovies and mackerel which flipped through the shallows had migrated there from the Mediterranean after the last Ice Age, when the Black Sea was merely a lake.[24] In spring, mackerel, the *scomber scombrus*, were in particular preponderance here, which was just as well because mackerel made the finest, and the most expensive salted fish sauce.

Bithynia and the Hellespont were famous for their salted fish. The Hellenes had feasted on pickled fish for centuries, and the Romans were fond of *garum*,[25] a coveted fish sauce that they consumed as a condiment with meals. Though it was expensive, watering it down with wine or olive oil meant that a little could go a long way. Most recipes only needed a splash, and not everyone was partial to it. Fish sauce had a habit of lingering on the breath and seeping through pores, and some men worried about whether they could sustain an erection if their girlfriends consumed too much of it.[26] Others complained that it gave them heartburn.[27] Rubbed on externally it was meant to have wide-ranging medicinal benefits, such as the wonderful ability to heal a crocodile bite.[28] It would have been wise to keep a bottle in the cabinet, as one never knew when such an eventuality might occur.

Making *garum* was a laborious process, as a surviving Bithynian recipe shows. It advises to take small fish, such as anchovies and mackerel, and put them in a bowl of the kind bakers used to knead dough, add six measures of salt per measure of fish, mix, and leave it in a clay pot, uncovered for two or three months – stirring occasionally. Then cover and store. To use it, add two measures of old wine per measure of fish mixture.[29]

Considering the intensity of the manufacturing process, it became increasingly attractive to import *garum* from sites where it could be made on a more industrial scale. The Valerii Catulli appear to have established themselves as importers of *garum* from Further Spain.[30] Catullus' descendants probably procured it from the first fish-processing plant there, which was situated at Baetica (Baelo Claudia) on the Atlantic coast. At the plant, the rooms for cleaning the fish received water pumped from underground pipes. Dirt washed down their sloping floors, and away. Near the shore, salting vats sat proudly in long lines, some rectangular, others cylindrical, each with smooth, mosaicked hollows. Men sold the salted flesh as it was. The rest — intestines, brains, blood — was piled into the vats and then fermented in the sunlight and great furnaces.[31]

As the salted fish fermented on the shore in the heat, the smell was indescribable. Only the 'polyp' did not seem to mind, as it snatched the odd fish prematurely from its vat and crawled off to enjoy it away from harm's reach.[32] What was left was carefully strained off into a sticky, viscous, but versatile sauce. With every drop of *garum* one mopped up with one's bread, it was possible to forget the stench of what went into it.

CANVAS

This bedspread,

Embroidered with the shapes of men

Who lived long ago, unveils the virtues of heroes

Through the miracle of art.

(Poem 64, lines 50–1)

THE BLACK SEA was more than a giant fishpond waiting to be drained. Men sailed its waters in the belief that they were reliving the adventures of heroes, feeling their pain at the oars and valour as storms tossed them off course. They strengthened their spirits with the promise of fulfilling immortalising deeds of their own on distant shores.

From Troy in the west to Colchis in the east, the coasts nursed rich mythological traditions. Catullus could almost taste them as he traipsed across Bithynia, the Roman province which remained decidedly pre-Roman in its details, the language its people spoke; the coins with thick Greek letters they passed between their fingers.

He had little reason to doubt that it was a place of immense literary virtue. His dear friend Cinna, with whom he was spending long days calculating taxes under Memmius' watchful eye, had done much to pique his interest when he returned from there a decade earlier, armed with the most exquisite literary affairs. In his hands he was carrying some dry mallow leaves, inked over with a Greek poem by a man named Aratus.[1] A few paces behind him stood a poet in the flesh, Parthenius. Cinna had found him working as a slave in Nicaea, where Memmius' cohort had their headquarters, and promptly freed him 'on account of his education'.[2] Some years from now, Parthenius would find himself tutoring a young Virgil in Greek.[3]

Catullus had to admire him. Like the poets of his set, Parthenius recognised the talents of the Hellenistic poets of the third century BC, and had proved himself their ally in his distaste for verbosity.[4] His poetry seemed to conform to what Callimachus preached: that a man should feed his sheep to be fat, but keep his verse slim. If they were not so long, perhaps he would have found Homer's *Iliad* and *Odyssey* somewhat better than 'pure filth'.[5]

Catullus would have been happy to welcome a man like Parthenius into his urbane coterie had he put Callimachus alone to heart, but the man's knowledge did not stop there. It was as though he had crept into Mithridates' private library in Pontus, the best part of which now lay on Roman floors awaiting reshelving, and absorbed its lessons until he was ready to make off on his own.[6] The books Mithridates owned included works of Stoic literature of the kind that would inspire Virgil when he came to write his great epic, the *Aeneid*. Parthenius was more interested in what love had to offer a broken soul and how much love he could pack into a compact verse. He had been busily engaged in composing a three-book work in honour of his late wife Arete.

Cinna had kept Parthenius close at hand ever since he freed him and embarked a short time later on a poem entitled 'Zmyrna'. He was still writing it, but already it was obvious that it was going to be perverse. Both Catullus' Bedspread Poem and Cinna's 'Zmyrna' were to be written in hexameters, as though they were epics. But war was the stuff of epic, not the forbidden, unnatural love affairs of princesses, the deeds of fallen heroes, forgetfulness, which filled the two friends' verses. Their comparatively short length would only undermine the epic form further. Both would be compact, such as Callimachus preached, and offer stories in miniature. Aspects of each would be obscure. Catullus and Cinna quite expected that commentaries would be written to render them more readable.[7]

The *miniature epic* seldom focused on the war and glory of Homer's poetry, but sometimes evoked it through its landscapes, characters, and details. Cinna's 'Zmyrna' described the birth of Adonis from a divinely inspired incestuous encounter between Zmyrna, a princess, and her father, the king:

Early morning Dawn caught you weeping

And the Evening Star shortly after saw you cry too.[8]

Cinna's Dawn was not 'rosy-fingered' like Homer's, but the picture of the stars watching the lives of men, found also in Catullus' Poem

7, evoked the spirit of his epics. That spirit faded as the story of Zmyrna's tear-wrenching predicament unravelled. After falling in love with her father in Cyprus, she metamorphosed into a tree. A first-century BC stone relief sculpture survives in a museum in modern Verona commemorating the life of a youth.[9] On horse-back, the boy approaches an altar and a tree that blooms with leaves, each of them pointing towards the sky. Cinna visualised in his 'Zmyrna' a tree that was pregnant with life. Adonis was born when the trunk split open after full term.

Cinna would only finish writing and editing 'Zmyrna' nine years after starting it. Catullus thought it was marvellous. While the *Annals* of Volusius, another poet, would go no further than the Po Valley and become 'shit-smeared sheets' (*cacata carta*) or wrapping for takeaway fish, Catullus boasted, Cinna's 'Zmyrna' was so compact and brilliant after so many years' editing that it would travel beyond Italy's borders to Cyprus, where it was set. 'The centuries grown old will still be reading Zmyrna' (Poem 95). He would be sorry to know that it is now lost.

'Zmyrna' would be the highlight of his career to date, but Cinna could not help but wonder what else was out there. A year abroad with Memmius was a valuable enough break from life in Rome, but would be far more valuable if used as a beginning rather than an end. If he was to have a political career, now was his chance to make himself look eligible, and this he did, with aplomb. Soon enough, Cinna would reach the tribunate at Rome.[10] If Catullus' father had similar ambitions for Catullus, now that his first son had died, nothing Catullus wrote suggested that he was remotely taken with the idea.

So there he stood, between Cinna and his political ambitions in Bithynia on one side, and the memory of Calvus on the other. Back in Rome, the diminutive poet of Io's metamorphosis was vainly searching for signs of hair growth as he galloped precociously forward in his legal career.[11] Proving himself an ever more capable orator through his dynamic legal speeches, Calvus showed that he had had little need of experiencing Bithynia with his two friends. Quite content to enjoy the region's exports from Rome, he thumbed Parthenius' scroll *On Painful Romances*, descriptions of unusual and tragic encounters.

It was comfort he sought from these passages, for sadly he had lost his beloved Quintilia before her time. Catullus must have felt a pang of guilt at having compared her so unfavourably to Lesbia: 'No grain of salt, in so large a frame.' As Parthenius mourned his wife's passing, so Calvus found himself trying to put into words his grief over the lover he had lost. He wrote a poem: 'Perhaps her very ashes may rejoice at this.'[12] Catullus, anxious to help, picked up the same metre, the elegiac couplet, and met him with a poem of his own to lament her death. For all his best efforts, he could not quite achieve the right note:

> If anything we place upon the silent grave
>
> > In our grief, Calvus, is ever received,
>
> Then through the longing with which we renew former loves
>
> > And weep for friendships once thrown away,
>
> I know that the early death of Quintilia is not so much
>
> > A source of grief but of joy for your love.
>
> (Poem 96)

A stable relationship was not something Catullus had known, nor, as far as he could imagine, would ever know. Parthenius might have written a wedding hymn that inspired Catullus' hymns of a kind (Poems 61 and 62); unlike Parthenius, Catullus had had no wife, but somehow he still felt like he had. He mourned her absence as though it was her loss.

His situation might not have been so tragic had the burden to prolong his father's line not fallen so desperately upon his loins alone. Many of the men he knew were married by now, fathers, too. No fears for them of growing infirm without a child to care for them in old age. As Catullus spent time in the place that Parthenius had once called home, he needed to accept that his future did not lie with Lesbia. While he gathered material for two highly erudite and compact epic works of his own, he had the opportunity to explore from a new perspective what love and commitment entailed.

———————

The starting point for Poem 64, his Bedspread Poem, lay between the landscapes and seascapes of the Black Sea coast and the Aegean, and Catullus' forebears' celebration of them in verse. He discovered particularly poignant episodes to draw upon in literature from the era following Alexander the Great. The *Argonautica*, an epic poem by Apollonius of Rhodes, was among the best of it. In wonderful verse it described the journey Jason and his Argonauts were said to have made across the sea in ancient times. The *Argo*, their ship, had featured in the poetry of Homer and Pindar, and took centre stage in a Latin poem by Varro, Catullus' contemporary and fellow Gaul.[13]

———————

Jason and his Argonauts were said to have plied the Black Sea, the 'Inhospitable', with cumbersome oars on a mission to steal the golden fleece of a ram once sacrificed to Jupiter. The fleece lay closely guarded in the coastal town of Colchis. At nightfall, the Argonauts reached the Caucasus nearby. Even if it had been light and Jason had craned his neck until his head rested on the burgeoning muscles of his back, their mountains would still have overwhelmed him. He needed to persevere. He knew that, should he make it back to his royal palace in Iolcus (Volos), south of Larisa on the east coast of Greece, he could present the fleece to the king and usurp him to become lawful ruler of his native land. To obtain the fleece, he would have to rely upon the help, the love, of the king of Colchis' daughter, Medea.

The story of Jason did not read like an attempt to glamorise an historical journey that no one remembered. History and myth were not necessarily so distinguishable. There were features on this landscape, aspects which were hard to pinpoint exactly, but lay over it like a fine fishing net, which made this part of the world look every bit the setting for Jason's experience.

There were, for example, men and women who rolled their leggings up above their knees and panned for gold using animal fleeces. The damp gold dust which clung to the coarse hairs of the sheep jackets made the myth of Jason's golden fleece seem rather more than mythical.[14]

Then there were the Caucasus, mountains so remote and fore-boding that it seemed plausible that they housed divine prisoners.[15] Jason and his Argonauts were said to have heard a terrible wailing as they approached them in their ship. Chained to the heights of Mount El'brus, in Greek *ho Strobilos*, 'the twisted one', the tallest mountain of the Greater Caucasus range, the Titan inventor god

Prometheus was believed to have been forced to feed his ever-regrowing liver to Jupiter's eagle for 30,000 years. He cried out in pain.

In earlier times, Prometheus was said to have stolen fire from the gods and carried it to earth inside the hollow of the fennel plant. Until that point, mortals had lived simple lives, with no work or illness. After Prometheus gave men fire, they worked and fended for themselves. He was remembered as the fire-giver and teacher of man's skills and, in a separate tradition, as a creator of men from clay.

Proving himself to be more cultured than many of his peers would give him credit for, Pompey was among the men who went in search of these ancient myths. The previous decade, as he made his pursuit of King Mithridates through the shadows of the Caucasus near Colchis, at the eastern extreme of the Black Sea, he had sought to learn about the place the Argonauts had visited. In particular, he wanted to see the spot where Prometheus was chained.[16]

The easiest way into the bowels of the Caucasus was via the Phasis river (River Rioni in Georgia), whose name evoked the pheasants (*phasianos* in Greek) which still visit its banks and turn the skies white with wings and errant feathers set loose in panicked ascent. Pompey crossed it.

Against these harsh rocks, he could picture Jupiter's ravenous bird flying overhead, as described by Apollonius of Rhodes, its beak dripping with Prometheus' viscous liver. Herbs grew here, watered, or so they said, by Prometheus' spilt blood.[17] Medea used them to concoct a balm to protect Jason's body from the monstrous creatures that guarded the fleece. Under Venus' spell, Jason and Medea became ill-starred lovers.

Catullus absorbed the mythological elements of the land-
scapes Pompey visited. He was intrigued also by the ship that
first approached them, the *Argo*, brimming with fine heroes, Jason
and his men. Its journey over the treacherous seas was difficult,
but humanly possible. The fifty-oared galley that Apollonius des-
cribed sailed up through the straits of Bosporus against a strong
counter-current to reach its destination.[18]

Catullus found himself struck by the image of the *Argo* crossing
the Black Sea in an age long passed. His predecessors, including
Apollonius of Rhodes, believed that other ships had sailed before
the *Argo*, but Catullus preferred to envisage the *Argo* as the first
ever ship. It might have sailed two centuries before the Trojan War,
in the fourteenth or thirteenth century BC, or centuries earlier.
Catullus could not have explored the bed of the Black Sea for evi-
dence of earlier ships, any more than a diver today can reach its
noxious depths to recover its ancient secrets.[19] He needed only to
imagine that there was a first ship like Jason's *Argo*, once. Between
the myths he had learned and his own taste of sea travel, he had
the material he required to describe what it might have been
like.

The flight of the *Argo* was only the beginning of a tale he had
been sowing, if only half-consciously, for years. In Rome, there
was admiration for the poet who could take a well-worn theme
and make it his own. During his travels across Rome's new empire,
Bithynia and its coastline, Asia, as well as the Cycladic-dotted
Aegean, Catullus saw first-hand the particular sights which drove
his story onto fresh ground. And it was in Poem 64, his greatest
masterpiece, that he gave them life.

They say that pines were born long ago

From the head of Mount Pelion in Thessaly

And swam the sea, its undulating waves

To Phasis, pheasant river, and

The land of Aeetes the king

As young men, plucked from the

Flower of Greek youth in a mission

To steal the golden fleece

Of Colchis

Dared to skim with speeding stern

The salt sea,

Sweeping turquoise waters

With oars upturned like hands.

Divine Minerva, her keep a citadel

In the city's heights

Streamlined the flying chariot to the breeze

Herself, weaving, joining the pines together

To form a curving keel.

She, the ship, inured the innocent sea

To the flight of ships.

No sooner had she torn the capricious membrane

With her beak and with a twist of the oar

Turned the waters white with foam

Than from the whitening whirlpool there emerged

The unpainted faces

Of nymphs glistening in brine and gazing

In wonder at so novel a contraption.

(Poem 64, lines 1–15)

Using the *Argo* as the starting point, Poem 64 opened with the vivid image of pine being born from the head – the peak – of Mount Pelion in Thessaly. The image of the birth of pine triggered the picture of the fabled birth of Minerva from Jupiter's head after he swallowed her mother to ensure that she could never deliver him a son to usurp his throne.

Minerva knotted together the Pelion-born planks of the *Argo currus*, 'chariot' – it was so novel that there was no word for 'ship' yet – which the sea would inure to water.[20] Catullus reflected the difficulty of a sea journey across the waves in the long, heavy pauses of the dactylic hexameter: *caerula verrentes abiegnis aequora palmis* ('Sweeping turquoise waters with oars upturned like hands'). It was the ship's maiden voyage, but the sea's maidenhead that was stolen by her flight. The lines echoed both Apollonius of Rhodes' *Argonautica*, and the *Medea* of Ennius, a Latin adaptation of the Greek tragedy, in which Medea ultimately came to wish that Jason had not sailed to her abode at Colchis.

Changing his focus from the *Argo* and its perilous voyage to one of its lesser-known sailors, a mortal named Peleus, Catullus soon found a fresh angle. In Apollonius' tale, Peleus had already married and had a son before he set sail. Catullus, by contrast, proceeded to describe the moment Peleus spied from the *Argo* a beautiful bare-breasted nymph, Thetis, emerging from the sea foam.

Her grandparents were Tethys, a water goddess, and Ocean, god of Oceanus, the river which men imagined encircled the perimeter of the earth. Poem 64 would be, in one part, the story of their subsequent marriage, and the prospective birth of their son, Achilles.

For centuries, the Greeks had celebrated the heroism of Jason and his Argonauts, and of Achilles and the warriors of the Trojan War. Through Achilles, Catullus would link the world of the Argonauts to that of Troy, as if creating his own epic, albeit in miniature form. The quests of these men belonged to the Heroic Age, the fourth in the sequence of five eras against which writers mapped their semi-mythical history.

Time, as Catullus and the ancient poets liked to contemplate, began with a Golden Age, an Edenic, peaceful paradise in which man did not work or venture overseas, but lived off the produce of the land which grew freely and amply. They lived in close harmony with the gods, free from disease, greed, and women.[21] There was no technology, so no agriculture, and no ships. Saturn was god and ruler.

Soon after Saturn's son Jupiter usurped him, the trickster Titan Prometheus intervened in the divine order by giving men fire and the means to acquire all skills, including shipbuilding. Catullus and later Horace believed Prometheus established seafaring among men.[22]

With his gifts, Prometheus symbolised the end of the Golden Age and laid the path for the next era, an inferior Age of Silver. This flourished until Jupiter felt compelled to overthrow it because its people failed to sacrifice to the gods. Following the violent Bronze Age was the Heroic Age, a respite from the downward spiral, welcoming the Trojan War and flight of the *Argo*. For all its glory, its Heroes perished, and the wretched Iron Age came about. It was in the Iron Age that the poets, from Hesiod, Homer's near contemporary, to Catullus and beyond, believed they lived.

When he came to write the end of his Bedspread Poem, Catullus chose to do so with imagery that evoked this miserable modern Iron Age:

> All things speakable and unspeakable, muddled together in evil fury,
>
> Have turned the just minds of our gods away from us.
>
> (Poem 64, lines 405–06)

Murder, adultery, injustice, and careless disregard for the gods were rife. Near the beginning of the poem, in contrast, Catullus praised the Heroic Age: 'Heroes, born in the moment most admired beyond measure of all Ages, godly race, offspring of a noble mother.' But he did not complete this work before he had experienced some second thoughts on the relative merits of each age.

Jupiter, Catullus remembered in his poem, had once desired Thetis, the alluring sea nymph, for himself. But as the playwright Aeschylus had revealed in a trilogy of tragedies put on in fifth-century BC Athens, Prometheus warned Zeus (Jupiter) of a prophecy that said that any son the nymph should bear him would be greater than him, and therefore capable of toppling his throne. In this family, sons had succeeded many times in usurping their god king fathers. Jupiter's father had castrated his father to snatch his throne. Venus was among the offspring born when his semen spilt in the sea. Saturn, after succeeding his father, swallowed most of his children whole so that none could usurp him. Jupiter, who was fortunate to survive when his mother concealed him in the cave, grew up to usurp his father Saturn. Against the backdrop of such a bloody family history, Jupiter was right to heed Prometheus' warning against coupling with Thetis. As it was, he had to swallow one wife and deliver their daughter Minerva from his head. Marrying Thetis off to a mortal was the only way he could ensure that history did not repeat itself.

The last time the divine order was overturned, with Jupiter's usurpation of Saturn, the Golden Age had segued to Silver. In Poem 64, Catullus flirted with the idea of what might have happened if Thetis the nymph had not married the Argonaut Peleus. Had Thetis had a child by Jupiter instead of Peleus, might another new age have taken root? The lavish wedding ceremony was taking place at a royal palace in Pharsalus, in Greece. Outside its grand walls, something close to a new Golden Age was beginning to unfurl:

Cieros was deserted, Phthian Tempe left behind,

The houses of Crannon, the walls of Larisa, empty;

They convened at Pharsalus, to Pharsalus and its homes

They flocked. No one tended the fields. The necks

Of bullocks grew soft through inactivity,

No curved scythe cleansed the soil beneath the vine,

No bull stooped beneath the yoke to cleave the earth,

No hook pruned the shade from the leaves of the trees,

Decay and rust overran the abandoned ploughshares.

(Poem 64, lines 35–42)

With his rich description and powerful tricolon 'no curved scythe . . . no bull . . . no hook', Catullus painted a teasing picture of the Golden Age trying, but not quite managing, to return. No one was tending the land, and the animals had grown idle, as they had been in the pre-agricultural Golden Age.[23]

No poet before Catullus had featured Prometheus at the wedding of Peleus and Thetis, but Catullus situated him prominently in the roll-call of guests, recently released from his chains on the Caucasus.[24] Before he gave men fire, they had enjoyed life free from work and travel. As an inventor of sailing, Prometheus therefore stood as a symbol of the post-Golden Age world.

Had Prometheus not interfered, and had Thetis married Jupiter instead, there might have been a new age. The moment just before the wedding that Catullus' poem was describing would have been the optimum time for such a change to take place. For all anyone knew, it might have been a new Golden Age that arose, albeit one that bore rust or tarnish like a memory of the bloodshed that had come before it. In subtle verse such as this, Catullus weighed the Heroic Age against the Iron Age present and Golden Age past.

The more Catullus thought about it, the more he determined to break away from his Greek forebears and their dogged admiration for heroism, or Heroism, at all costs. As he came to imagine in his Bedspread Poem, the *Argo*'s crossing might rather have been the beginning of the end. Thetis was not particularly enthusiastic about marrying a mortal when she could have had the king of the gods himself. She might not have had to wed Peleus if the *Argo* had not come. With every ship that sailed in the *Argo*'s wake came the risk of deaths at sea and beyond, of luxury sown by the desire and newfound ability to sample another land's treasures, and the need for men to labour at construction. If ships had never been invented, Catullus realised, life might have been simpler.

Set inside this story of marriage and decline, Catullus wove another layer of mythology. He digressed from the wedding to describe in a lengthy *ekphrasis* (literally 'a speaking out', a vivid description that formed a digression) the story embroidered on the *vestis*, the bedspread that covered the wedding bed of Peleus and Thetis. Its protagonists were a young princess Ariadne and the wine god Bacchus.

In the great treasure trove of myths Catullus kept to heart were tales of the fear Bacchus could instil in mankind. The kings of ancient myth shuddered at his wild influence over their subjects. In India, he quelled all who resisted his lifestyle. In Thrace, he experienced so violent a reception that he had to find solace in the lap of Thetis.

Catullus' bedspread was coloured brilliant purple with dye extracted from murex molluscs. Woven upon it were Bacchus arriving on the island of Naxos, and Ariadne, daughter of King Minos, gazing forlornly out to sea. The hero Theseus had abandoned her on the lonely island after she helped him to navigate the maze in which the Minotaur was imprisoned. Ariadne was mourning the sudden departure of the man she had loved. Bacchus had come to convince her to love him instead.

The bedspread was a visual web of words. It even had its own frame, adorned with the wedding tale of Peleus and Thetis. Few readers could picture a bedspread embroidered with as much detail and emotion as he described, but Catullus wanted to evoke more than two dimensions; he wanted to evoke an entire world. His bedspread wrapped around the ivory wedding bed of Peleus and

Thetis, ready for a night of passion. In true Alexandrian fashion, Poem 64 had become a story within a story: erudite, compact, a miniature epic of the type Parthenius and Callimachus and Cinna admired.

Poets before Catullus and poets after him might have viewed Theseus' desertion of Ariadne as the necessary sacrifice of a hero. In his Latin epic, the *Aeneid*, Virgil would have Aeneas make love to the beautiful Dido of Carthage and abandon her to complete his quest to found a new city for Troy's refugees. The episode would result in Dido's suicide, but underline in the course of the poem Aeneas' commitment to his people's future. The story of Ariadne's own sacrifice for Theseus had already become proverbial. In Apollonius' tale, Jason quoted it when he met Medea in order to persuade her to help him to acquire the golden fleece. Medea followed Ariadne's example, and even killed her brother herself in the process of aiding Jason. Catullus took a more revisionist view of the relationship between hero and lover. He could not help but sympathise with Ariadne's plight. The princess had abandoned her whole family to help a stranger she loved to achieve heroism.

Catullus described in his poem the moment Ariadne woke at dawn to witness Theseus' ship departing over the distant horizon. Her skin turned to stone and her heart to a tambourine. She was, Catullus said, 'like a stone sculpture of a bacchante'. She was the sorrowful inverse of Bacchus who arrived on the island of Naxos with a noisy throng, which Catullus described in a cacophony of heavy consonants and onomatopoeic frenzy, hurling the severed limbs of animals, beating shrill cymbals, *tereti tenuis tinnitus*, and drums, blowing horns.

He attributed to Ariadne a long speech, which his reader was to imagine was transposed upon the design of the bedspread. She prayed that 'with the kind of heart Theseus had when he left me', he might destroy himself and his family. Theseus had promised his aged father Aegeus before leaving on his quest that if he survived, he would change the black sails of his ship for white ones, so that his father could watch from the cliff tops and know that the returning vessel was carrying him home safely. In Catullus' poem, satisfying Ariadne's prayer, Theseus forgot these instructions, his father saw his black sails, and 'threw himself headlong from the top of the cliffs'.

> So savage Theseus entered a household
>
> Decked in mourning for his father's death
>
> And caught the same sort of grief
>
> He had imposed on the daughter of Minos
>
> Through the neglectfulness of his heart.
>
> (Poem 64, lines 246–48)

When he wrote poems for friends in the wake of his brother's death, Catullus had had to contemplate the kindred nature of love-loss and death. The fulfilment of Ariadne's prayer in Poem 64 equated again the death of a family member with the loss of a lover. In the earlier part of her soliloquy, Ariadne wept that Theseus had thrown all his 'promises unfulfilled to the tempest that is stirring'.

> These were not the promises you once made
>
> Me in a warming tone, these are not what you bade
>
> My wretchedness to hope for, but a happy marriage,

Longed-for wedding songs, everything
The errant breezes have scattered vain.

May no woman now believe a man when he makes a promise,
May no woman hope the words of her man are true.
While their minds are desirous, desperate to obtain something,
They are afraid of swearing nothing,
There is nothing they won't promise.

(Poem 64, lines 139–46)

Her sorrowful speech closely echoed the words Catullus put in Lesbia's mouth in a separate poem:

My lady says that she would rather marry no one
    But me, not even if Jupiter himself were to ask her.
She says, 'But what a lady says to a lover in the moment
    Ought to be written on the wind and running water'

(Poem 70)

Here Catullus is like the wounded Ariadne, while Lesbia is the callous Theseus figure.

On Catullus' bedspread, Ariadne was blinded by love. So, in the myth that inspired Apollonius and the poet Ennius, was Medea. But the whole world was blind to what it meant to love a hero, or a god. In some myth traditions, Bacchus, Ariadne's saviour, gave her a crown of stars, a constellation, then left her for another lover. Catullus alluded to the constellation in his poem about Berenice's lock of hair. In other myth traditions, Ariadne threw herself from a cliff. Even in myth, Catullus discovered, relationships seldom ended happily.

In the outer ring of his Bedspread Poem he found himself unable to remain optimistic about the future for Peleus and Thetis. According to most myth traditions, Thetis bore Peleus a son destined to be the envy of men for centuries to come: Achilles. But the whisper of divinity that flowed through Achilles' bloodline, Catullus showed, was also what caused mothers in their thousands to weep.

Catullus preferred to linger over Achilles' violence, not his Heroism, because in his eyes, the two were not necessarily connected. Homer and Homer's admirers might have upheld the glory of war, whilst recognising also the pain it inspired; but like the Greek tragedians, Catullus found in it something less than heroic. Just before the concluding encomium of the wretched Iron Age, the Fates appeared in his poem – hoary personifications – to sing a wedding hymn. At its heart was a warning for the havoc Peleus and Thetis' yet-to-be-born baby would grow to wreak. Mothers would beat their breasts in bereavement as Achilles hacked down young Trojans, 'as a reaper picks thick bundles of corn'. The Scamander river, which flowed into the Hellespont, would grow still narrower by the corpses Achilles would see pile up there. He would slay a virgin at an altar.

Achilles would never have been born had the *Argo* not sailed. Had Prometheus not reported the prophecy that warned Jupiter away from Thetis, perhaps their son would have toppled his father then spread not warfare but peace in a new Golden Age. With the coming of Rome's first emperor, Augustus, Virgil would draw upon Catullus' lines to pronounce a return of Saturn's glorious

Golden Age. Catullus' Bedspread Poem was panegyric in reverse. He entertained little optimism for the present or future, but little optimism for the second-best Age of Heroes in the past, either.

The greatest symbol of decline remained for him the ship. At the beginning of his poem, Catullus was explicit in describing the *Argo* as the first ever ship. Yet, on his bedspread, Theseus sailed away on a still earlier craft.[25] Ariadne wished this ship had never come. Catullus subtly placed his focus here, urgent for all to know that ships, symbols of the end of Golden Age living, could never truly bring glory or love, assurance of survival, or even, as he discovered at the end of his year in Bithynia, true material gain.

Carried through many nations and over many seas,

    I have come for this sorrowful funeral, brother,

To give you the final gift of the dead

    And to address your mute ashes. There will be no reply,

Since fate has stolen you from me.

    Poor brother, snatched from me unworthily.

But accept these sad offerings now, which are handed

    To the dead, in the ancient custom of our elders,

Much moistened by a brother's tears.

    For now and forever, brother, farewell.

(Poem 101)

THE BOXWOOD
ARGO

And so he put his trust in a light ship and gentle breeze

And came before haughty Minos

And his magnificent enclosure.

(Poem 64, lines 84–5)

AFTER HE HAD PAID his brother his last respects, Catullus made his way inland from the shore of Rhoeteum until he reached the belly of Asia. He had about his shoulders a large woollen cloak, which rode up as he walked and brushed obtrusively against his neck. His shoulders felt the weight of his baggage, in which he had stored his money, maps, and wax tablets. His bread had crumbed in its corners, and clung rudely to his fingers each time he reached inside.

It was a pity that he had such coarse fabrics and painful blisters to distract him from the beauty of the land. Without them, he might have forgotten he was mortal at all as he wandered over the vast, sheep-rearing country, dipping his toes into the River Lycus before it vanished into the earth, only to reappear several *stadia* away.[1] While Mount Ida thundered morosely into the sky, no wanderer could doubt that the stories men told were true: a formidable goddess drove a chariot through its luscious glades.

Cybele, the Great Mother, had been worshipped in Smyrna (Izmir) and across Asia since very ancient times as a bountiful earth goddess. The Romans had regarded her cult with varying degrees of reverence and abhorrence ever since they established it in their city in 204 BC in a moment of desperation. They were at war with Carthage (in modern Tunisia) at the time, a great power that had formerly controlled much of Sicily. The Romans had since taken the island and transformed it into a Roman province. Carthage's forces expanded into Spain while Hannibal, one of Carthage's most able generals, invaded Italy with a large army and elephants. Over many years, his forces had slaughtered tens, perhaps even hundreds of thousands of people across Italy. The Romans had been at a loss as to how to extricate themselves from his grip.

An oracle told them that, if ever a foreign enemy should invade, it could be overcome if the Mother was carried into Rome. No strangers to oracular riddles, the Romans understood that they needed to welcome the Great Mother into the city. While her spirit wandered Mount Ida, her body rested in Pessinus, in Asia, in the form of a stone.

They needed to receive the goddess in 'chaste hands', the oracle blithely informed them.[2] So they carried her over high seas past

Rhoeteum, Tenedos, Lesbos, Crete, skirted Hannibal's Africa, and passed into the mouth of Italy's Tiber at Ostia. The city's best men were waiting there, ready to beach her, but suddenly her ship faltered, trapped knee-deep in mud. It settled, Ovid said, 'like an island fixed, balanced, on the middle of the sea'.[3] A girl stepped forward. She was beautiful, though blighted by rumours of easy virtue. With a hearty tug at the rope, the girl succeeded in dislodging the heavy vessel and carrying the Great Mother safely to land.

The entrance of the strange, eastern goddess confirmed that the hands of the young woman were unsullied by any man. The Clodii Pulchri were said to be her descendants, as Ovid later acknowledged by describing the 'ready tongue' with which the beautiful girl spoke to 'severe old men', an allusion to Catullus' kiss poems for Lesbia.[4] It was a pity that Clodia did not have the same opportunity as her forebear to shed her own lascivious reputation.[5]

The Great Mother, whose powers were such that the Romans ultimately defeated Hannibal and the Carthaginians, travelled by chariot with lions and *Galli* — a rowdy band of self-castrated priests. With the exception of the goddess' eunuch priests, few could countenance such fanaticism as this. Instead, they celebrated the cult each April with an optimistic but comparatively restrained religious festival. The Great Mother's temple stood beside Clodia's villa on the Palatine Hill, but greater excitement was to be found at the games and lavish feasts around the city.

How a man could castrate himself was something Catullus

struggled to understand. The absolute commitment of the eunuch priests to the goddess' cult perturbed him, repulsed him, fascinated him. And to think that Clodia's family played a part in the cult's history. In Poem 63, Catullus took one of the goddess' followers, Attis, as his subject. In a rare and curious metre, 'galliambics', he captured the frenzy with which Attis castrated himself in logic-defying reverence to the cult, only to wake the next morning to regret it. As in his Bedspread Poem, Catullus drew heavily upon the strangeness of fresh landscapes and the ease with which they complemented the emotions of loss and heartbreak. As soon as Attis castrated himself to become the goddess' servant, Catullus stopped referring to him as a man. 'He' became 'she':

The moment Attis replayed in her mind what she had done

And clocked, clear-headed

    Where she was

What she lacked

She made her way back to the shore again.

Her heart was rippling.

Watching, there, a desert of sea with tears in her eyes

She spoke to her country in a voice that was sad, miserable, like this:

    'Oh my country, my maker, my mother, my country oh

How rueful when I left you, as runaway slaves escape their masters

So my feet took me to Mount Ida's groves,

To be mid-snow and ice-riven beast lairs

And to approach, quite witless, their dens in the shadows.

Where do I believe you lie, my country? Or on which plots?

My very pupils burn to turn their gaze to you

While for sharp season my mind is free of rabidity.

Am I to be uprooted from my home to these backwoods?

Am I to retire from my country, possessions, friends, parents?

Am I to retire from the forum, palaestra, racecourse, gym?

Helpless, helpless, heart, more, more, must you weep.'

(Poem 63)

In the frenetic rhythm of the piece, the play of short, light syllables upon the tongue and unexpected heavy beat intruding like a distant drum upon an orchestra of cymbals, a reader or listener could feel Attis' terrible sense of displacement. In severing a part of his body he had severed himself from himself and from the only life he had known. There was no way out, no way back. She could rove Ida's groves in despair, but could never escape from herself, her lack of self.

Catullus brooded empathetically on the inevitability of Attis' future, in service to an unfeeling female. He found again the sympathy he had felt over the plight of Ariadne as he pictured emasculated Attis dripping blood over the grasslands of Asia. In myth, one character had always to suffer in subservience to another, and Catullus had learned by now which pole he was more likely to be attracted to.

He might have taken years to finish composing and editing Poems 63 and 64, refining his allusions and inhabiting the world of his characters. In these poems, the landscapes of Asia and the Black Sea remained trapped in their past. Only when Attis lamented her departure from 'the forum, palaestra, racecourse, gym', did Catullus allow the landscapes of the civilised world to encroach upon the otherness of Phrygia. Although he might never have been able to write of these exotic places with such precision and passion had they not fallen to Roman control, he preferred to describe them as though he had experienced them centuries before they came within the burgeoning sphere of empire. In a later poem, he would document Rome's expansion across the globe with some excitement. For as long as he travelled the provinces through the lens of his mythological characters, however, he seemed to find no glory in their newfound Roman identity.

In the short term, his work under Memmius might have killed off any enthusiasm he might have learned to acquire for Roman expansion and conquest. While travels across Asia provided him with rich literary material, the work he carried out under Memmius did not interest him sufficiently to inspire a single poem.

Whatever his cohort achieved during its year on the Black Sea coast, the Senate decided not to extend Memmius' command there, as they had that of his predecessor, who had remained in Bithynia for up to three years.[6] Catullus did not care. Memmius had long struck him as a selfish leader, a man who would do anything to protect his own interests. Why, he had prevented his men from making any profit at all from the province. By his own admission, Catullus had taken to recording his expenses as profits in his account books, as if to make himself feel better when he looked at them (Poem 28). He did so, he wrote, 'following my praetor's example'. It later transpired that Memmius had a habit of fiddling his own accounts. In 54 BC he would attempt to bribe his way to a consulship for the following year. The bribery would be uncovered when he presented his account books before the Senate.

Catullus was prone to exaggerate, but could not help but liken his service under Memmius to oral rape: 'Oh Memmius, for long now you've excelled at slowly inserting the length of that pole of yours into my face' (Poem 28). So it was that when the moment came for Catullus to return home, he was anxious to go. That opportunity came with the first signs of spring in 56 BC.

The new season revealed itself in absences. Gone were the anchovies which had flooded the shallows in the winter months. Gone the foolhardy locals who dared to skid over the frozen sea in carts, to dig them from icy slurry.[7] Urgent to follow the fish into water that was deep enough to sail over, Catullus expressed his excitement at leaving in brilliantly concise verse:

> Goodbye, sweet crowd of friends, we set out
>
> Together from home far away, but
>
> Different and varied are the roads that carry us back.
>
> (Poem 46, lines 9–11)

In Latin, line 11 read merely *diversae varie viae reportant*. Catullus' words were clipped, which befitted an authoritative governor like Memmius better than the average subordinate. Leaping to his feet and separating himself from the group, Catullus finally took control. His homeward path was the one that mattered.

Among his 'sweet crowd of friends', Cinna would follow him in a different boat. He would be safe. He knew well from experience that only 'the strongest sail rope will guide a stable course' over the sea.[8] Following his tour of 'the distinguished cities of Asia' as well as the promontory of Rhoeteum, Catullus boarded his own vessel home.

The boat he procured came from Amastris, a city on the Black Sea coast. It had formed one of the western points of Mithridates' kingdom while he was alive. There were two harbours here, and a proud heritage, which men traced back to Queen Amastris, niece of Darius III, whom Alexander the Great famously pursued soon after invading the Persian Empire.[9] It was marred only by a long, open, reeking drain, which wafted its toxic fumes across the city's rooftops.[10] Its great mountain, Cytoris, grew what Catullus described as a 'long-haired forest', so thick was its carpet of leaves. Boxwood trees were in particular preponderance.

Catullus found a second-hand yacht made from Cytoris' boxwood. This timber was better suited to the construction of small objects than to shipbuilding, for which pine was the preferred material, but boxwood was hard, easy to carve. The resulting boat was, Catullus wrote, a *phaselus*, a 'kidney bean', named after its shape. Bean ships were sometimes made from clay. Men painted them and often relied on sails alone to carry them over the water.[11] Catullus' wooden yacht had both sails and oars.[12] It had probably been constructed in the traditional Greek 'shell-first' method. It was worn, its timbers clogged with salt.

Jason's pine-built *Argo* might have been born from Mount Pelion's head, but Catullus' *phaselus* would not consider itself in any way inferior for being born from boxwood on Mount Cytoris in Amastris. Catullus had lingered over the troubles boats caused in his Bedspread Poem, but allowed his latest yacht to sing its own virtues. While the *Argo*'s flight had been one of determined necessity, he classed the yacht's joyride in similar terms: 'No vows were made on her behalf to the gods on the shore when she set out . . .'

Diving in and out of the Aegean, his boxwood *Argo* sped past Lesbos and Rhodes and the long-ridged island of Naxos. It passed the fair isle of Apollo and Artemis, Delos. Mithridates might have despoiled it, but high on one of its hills stood a splendid Doric temple, gleaming in honour of the Egyptian gods Isis, Serapis, and Anubis. An ancient line of sculpted lions, holy to Apollo, stood proudly on their pedestals, not quite the fearsome monsters Odysseus encountered on his journey home, his famous *nostos*, but majestic in their own way. The ship passed Mykonos, where rounded rocks bore out the myth that Heracles had defeated Titans here and turned their testicles to stone. On it swam to the Adriatic.

Brimming with confidence, the personified yacht of Poem 4 in Catullus' collection recounted the journey from mountain forest to water, the very first movement of her oars across the Black Sea, her progress through the Propontis, and the speed with which she travelled the Aegean – she merely listed the sights she saw, the Cyclades, Rhodes, as if she could barely glimpse them. Whether this was her very last voyage, or merely her most recent (the Latin could mean either), Catullus dedicated her to Castor and Pollux, the twin gods of travel, once he reached the final port, 'this limpid lake'.

The lake might have been in the south of Greece, or the beginning of the Adriatic, where Catullus could board a second ship to complete his journey home, or it could equally have been Lake Garda. A kidney-bean boat sounds fragile by nature, but might have been strong enough to carry him over the seas before darting lithely up the Po.[13] After all, in Catullus' poem the yacht recounted her journey with smooth continuity, and backwards: lake, Adriatic, Aegean, then Black Sea and her origins in Amastris.

Wherever the bean boat first landed, Catullus hastened to Lake Garda shortly after his return from Bithynia. If even the thought of disembarking after so long a journey demanded much of his sea legs, then he could find comfort in the fact that no place could ask less of him than beautiful Sirmio (Sirmione), the narrow strip that divided the waters of Lake Garda like a tongue that split a heart in two. To rest here, midway between Verona and Brixia, was like being back on a large steady deck, only one strewn with cobbles and olives. Jutting into the majestic blue lake, framed by the Alps, of which Monte Baldo loomed largest, Sirmio lingered between water and land.

At barely a hundred metres wide, the strip of peninsula nearest the mainland was too narrow to hold a villa sufficiently large to have been his. Catullus' house stood rather on Sirmio's endpoint, surrounded by the waters of Garda. From a boat on the lake, this part looked particularly like an island. A stream divides the narrowest section of the aquiline peninsula by which Sirmio is connected to Italy so that the bulbous nose of land at its end seems to float like an independent landmass. So Catullus described it:

> Paene insularum, Sirmio, insularumque
> Ocelle, quascumque in liquentibus stagnis . . .
> marique vasto fert uterque Neptunus

Eyelet of almost islands, Sirmio, and of islands,

And whatever each Neptune balances on

Pure waters and expanse of sea

(Poem 31)

He intended these lines to be seen as well as heard. 'Sirmio' floated in his first line between two words that were the same. In that way, it looked like an island, marooned and sprayed by water on every side. He placed the word 'Sirmio' between *insulae*, islands, because while it felt like an island, it was caught between being and not being one. What Catullus called 'the eyelet of almost islands' became for Alfred, Lord Tennyson 'Sweet Catullus' all-but-island olive-silvery Sirmio!'[14] Ezra Pound obsessed still more fervently over Catullus' Sirmio in his *Cantos*, 'and the water flowing away from that side of the lake/is silent as never at Sirmio . . .'[15] He heard it with the ears of Catullus, and saw it with his eyes.

Sirmio's eyelet could accommodate only a small number of estates, perhaps just one. A monumental villa was built upon it, which exuberant travellers established in the fifteenth century as the cave-like remains of Catullus' home; its earliest parts in fact dated to the era of Augustus, perhaps forty years after Catullus lived.[16] It elegantly traced the outline of the coast with its baths, cryptoporticus, workshops, countless bedrooms. Under later emperors, it grew to three storeys high.

Catullus' house was buried beneath it. On the south-east side of the peninsula, near the later villa's entrance, remains of inter-connecting cobble walls were discovered underground, rooms which dated to the first century BC. The cobbles of its walls were reused in the southern sector of the new building.[17] The earlier villa was no farmer's hut. There were brick columns, and painted plaster. Among the objects discovered from the same century across the peninsula were coins, ceramic cups, and shiny, black-glazed plates of the kind Catullus and his family dined off before the sun set over the lake.[18]

The house was angled, precisely as the later villa was, to make the most of the views. Catullus perched here on higher ground, before the promontory dropped down a level towards the water before it. The lake felt so close that he might legitimately fear a deadly tumble onto the beaches it lapped.

Richly coloured wall paintings of daisies and fruit, ferns and garlands, and human figures – including that of the poet with the lazy eye – adorned walls. Paint layered on plaster with lime and quartz made each surface glisten.[19] Perhaps Catullus came home from his worldly travels and commissioned the scene of blue-grey sea filled with ships, one manned by oars alone, the other by sail and oars, both filled with men. The ships were near a coastline dotted with rocks. A man sat (his limbs alone survive) and tossed his line out to sea, confident of his catch. Another, wearing linen like a loin cloth, waded through the shallows to fix his net upon the still water's surface. Or perhaps the family of Catullus, or Sirmio's next residents, chose to commemorate the poet's life with a scene that evoked his travels, and his charming portrait, too.

Catullus' mind was still cloaked in the canvas of Bithynia when a line of olive trees threw its familiar shadow upon him. Balls of leaves pixelated the horizon over the lake, making an artist's palette of the sky and water, grass and Alpine snow. He made his way up towards its tip, where the opening out of the land encouraged a more leisurely pace than the narrow thoroughfare hitherto. It was no accident that he wrote his poem in 'limping iambics', a metre which dragged at the end of each line, like a man's wearied feet.[20] Catullus limped over the threshold of his home, greeted his household gods, and inhaled the familiar smells of home:

> How gladly, how happily I look upon you,
>
> Hardly even believing that I have left Thynia
>
> And the Bithynian plains and see you in safety.
>
> Oh what is happier than when the mind
>
> Releases its worries, lays down its burden, and
>
> Wearied from foreign labour we come to our hearth
>
> And find repose on the bed we have longed for?
>
> This alone is worth struggles so great.
>
> Hello to you, charming Sirmio, and rejoice as I,
>
> Your master, rejoice. And you, Lydian waves of the lake,
>
> Laugh with all the laughter we have at home.
>
> (Poem 31)

As with all travel, but particularly far-flung protracted travel, time had gone awry. Catullus' memories of Bithynia were suddenly those of a parallel life, one not quite his own. He caught an essence of them in the 'Lydian' waves, which evoked the Etruscans' escape from Lydia in ancient times. On returning from Asia, Catullus, in a sense, had come full circle.

He bade the waves of his ancestors 'laugh with all the laughter we have at home', *o Lydiae lacus undae, / ridete quidquid est domi cachinnorum.* He expected not merely a smile, but a hearty guffaw like a crashing wave, *cachinno.*[21]

He did not need to imagine the waves laughing, because they were laughing in their very depths, carrying each laugh to the surface with a bubble. Thermal springs lie on the bed of Lake Garda, and bring bubbles to its surface. Their healing vapours escape to lend Sirmio's air a heady, sulphuric oppression.

As the sulphur of Sirmio was carried through Catullus' dining room, he could well picture Clodia bathing elsewhere. She had her pick of naked bathers at her gardens on the Tiber's lower bank, as Cicero cuttingly observed.[22] And then there was Baiae. A more extravagant but less charming thermal resort than Sirmio, Baiae was a great attraction for the posing elite. Its natural springs ranged from the sulphur-rich to the aluminous; each treated a different disease.[23]

The coastline of Baiae was overhung with sultry heat haze. Each day, the haze lifted over the sand paths and hill-chiselled caverns, half consumed by sun and half holding out to witness who would come. The rich descended here from Rome each spring, some trailing ailing limbs to bathe in the healing waters, others simply trailing. As they knew, there was fun to be had at Baiae, for which clothes were superfluous.

Cicero could not stand the place. Between the giant dome-roofed baths and the pleasure boats piled up on the sands, it posed a risk to self-restraint. No wonder, he supposed, that Clodia loved it. The place had no local politics or trade to speak of, no particular fingerprint aside from its beauty and the people it attracted to define it to the outside world.[24] Without purpose beyond its fuel for pleasure, it fell victim to the charge of excess, something it only half fulfilled by failing to convince people of a greater purpose. Baiae became what they imagined it to be.

Those who frequented it were not just trendsetting for their own age, but for future rulers, too. 'No bay in the world outshines gorgeous Baiae,' wrote Horace decades later, quoting the rich man of his day.[25] Caesar and Pompey purchased villas up in the hills, and later the most licentious emperors, Caligula and Nero among them, lavished their riches on grand properties overlooking the sea. By then, Baiae was a noted 'inn of vice'.[26]

Catullus disliked the extravagance that Baiae typified. That was not to say that he wanted to be perceived as penniless. Although he saw poverty as a rich man's fashion, he liked to think that people knew he only cultivated it from a position of wealth. More, he recognised that a man's display of ostentation could be construed as an invitation to engage with him in a dull manner. Back in Rome after Sirmio, he wrote a poem in which he demonstrated how pandering citizens could be towards the rich. He was entering the Forum where he caught the attention of his old poet friend Varus and a woman he presumed to be Varus' new girlfriend. They asked him eagerly how he had fared in Bithynia, and how much profit he had made:

I was idling in the Forum when my friend Varus

Saw me and led me off to the home of his lover,

A little tart (as she immediately struck me),

Though not obviously inelegant or lacking in charm.

When we arrived here we got lost in conversation,

One topic, then another, such as what Bithynia

Was like today, and how it had gone,

And how much profit it had made me.

I told it as it was – it brought nothing for the natives

Or the praetors or the cohort,

Which was why no one's head was any glossier –

Particularly for those who had a fuckwit as a praetor,

Who split not a hair over his entourage.

'But surely,' they said, 'You procured litter-bearers there,

Which they say are native to the region.'

To make myself singularly more attractive to the girl

I said 'Although it was a bad province

Things did not go so badly for me

That I could not obtain eight straight-backed boys.'

(But in fact I had no one from here or there

Who could lift even the broken foot of an old bed

Onto his shoulders.) And she, as sluttier girls will, said,

'Will you lend them to me a while, dear Catullus,

I want to take a ride to Serapis.'

'Wait,' I told her,

'What I said I had a moment ago . . .

My mind flew – my friend,

Gaius, Cinna – obtained them as his own.

But what difference does it make if they're mine or his?

I use them as if I bought them myself,

But you, you are so vulgar and meddlesome

That I can't be off my guard at all!'

(Poem 10)

With great wit and insight, Catullus made fun of his friends' ignorant assumption that province-hopping guaranteed a man wealth. All the while, he tried to save face. He knew as well as Varus' girlfriend did that Bithynia had traditionally been famed for its export of slaves, so much so that its penultimate king, Nicomedes III, had once said that he lacked the men to support Rome's battles against certain Gallic tribes, because they had been taken as slaves by Roman tax collectors.[27] For all her charm, Varus' girlfriend would not visit the temple of Serapis, the Graeco-Egyptian god of healing. The joke was on Catullus. The Bithynian litter-bearers? Oh, he backtracked pathetically, they were not his to lend. To the average Roman, it was incredible that when a cohort returned from one of the provinces it should do so without having earned enough for hair oil, 'no one's head was any glossier'.[28] Catullus found the girl's persistent questioning of his finances tiresome.

Privately, he sought consolation for his lack of earnings elsewhere. He turned to two dear friends, Veranius and Fabullus ('little bean', surely a nickname much like 'old bean' today), who had seen overseas service of their own. In a poem, he asked them whether they did not become fed up with the cold and hunger brought on by their own thrifty commander, Piso, and whether their accounts in any way resembled his.

If their tour overlapped with his in Bithynia, as Catullus' poems imply, they were probably stationed under Lucius Calpurnius Piso Caesoninus, Caesar's father-in-law, in Macedonia. Following his consulship of 58 BC, Piso enjoyed a protracted governorship there until 55 BC, providing his men with ample opportunity to shudder at his yellow teeth.[29] The man had little talent, if Cicero was right, and had achieved his magistracies merely as a result of other men's mistakes. Catullus had little reason to dislike the general, unlike Cicero, who suffered his exile under his watch; but that did not stop him from characterising Piso just as negatively.

Aligning him with Memmius as a man who 'screwed' his subordinates, Catullus bemoaned how Piso, 'that erect Priapus', flaunted 'sumptuous dinner parties' before the empty-bellied Veranius and Fabullus. So disgusting was Piso's greed, that his dinners took place early in the day, while his friends were left outside, scavenging for invitations of their own (Poem 47).[30] Drained by the injustice, Catullus sighed over the emptiness of his elders' advice: 'Seek noble friends, they say,' he scoffed with an ironic splutter (Poem 28).

Fortunately, Veranius and Fabullus were capable of inspiring more jubilant verse than this. They were experienced travellers, who had spent time in Spain as well as Macedonia. Catullus wrote a poem in which he expressed how much he was looking forward to seeing Veranius speak 'of the landscapes and habits and nations of the Spaniards the way you always do' (Poem 9).

Basing his beliefs solely on his observations of a certain hairy, 'rabbity' and unrefined Spaniard named Egnatius who had set up home in Rome, Catullus considered Spain a place of curious people and customs.[31] Catullus disparaged Egnatius' red-gummed toothy grin, which was framed by a thick beard (Poem 37), and wrote that he smiled toothily regardless of the occasion – in court, at funerals, among mourners – because he was proud of his teeth, which he polished with urine 'in the Spanish way' to make them sparkling white (Poem 39). Rome was home to many 'fullers', whose job it was to wash clothes in urine, but Catullus perceived little similarity here with the Spanish tooth habit.

While his friends recounted old tales, Catullus observed the women at the table. One lady made an effort at old-fashioned decorum and sat upright beside her husband. Other guests slipped steadily onto their elbows as the dinner progressed, and picked at the fruit which dripped honey over the tabletop. Reclining on a bench, resting on a cushion, Catullus reached for olives and eggs, shellfish, crudités, and washed them down with wine. He mopped his fingers with a napkin as he ate, and drank and jested with his friends. There were knives to slice the meat and poultry, but no forks yet in Rome to lift them from the thick sauces in which they were served.

Catullus delighted in the simple Spanish napkins Veranius and Fabullus had given him as a gift: such napkins were inexpensive, but Catullus was sentimental. Men usually brought their own to the dinner table. When some boys tried to steal one from him, Catullus practically exploded in fury. The first incident occurred while he was distracted by laughter and wine, *in ioco atque vino.* The assonant Latin in which he described his state amply conveyed his slurred speech and stupor.

'Do you think it witty?' Catullus barked, as one Asinius Marrucinus secreted it away (Poem 12). Threatening him with rude verses, Catullus compared him unfavourably with his elder brother, Gaius Asinius Pollio,[32] 'a boy who brims with grace and wit'. Pollio would one day become the patron of both Virgil and Horace, and found Rome's first public library. He was little more than a boy, but Catullus saw in him the makings of some-thing special.

If only Catullus could say the same of young Thallus, another boy who decided to tuck into dinner and, aping Pollio's brother, steal not just Catullus' Spanish napkin, but also his cloak and *catagraphos Thynos,* 'Bithynian sketches' — artworks or writing tablets he had purchased there (Poem 25). By now exasperated, Catullus declared Thallus softer than 'an old man's floppy penis'. Guests might laugh at his fury, but then they did not understand what these objects meant to Catullus. The loss of a piece of cloth was the loss of a piece of friendship, and the loss of a piece of the world beyond. Something as mundane as a napkin could ground him when nothing else could.

XII

GODLY RUMBLING

But after the earth was infected with unspeakable crime

And everyone put justice to flight from his grasping mind,

Brother drenched hands in the blood of brother,

Son ceased to grieve for the death of father and mother,

Father longed for the premature death of his son

So freely he could get purchase on the flower of a new wife,

Mother lay herself down beneath her naïve son,

Wrongful and unafraid of doing sacrilege to her household gods –

All things speakable and unspeakable, muddled together in evil fury,

Have turned the just minds of our gods away from us.

So they do not dignify our assemblies with their presence,

Or even bear to touch the clear light of day.

(Poem 64, lines 397–408)

WHILE CATULLUS HAD BEEN IN BITHYNIA, Cicero had languished in exile. The long, lonely days might have suited him, had he not been so in love with Rome. He had always valued opportunities for contemplation and private study, opportunities to gather his thoughts. In the isolation and frugality, the clarity that distance provides, he might have taken greater pleasure in observing that while Clodius Pulcher's law had made him a physical outcast, it had not rendered him a forgotten man.

Cicero, however, had as good as given up. He wept bitterly for his wife and his children. He dreamed longingly of being back in their arms in Rome, where people made fiercer attempts than he realised to call him home. His brother and son-in-law rallied heartily on his behalf. Even the Senate and certain tribunes were seeking to arrange his return, a clear message to his relatives that few had willingly supported his exile after all; they had been only too weak to act against it. And so they tried, and tried again, but there was always another tribune loyal to Clodius waiting to impose his veto.

Cicero could cling to his disappointment over his desertion by the triumvirs, Caesar, Pompey and Crassus, but they had only repeated a mistake he had made himself. He had never imagined that when he stood up to Clodius in the Bona Dea trial the young man would pursue him so savagely and for so long. Nor had the triumvirs considered the repercussions when they supported Clodius' adoption into a plebeian family, happy at the prospect of silencing Cicero's criticism of Caesar's popular legislation. Cicero in exile and the triumvirs stood united at last, if only in their disastrous underestimation of Clodius Pulcher.

While Cicero blamed many people for the shame of his exile – his friends, his enemies, himself – he could not have known, any more than the triumvirs did, that a member of one of the noblest families in Rome, the brother-in-law of a recent consul – brother, indeed, of a staunch optimate senator – would resort to the actions of a street urchin. Whether he hungered for a dictatorship, or the opportunity to destroy the Republic forever to hand power to the masses, Clodius had succeeded in stunning the elite.

Catullus' sabbatical from Rome could not have been better timed. Both consuls for that year were connected to Clodia: the brother of her late husband, Metellus Nepos, a former tribune who had feuded with Cicero over the Catilinarians years ago; and her son-in-law Publius Lentulus Spinther. It would have been impossible for Catullus to forget Clodia while her relatives filled such prominent seats. But Catullus' loss was Cicero's gain. Time, it transpired, had so healed Metellus Nepos' wounds that, when Lentulus put forward a proposal for Cicero's return, he supported it, along with Pompey, who had cowered so wretchedly behind his door on the eve of Cicero's exile.

Clodius, however, refused to give in. He had risen to the office of *aedile* while Catullus was abroad, the perfect base from which to draw upon his popularity among the free poor, including those who had come to Rome as immigrants and failed to find work. Gasconading through the streets, he issued instructions for a mob, supported by gladiators, to ensure that the bill for Cicero's recall was not carried to the vote. Aediles were supposed to organise public entertainment and keep the peace, but Clodius was doing the reverse. Rival street gangs had emerged, the most prominent under the leadership of Publius Sestius and Titus Annius Milo, the fervent young tribunes of 57 BC. The struggle over Cicero had become a struggle over justice. Tensions which had been lingering for years between the most stalwart optimates and the populares who pledged allegiance to Clodius spilled over. Riots had already erupted when Clodius freed a hostage Pompey had kept from the East, and Pompey's supporters sought to recapture him.[1]

Cicero was not exaggerating when he later described the continuing violence: 'the Tiber was filled with the bodies of citizens, the sewers were clogged, blood was wiped from the Forum with sponges . . .'[2] He might as well have quoted from Catullus' Bedspread Poem, where, in the Heroic Age, the Scamander river was narrowed by the bodies piled up in the wake of Achilles' spate.

Catullus was still in Bithynia when Cicero finally won the right to return following a near-unanimous vote (Clodius alone opposed). When Cicero re-entered the city, he found that the huddle of houses on his corner of the Palatine Hill had swollen into a complex, with one property spilling over into another. The late Quintus Lutatius Catulus' monumental portico had been wrecked; Cicero's own house was gone: Clodius had seized it and, feigning reverence, transformed the site into a shrine dedicated to the goddess Liberty.

By the time Catullus returned to Rome in 56 BC, Cicero had managed to reclaim his plot on the Palatine and the city felt comparatively calm. No sooner had Cicero begun to settle back into life in Italy, however, than reports started to come in of a series of troubling incidents across the country. High on the Alban Mount (Monte Cave, near Rome) stood a small temple of Juno. It had been built to face east, but had now mysteriously turn-tabled to face north. Strange lights and lightning strikes lit up the sky, killing more than one Roman citizen. A lone wolf was seen wandering into the city. Most frightening of all had to be the rumbling: a loud, bellicose sort of groan issuing from the surrounding countryside.[3]

The Romans knew that the gods voiced their displeasure at men's ways through nature, and shuddered at what it all meant. Clodius was not an augur or haruspex, whose right it was to interpret the messages of the gods, but belonged to a priesthood, and identified Cicero's reclamation of his property from the hands of the goddess Liberty as the obvious cause for the godly earthquakes. Cicero would not stand for this. He worked himself into a rage, marched across the city and tore down the plaques Clodius had erected in celebration of his exile. This – his exile – he said, was the reason the gods were rumbling. No, Clodius argued: the gods were angry because he had *returned* from exile.

Between the bloodthirstiness of Rome's gangs, the riots, the turning upside down of political order, a reader of Catullus' poetry had every reason to believe that the darkest days of his Iron Age had arrived. Mob rule, as everyone knew, was fertile breeding ground for a dictator. The fear of one-man rule was something that had been passed down the generations, from those who had experienced the uprising against the rapist son of Rome's last king. The Republic had been founded on the very principle of shared rule, and that was precisely what Cicero had dedicated his life to championing. He was not about to stop now. As he fumbled for a convincing explanation for the earthquakes, he cast his eye towards the Clodii Pulchri. Spring 56 BC had been quite a time for them.

Catullus might just have been back in Rome in time to catch the last days of spring, even if he missed the April festival when the situation had erupted. He wrote nothing of this festival, the

Megalensia of the Great Mother, despite his experience of the cult in Asia. He much preferred the Saturnalia – 'the very best of days' (Poem 14) – the midwinter festival during which people exchanged gifts, played tricks on one another, feasted, and masters and slaves swapped roles (Catullus always had loved role-reversal).[4] When he discovered that the Megalensia of 56 BC had brought Clodius and Clodia into the limelight, he had even greater reason to express a preference for other public holidays.

Clodius was responsible for overseeing this year's Megalensia celebrations, and if he was capable of organising anything, he should have been able to organise these. He barely had to get out of bed in the morning before he was confronted with the Temple of the Great Mother, which stood a matter of steps away from his house on the Palatine Hill. His very soil was soaked through with memories of her cult's foundation in Italy. Every so often, terracotta statuettes of her worshippers poked their heads up between the poppies in his forecourt. Shards of one-time props from plays performed by her temple lay just under foot. But Clodius' proximity to the cult proved to be no guarantee of his ability to orchestrate events. The theatres in which the festival's plays were performed were overrun with rioting slaves – proof, Cicero said, that Clodius was intent on provoking a revolt.[5] In the despoiled games of the Great Mother, Cicero found further explanation for the godly earthquakes:

And if we care to remember those traditions which have been handed down to us about the gods, we have heard this Great Mother, whose games were violated, polluted, almost turned to the massacre and burial of the citizen body, this Mother, I say,

wander across the fields and groves with sure shriek and groan.[6]

While revellers tried to make the most of this year's Megalensia, Cicero was in court delivering a defence speech. The law courts were supposed to be empty during festival time, but a jury had been summoned to deliberate over one man's innocence. Standing there was Caelius Rufus, the brilliant young orator whom Clodia Metelli had taken into her bed. Contrary to Catullus' earlier assumption, Caelius' involvement with Clodia had been, at best, a dalliance. Had been, because Caelius' mind was now raking over their ruined romance while he stood accused of a list of criminal charges.

While Catullus was in Bithynia, Caelius had been accused of playing a part in the attack on a deputation of Alexandrians, who were attempting to prevent their Ptolemy from regaining his throne.[7] Caelius had allegedly taken property from a woman named Palla, borrowed gold from Clodia Metelli, and used it to pay slaves to carry out the assassination of Dio, the deputation's leader. Some even claimed that Caelius Rufus had procured poison with which to silence Clodia.

Catullus could not let this opportunity slide. Turning to his writing tablets on the eve of the trial, he set about documenting Caelius' fall in the most spectacular way. For years, he had taken pleasure in mocking the unpleasant habits of others – the father and son at Rome's baths, the woman snatching bread from a blazing funeral pyre, toothy Egnatius smiling in solemnity, the young boy masturbating before his eyes. As he drafted two poems on Caelius Rufus, he sought the same tone:

Don't be bewildered, Rufus, as to why no woman

    Is willing to lay her delicate thighs beneath you

Even if you ply her with gifts of fine clothes

    Or splendid gleaming gemstones.

There is a cruel rumour that does you discredit, according

    To which you house a wild goat in your armpits.

Everyone is afraid of it, and no wonder: for it really is

    A bad beast, not one a beautiful girl should bed down with.

So either kill the harsh assault on our noses

    Or stop wondering why they flee.

                                    (Poem 69)

In his second poem, Catullus described how, against the odds, stinking 'Rufus', who he claimed suffered from gout, found himself a girlfriend. When the woman betrayed him with another man, she passed on to him Rufus' gout (Poem 71). In the poetry collection, the two poems are settled between those in which Catullus wrote of a woman's words being written on running water, and his love for Lesbia as familial.

As witty polemic, these verses might have held their own, but Catullus embedded within their Latin a still more threatening warning to Caelius Rufus. The young lawyer had recently attempted to prosecute a certain Lucius Calpurnius Bestia for bribery during his campaign to become a praetor. Caelius and Bestia were on familiar terms when the case began. They had formerly been members of the same priesthood, whose responsibilities involved performing a ritual sacrifice of a goat each February. Sparing no thought for their earlier kinship, Caelius had used the case to accuse his former colleague of killing his own wives by poisoning them vaginally with the aconite flower while they slept.[8] For all his determination, he lost the case to the more qualified lawyer: his former mentor Cicero.

The 'bad beast' which Rufus kept beneath his armpits in Catullus' poems was Bestia ('beast' in Latin), the man he had faced in court. The 'wild goat' Catullus described as causing the stench was little more than a veiled reference to the two men's former involvement in the annual goat sacrifice.[9] The belied simplicity of these polemics showed how masterfully Catullus could communicate on two levels, with the man in the street, and with the people who were sufficiently involved in public life to understand his subtle references. There was much his later reader could miss between the lines of his invective.

Catullus might have been insinuating that Caelius' professional failure had made Clodia flee, but his more pressing point was that Caelius Rufus was about to receive his comeuppance for the two misdeeds: his contretemps with Bestia and his relationship with Clodia. The chief prosecutor at the trial that was about to start in the Forum was none other than Bestia's young son, Atratinus.

In his poetry collection, Catullus left his reader here, in the forecourt of the tribunal, on the eve of Caelius' trial on 3/4 April 56 BC. He did not want to enter the open-air court, where a crowd had gathered. He was not of a mind to join the spectators as they gazed expectantly at Caelius Rufus. While Clodia entered the court to witness the prosecution, he stepped back, and left Caelius in the hands of his lawyers.

After Atratinus and two junior lawyers delivered their damning prosecution, Caelius and the defence lawyers braced themselves to speak. How fortunate Caelius was that he had his two former mentors, Crassus and Cicero, speaking on his behalf. No one was better placed than Crassus to testify to his character, and convince the jury that he was not the kind of man who stole from women.

Cicero, for his part, saw this as little more than an opportunity to incriminate the family of Clodius. Caelius might have been guilty of all or some or none of the crimes of which he was accused, but Ptolemy might well have employed him indirectly to overthrow his Alexandrian enemies. Cicero decided not to trouble himself with that possibility.

Approaching the platform, he claimed with a mischievous glint in his eye that he would say nothing of Clodia except what was necessary to counter the charges against his client. A few moments later, and he had 'made a slip' and referred to her incestuous behaviour, and accused her of participating in all manner of lewd outdoor activities in the debauched resort of Baiae. As if in a play, he adopted the role of her severe old bearded ancestor Appius Claudius Caecus, and taunted her over why she had been on such familiar terms with the young Caelius that she could lend him gold, but also fear poison. He veiled the matter of Dio's assassination so tantalisingly with his talk of gold and poison that his excitable audience of jurors might easily have forgotten what they had come here to deliberate over.[10] With his spiteful tongue, Cicero made Clodia out to be a prostitute with whom a young man was quite free to sport. After one such liaison, he insinuated, Caelius Rufus had spurned her, providing her with the incentive to make false allegations against him.

As Catullus might have observed, it was rather more likely that Clodia had spurned young Caelius. It was with great petulance, after all, that the young man stepped forward to declare her a *quadrantia Clytemnestra*, a 'penny Clytemnestra', a prostitute and a murderess.[11] This delighted Cicero, who then exclaimed before the gawping jury that, despite her inheritance and noble birth, Clodia Metelli could be bought for a *quadrans*, the price of entry to the cheap Roman baths.[12] She was cheap, indeed, and she was as much a murderess of her husband, Metellus Celer, as Clytemnestra was of hers, the Homeric war hero Agamemnon. Revelling still further in myth, Cicero called her a 'Palatine Medea'[13] – the woman who, according to Euripides' drama, killed her children to spite Jason after he deserted her.

If Clodia *had* lent Caelius gold, ignorant of the murderous use to which he would put it, then she might have been only too happy to play a part in the trial and watch him suffer. She could hardly have anticipated that Cicero would turn the situation on its head and suggest that, like Medea spurned by Jason, she had fabricated the story, the poison and gold, to seek vengeance against the man who left her. A part of Catullus must have appreciated the comparison made between his former lover and the murderesses of myth. And yet, Clodia Metelli emerged from Cicero's account as a figure of myth herself. Between the lines of his character assassination there was a hint that she was as vulnerable as any lover was.

When he likened her to Medea, Cicero might have quoted from Euripides' *Medea*, but instead chose the very passage from Ennius' Latin version that had inspired the beginning of Catullus' Bedspread Poem:

Utinam ne in nemore Pelio . . .

If only in the forest of Pelion [the ship] had not[14]

In his poem, Catullus had drawn a comparison between the plights of Medea and Ariadne, who regretted the time that Jason and Theseus respectively crossed seas to acquire their help in achieving Heroism. In his defence speech for Caelius, Crassus drew upon Medea's wish that from 'the forest of Pelion' the *Argo* had not sailed the Black Sea. His wish was that Ptolemy Auletes had never come to Rome, like a new Jason, to ask for help in reclaiming the kingship from which he had been expelled. Perhaps it was only now, as Cicero wove the myths together before the court in a new context, that Catullus appreciated how far the unhappiness he had perceived in the Heroic Age coloured all of contemporary Rome. In Cicero's springtime law court, it was as though his Bedspread Poem had come to life.[15]

The flight of justice and refusal of gods to 'dignify our assemblies with their presence' in the Iron Age, which Catullus described in his Bedspread Poem, were there in Rome for all to see when Caelius was acquitted, free to pursue his legal career, quite unscathed. Cicero had done little to address the main charges. He had put far more energy into blackening Clodia's character, and providing a theory about how she foiled Caelius' plot to silence her with poison. The scenes he painted had been pure farce, with Clodia instructing her slaves to hide in the baths in order to catch the slave Caelius had employed to do the terrible deed. The defence had succeeded in offering the crowds a greater spectacle than that which Clodius had put on in the theatres for the festival of the Great Mother. Hosted so soon after his return from exile, and against the troubling background of supernatural occurrences in Italy, the trial had provided Cicero with an opportunity to persuade Rome that the source of the city's moral depravation lay in the blood of the Clodii Pulchri.

As Catullus turned his angry hand again to his wax tablet, he offered his readers little reason to deviate from that view:

Caelius, our Lesbia, the Lesbia,

That Lesbia, whom Catullus loved alone

More than himself and all his family,

Now on crossroads and in alleys

Wanks the descendants of great-hearted Remus.

(Poem 58)

Many a Latin poet used *nostra*, 'our', for 'my', but when Catullus used the word in the first line of his poem he seemed to want it to be read as 'our'. For here he stood with Caelius Rufus, both united in a victory of sorts, but convinced still that *his* love for Lesbia had exceeded that of any other man in the world. That very devotion had been his destruction:

My mind has been reduced to this because of you,

   Lesbia, and so destroyed itself through its devotion to you

That it could not now think well of you if you were exemplary,

   Nor stop loving you if you did everything.

(Poem 75)

Catullus' Bedspread Poem and its quite coincidental reminiscences in Cicero's rhetoric had shown that it was easier to situate the beginning of man's fall in the Heroic Age, when the myths themselves provided tales that could be used to demonstrate heroic failings, than it was to accept that the disease of the times was purely endemic to this point in the Republic. Placing blame for man's demise on the ancient Greek myth of the Ages diminished the culpability of the people who inhabited these times – people like Clodia, who was at once a victim of the age in which she lived. Yet at heart, Catullus believed as much as Cicero that the gods were not to blame for this, only those who failed to worship them. They were all just victims of each other's transgressions and mistakes.

THE ROMAN STAGE

Calling upon the shining temples

When the annual rites of festival days arrived

The father of the gods would watch one hundred

Bulls fall prostrate in sacrifice.

Often wayfaring Bacchus led from the high summit

Of Parnassus his Euhoe-crying, wild-hair flowing

Bacchantes, when all of Delphi rushed from the city at once

To welcome the god, rejoicing, with smoking altars.

(Poem 64, lines 387–93)

THERE MIGHT HAVE BEEN evenings since the trial when Clodia longed to find comfort in the arms of Catullus as they flapped open and closed like a bird. All the while he clung to the image of

---

her depravity, 'as a mule does her iron slipper in a sticky chasm' (Poem 20).[1]

He could hardly bring himself to say her name. If ever he began to fantasise about her, he hated himself for it. The more he pulled himself away from her, the more he thought about her. He wanted nothing more than to be free of her. He opened his eyes to the growing architecture of Rome's empire, and began to notice how the city emulated that growth. But each time he looked, there she was. He found her in nascent buildings, old structures, and crumpled world maps.

Catullus watched as Caesar, Pompey, and Crassus set their sights on three different parts of the globe. The coalition that still tied them was not unbreakable. They could taste their un-popularity in Rome, where voters had asserted their right to steer politics by electing as praetors two men who despised them. Even from his quarters in Gaul, where he was waging his wars, Caesar could feel that they would suffer still worse the following year.

In the heat of summer, dour Cato, the obstructive optimate senator who had so bitterly thwarted Caesar's ambitions for a triumph, returned from Cyprus. He and his fellow Romans had succeeded in reducing the island to form part of their province of Cilicia.[2] Cato was determined that 55 BC would be his year. He made no delay in announcing his candidature for the praetor-ship, while one of the candidates running for a consulship had connections in Transalpine Gaul, and looked certain to want to supplant Caesar there should he be elected.

Startled, Caesar called two summits, one at Ravenna, another at Lucca. He was aware of how strained the relationship between Pompey and Crassus had been. Between its cracks and the external pressures of the magistrates at Rome he discerned disaster. Fearful of losing his hold on Gaul, as well as Rome, he renewed their agreement and told Pompey and Crassus that they were to do all they could to ensure that they were elected as consuls for 55 BC. His own command in Gaul would be renewed by five years, long enough, he hoped, to complete its annexation to Rome. Following another shared year in office, Pompey and Crassus would be rewarded with five-year commands of their own, in Spain and Syria respectively.

Caesar brushed his fingers across the bags of money he authorised as bribes. Like Jupiter nodding assent to the plans of some minor god, he signalled for the military to whisper words of intimidation in the ears of Rome's voters. Cowering under duress, they elected Pompey and Crassus, who wrapped their arms across the shoulders of the man they backed against Cato: Publius Vatinius – an unappealing man with unsightly growths on his neck who bragged about achieving a second consulship before he had completed his first junior magistracy. In Caesar's eyes, Vatinius was a safe choice. He had already proved himself his ally by helping him to acquire his position in Cisalpine Gaul when the Senate had allotted him merely the *silvae callesque* of Italy. Vatinius waltzed triumphantly into the Senate House, leaving Cato crestfallen at the doors. Eight of the ten elected tribunes were loyal to the triumvirs.

Pompey longed to be appreciated again on his own merit rather than as one wheel of an uneven wagon. While Crassus would dedicate much of his time to preparing himself and his army for Syria at the end of the year, Pompey was standing joyfully on the Campus Martius in the north-west of the city. A structure was rising beneath a giant web of scaffolds. This year, he would unveil it: Rome's first stone theatre.

He remembered how excitedly he had gazed at the Greek theatre of Mitylene on Lesbos during an earlier trip there. Over time, he had accumulated funds to construct a building that rivalled it not only in size, but in sheer splendour. As he stood in the middle of the Campus, he surveyed the erection of his ninety-metre stage, its seats stretching in a wide convex bow.

Some of the older, more traditional residents, not least of them Cicero, looked askance at the size and permanence of the new building.[3] They were used to wooden, temporary structures, not monstrosities like this. But as curious spectators perched upon steps which led up to a new Temple of Venus Victrix (the goddess in her guise as bringer of victory) to the theatre's west, Pompey assured them that this, the religious centre, was the true highlight of his seminal complex. Bookending the vast stage was a new meeting house for the Senate and enormous portico leading to four further temples in the east.

It was the portico that obsessed Catullus. It formed a grand colonnade filled with plants, sculptures – and shade, the one key aspect that undermined the religious decorum Pompey sought by embedding his theatre within these temple precincts. Catullus wrote nothing to praise the ingenuity of the structure, or to commemorate the grand opening; these shadows fascinated him more.

In Poem 55, he described how he lost a poet friend Camerius in the city one day, and wandered over to Pompey's portico to try to find him. Catullus was in his late twenties, but seemed like a child as he despaired over the disloyalty and arrogance Camerius had showed him by disappearing from sight. Catullus searched the portico frantically: 'I grabbed all the young girls . . . gathering in the colonnade of Pompey the Great,' before one of them bared her breasts and asked Catullus to search her cleavage for his friend. 'Pompey's portico with its shade-giving columns, famous for its exotic woven canopies and rows of plane trees growing in unison' would prove no less convenient a location for sourcing lovers when Ovid, Propertius, and Martial walked through it later.[4]

The portico with its soliciting prostitutes and dishonourable chancers was where Catullus' search for Camerius ended, not began. It was an afterthought. Pompey had hoped that it would encourage people away from the cramped city centre, but this part of the Campus Martius still felt to Catullus like an outpost, a suburb to the hotspots he and fellow poets like Camerius had been in the habit of visiting: the Circus Maximus, the large sandy racetrack in the shadow of the Palatine Hill; the Forum's bookstalls; and the Temple of Jupiter on the Capitoline Hill.

Caesar hoped to change that. He had seen for himself how crowded the Forum's law courts were. He would not allow Pompey to cast him in shadow. He hoped to amass enough money in Gaul to begin next year a project of his own, a new forum to be situated next to the existing one. Like Pompey's complex, it would have porticoes and a temple to Venus, and he would name it after himself.[5]

Catullus, who would not live long enough to see the new forum rise, paid witness in a poem to the old centre in its sorry state. He looked up at the Temple of Castor and Pollux; where before he might have found inspiration from the twin gods of travel, he saw now merely emptiness. Clodius Pulcher had transformed the building into a storage shed for his weaponry and destroyed its grand steps. It stood like a tomb on a hillside, leaving his eye to fall solely upon a *salax taberna*, a seedy inn, situated nine pillars away from it.[6] Catullus describes the *taberna* in Poem 37 — bursting to the seams with drunken idiots and horny desperadoes, the white-toothed Egnatius among them. Catullus threatened to scrawl penises all over its walls in anger. For there, awaiting a queue of men desperate to have their way with her, was the girl who was 'loved as much as no other girl will be loved': Lesbia.

An inn of rowdy men remained for Catullus an inn of potential suitors for Clodia's hand. The sight of it persuaded him to revisit the strength of the lover's pact he had once made:

> No woman can truly say that she was loved
>
>> As much as my Lesbia was loved by me.
>
> No faith in any pact was ever as great
>
>> As that discovered on my part in my love for you.
>
> (Poem 87)

Catullus turned from addressing his words to the world in the first couplet to addressing Lesbia directly in the second. He had been so active in loving her, but she had never been anything more than passive: 'was loved'. Passive was how he now felt. His words were eloquent, but they served as an entrée for the deeper emotions he conveyed in another of his poems, Poem 76. In this piece he looked back from the same vantage point in order to recount his loyalty to his lover alongside his religious and familial devotion:

> If a man can take pleasure in recollecting former acts
>
>> Of kindness, when he considers himself to be moral,
>
> Not to have broken trust that is sacred, not to have
>
>> Abused in any pact the gods' sanctity in the interest
>
> Of deceiving people, then many joys lie ahead over

A long life, Catullus, grown for you
From this love that was rejected.

For whatever men can say or do to be kind
To someone, it has been said and done by you.

All your kind gestures have perished for being entrusted
To the heart of a woman who did not care for them.

So why torture yourself any longer?
Why not take stock in yourself and turn away

And stop being miserable when the gods do not desire you to be?
It is difficult to relinquish suddenly a love that long endured.

It is difficult, but you must accomplish it somehow:
This is your only hope, this is what you must overcome,

You must do this, whether it is possible or not.
Oh gods, if you can take pity, or if ever you have brought

Ultimate deliverance to anyone on the very verge of death,
Look upon me in my misery and, if I have lived my life faithfully,

Seize this plague and contagion from me
Which, like a torpor creeping deep into my limbs,

Has driven every happiness from my heart.
I am not now asking that she might love me back,

Or for the impossible – that she court chastity.
But I wish that I could be well and rid of this terrible sickness.

Oh gods, grant me this in return for my morality.

(Poem 76)

In light of everything he had done, all that was left to console himself with was the knowledge that he had acted in good faith and honour. Should he have had to face his day of judgement there and then, he was confident that he would be received favourably. If it could be agreed that he had never broken faith, or abused his relationship with the gods – his reference to a pact, *foedus*, was more fitting here than it was in relation to Lesbia – then he believed, alas misguidedly, that he should have a long life ahead of him, touched by happiness that would grow from the love he had seen rejected. The poem was all the more melancholic in Latin, where his words meandered like broken thoughts.

The question that plagued him here was not where had *it* all gone wrong, but rather where had *he* gone wrong. He had run through Lesbia's faults and he had run through his own faults, but never did he put to poetry a straight examination of *their* faults. There was the subtle moment of recognition of the inadequacy of his station, but no line-to-line study of their mutual incompatibility. The poems showed that he was not over her. When he came to contemplate the triumvirs' progress across the furthest reaches of the known world, she remained constantly on his mind.

While Rome was in chaos, Julius Caesar ventured like an athlete across the Alps, and repaired his strength in the dining rooms of generous hosts. His etiquette and manners were exemplary. He liked meals to be served in two separate rooms: one for his officers and any Greek friends who happened to come calling, the other for Roman citizens and important provincials. After that he was an amenable guest. He needed little wine, and was too polite to decline even the stalest of dishes.[7]

Almost every winter since he had arrived in Cisalpine Gaul, Caesar had established private military quarters for himself and his men, and during these times he had the chance to develop his friendship with Catullus' father.[8] Dinner at the home of a wealthy Gaul was a luxury to which he had seldom been averse. He was treated to the best of local produce: fruit, fresh fish. The two men talked between mouthfuls about Pontic fishermen and boats, aged Transalpine Gauls who still wore leggings not togas, the Britons with their skin dyed deep blue whom Caesar longed to see for himself.[9] Their friendship flew in the face of Catullus' efforts to remain aloof from Caesar and his coterie, but there was nothing he could do to stop his father from welcoming the vain commander into their family home.

Catullus had written nothing of his Gallic War up until now, the battles coinciding with Bithynia and the obsessions of youth. But as Caesar ventured across the Alps and beyond the Rhine, he knew that other writers, including his rival Furius Bibaculus, were turning to Caesar's exploits for inspiration. Much to his pleasure, Furius' long poem on the Gallic War was not entirely successful. (Horace would later deem Furius a 'Turgid Alpine' for his verbosity and provincial interest.[10]) But as the wars carried Caesar into unknown worlds, it became increasingly difficult for Catullus to ignore them.

As it was, Caesar himself was providing regular written dispatches, and composing a seven-book commentary (eight, if counting the one a friend was writing for him) on the *Gallic War*. Catullus could not overlook his writing or the high regard in which his contemporaries held his penmanship. Cicero was full of praise for the clarity and elegance of Caesar's prose. It was to-the-point, never entrenched in grandiose rhetorical flourishes, a generous compliment considering Cicero's profession, but one that could just as well be applied to his own oratory.[11] As a young man, Caesar had taken a course in rhetoric under the celebrated Greek orator Apollonius Molon, who just happened to have been one of Cicero's tutors, too.[12] When he travelled between Rome and Spain, Caesar wrote an essay he unimaginatively titled 'The Journey'.[13] In addition to his military reports, he also later found time during his tedious trips back and forward across the Alps to write an essay 'On Analogy'. His diaries of the Gallic War were another literary offering.[14]

When it came to other people's writing, Catullus never hesitated to offer a critique, which normally took the form of a barbed attack. Caesar's talent as a writer proved to be the one thing about him he could not criticise. The same could not be said of his chief engineer in Gaul, Mamurra.

Catullus wrote several poems about Mamurra, whom he tended to call 'Mentula' – a sobriquet that could mean 'penis', or something less anatomical in nuance. He was of equestrian stock and a famous resident of Formiae (Formia), on the west coast of Italy.[15] A thousand years later, the locals still knew the area as *Mamorrano* after Mamurra's wealthy relatives.[16] Catullus knew of an estate Mamurra owned containing 'every breed of fowl, fish, meadows, fields and game' (Poem 114). He begrudged him his money, but not the way he squandered it. Mamurra's family owed nothing of its enduring reputation to Catullus. As Caesar went about his province and made known his intentions to carry Rome to Britain for the very first time in its history, Catullus embarked upon a quest to savage his man in Gaul.

He battered Mamurra on so many fronts that, had it not been for his tough military armour, he should have been left a wreck. First, Mamurra had the presumption to think himself a poet when he had scant talent. His writing was atrocious:

Mentula tries to scale the mountain of the Muses.

The Muses hurl him headlong with pitchforks.

(Poem 105)

As if this was not bad enough, Memmius was 'shagging around' (Poem 94): Catullus wrote viciously of his girlfriend Ameana, 'a girl fucked by everyone', whose big nose, ugly feet, pale eyes, stubby fingers, saliva-drenched lips, inelegant tongue, were still nothing on her choice of Mamurra as a lover (Poem 43, Poem 41). Her name suggested she was little more than a slave, some-one Mamurra had just picked up during his travels.[17] She even had the cheek to seek 10,000 *sesterces* from Catullus himself (Poem 41). In Gaul, they called her a beauty; when Catullus heard that the Gauls compared her looks to those of Lesbia, he could only exclaim: '*O saeculum insapiens et infacetum!*' ('Ignorant and dull-witted is our age'), in clear echo of Cicero's seminal outpouring during the Catilinarian fiasco not ten years earlier, '*O tempora, o mores!*' ('Oh the times, oh the customs!').

There was room for exaggeration in an epigram, but when the source of Catullus' anger concerned Mamurra, he felt justified in believing that the world had lost its senses. As far as Catullus was prepared to respond to the Gallic War poetically, Mamurra would be his scapegoat.

A jibe at Mamurra proved often to be a veiled criticism of

Caesar. The Mamurra Catullus described in his poems dallied with the common, money-seeking girl Ameana from Gaul. And so Romans at home composed frivolous little rhymes in which they imagined Caesar cruising Gaul for prostitutes, a fine way to spend their taxes. Hostile to Caesar personally, if not professionally, for the control he operated over the city from Gaul, these men and women played upon his popular image as a womaniser. When, years later, Caesar returned from Gaul in triumph, many greeted him with virtuosos in the same fashion.[18]

Through Mamurra, too, Catullus found occasion to criticise Caesar's foreign expenditure. Unusually for a man with money, especially new money, Catullus knew its value. As in Spain, so in Gaul, Caesar was plundering and pillaging whatever he could, anxious to repay his debts, anxious to accrue greater influence, not least by earning enough to pay for his own forum. In Britain, he hoped to find exquisite pearls to add to his personal collection of fine luxuries.[19] The poor felt certain that they would be the last to see a crumb of his wealth. True to expectation, Caesar took so much gold from Gaul that he flooded the market in Italy, causing its price to plummet.[20]

In an attack on such profligacy, Catullus characterised Mamurra as the king of rakes. He made an example of Mamurra because he disliked him – and he disliked him in large part because he failed to learn from his mistakes. The man was born to money, but spent it; he profited in Pontus under Pompey, but spent it, and in Spain under Caesar, but . . . the cycle went on. In several of his poems, Catullus called him 'bankrupt', yet he also described his expansive lands (Poem 115). Asset rich, but cash poor, as *praefectus fabrum*, or chief engineer, to Caesar once more, Mamurra clearly had his eye on one thing only.

Like Calvus, who scorned a man 'learned at dice', Catullus hated chancers; and gambling was illegal.[21] In one particularly vituperative poem he blustered:

Who but a shameless, grasping gambler

Could look on, who could endure it,

As Mamurra acquires the riches Long-Haired Gaul

Once had, and remotest Britain, too?

(Poem 29)

Catullus' chief fear was for his native Cisalpine Gaul, more than 'Long-Haired' Transalpine Gaul or Britain, but with Caesar's gaze cast sternly across the English Channel, Catullus knew that the kind of conduct typified by Mamurra could seep into the new world. As it was, Mamurra's greed had made prisoners of Asia Minor, Spain, and his homeland Formiae. If Caesar could not hold his men in check, it seemed that there was little chance he could hold his own greed in check either.

Catullus had seen that the path was ready for Mamurra to take his foul habits across the mysterious seas to Britain, 'the remotest island in the west' (Poem 29). By August 55 BC, Caesar had subdued most of Transalpine Gaul. The Romans had enjoyed victory over the tribes of Normandy and Brittany, clearing the coasts nearest the Channel for an imminent attack.

Catullus turned his hand away from Mamurra to unmask the roots of his displeasure: Caesar and Pompey, the 'shameless, grasping gambler' and his partner in crime:

Why nurture this disgrace? What are his strengths,

Other than devouring inherited wealth?

Was it on his account, most dedicated men of the city,

Father- and son-in-law, that you lost everything?

(Poem 29)

Sparing no thought for the prospect of Roman glory, or the need for stability on Italy's borders in the face of ever-migrating tribes, Catullus could discern no greater reason for the Gallic War than his leaders' unquenchable avarice.

Perhaps it came as a relief to him to find that, for all Caesar's hopes, the initial crossing to Britain proved anticlimactic. The British felt no real urgency to mass a large attack against their Mediterranean visitors. Documenting the landings in his *Gallic War*, Caesar even described the people of Kent as being particularly civilised.[22] The few bloody engagements that did take place lacked finesse, and atrocious weather led to an early and swift withdrawal by Roman troops.

For the moment, it did not matter that Caesar had not achieved war. For Rome it was enough that he had dipped his toe in British slurry. At news of his landing, the Senate decreed a twenty-day period of thanksgiving in recognition of the undertaking.[23] Once back in Gaul again, Caesar set his men to preparing ships and supplies for a larger and more intimidating invasion the following spring.

In a poem, Catullus expressed wonderment at recent events, 'the monuments of great Caesar, the Gallic Rhine, and terrifying and far-off Britons' (Poem 11). What must have struck his friends as a puzzling volte-face perhaps concealed a subtle dig at Furius, who had written offensive poems about Caesar in the past, but was now providing Rome with such earnest and verbose *Annals* in praise of his Gallic War. Perhaps Catullus' words drew on those Furius wrote about 'the wintry Alps' and 'head of the Rhine'.[24]

Easy as it was for him to mock Furius' duplicity or sudden admiration for Caesar, Catullus never questioned the accuracy of Caesar's reports. While it was true that the mighty triumvir had penetrated far enough to confirm Roman rumours that Britons were huge and 'terrifying', even by the start of 54 BC, only limited inroads had been achieved there. Shortly before his first British invasion, Caesar had indeed made a bold venture across 'the Gallic Rhine' via an impressive yet rapidly constructed bridge, but he also wrote that he had to have that bridge destroyed merely weeks after it was completed to protect his men from future assault after he found the Germans reluctant to fight on the other side.[25] In the summer of 55 BC, neither Britons nor Germans could yet countenance the full force of Caesar's ambition. But Catullus, by listing these places, clearly could.

The fears Mamurra had embodied, about Roman greed for the world beyond, proved prescient. Mamurra appeared to profit from all that Long-Haired Gaul possessed. His house on Rome's Caelian Hill became the first of Rome's residences to have its walls encrusted entirely in marble.[26] The dedicatee of Catullus' poetry book, Cornelius Nepos, added that it was also the first to have all its columns built from solid Euboean or Luna marble, which everyone knew was very fine indeed.

Mamurra emerged from Catullus' poems as a symbol of not only everything he detested about wastefulness and the Gallic War, but also as the ugly underbelly of the coalition. He was as if an alter ego to its most ambitious member, and for all Caesar's accomplishments, Catullus was not to let him forget it. Calvus once wrote a poem lampooning Pompey, 'the Great man everyone fears', for scratching his head with one finger, a gesture taken to mean that he desired a male lover. He had also written verses mocking Caesar, and now Catullus did the same. Mamurra and Caesar, he decided, were united by more than their greed:

> A beautiful meeting of shameful lovers,
>
> Mamurra and penetrated Caesar.
>
> It's no surprise: there are similar stains on both,
>
> The one a City dye, the other Formiae,
>
> Stamped on them and not removed.
>
> Equally sickly, twins, the two of them,
>
> Both delicately versed on one little bed,
>
> One no more voracious an adulterer than the other,
>
> Allied in their rivalry over little girls.
>
> A beautiful meeting of shameful lovers.

(Poem 57)

> Was it on his account, unparalleled commander,
>
> That you were on the remotest island in the west,
>
> So that your overindulged Cock, Mentula,
>
> Might absorb twenty or thirty million sesterces?

(Poem 29)

When Caesar came by these poems for the first time, there was no pausing to consider their poetic significance.[27] He could not have needed any more than a fleeting glimpse at a single page, or a whispered paraphrase of what he could only imagine the world had already put to heart, to know that his honour was again at stake. His eye might have lingered momentarily over Catullus' phrase *unice imperator*, since it meant 'unparalleled', but could also offer a hint that Catullus saw him as *the unique* leader, the dictator. But the more offensive part came in Catullus' suggestion of his erotic activity with other men. To be called a *cinaedus*, a penetrated man, was among the worst insults imaginable.

Caesar had not been able to live down the verses Calvus had written mocking him over his supposed liaison with the late Bithynian king.[28] Driven either by a sudden crisis of conscience or a bid to further his legal career, Calvus had, through mutual friends, made an appeal for forgiveness to Caesar. Pre-empting his apology, Caesar wrote him a letter to convey his forgiveness for his indiscretions.

As far as anyone could see, Catullus followed suit. He issued Caesar with an apology, and in return he received not only his forgiveness, but an invitation to dinner. Catullus arrived at Caesar's residence one evening, and joined him for a spot of feasting, some cups of wine, and entertainment, as his father did so often. Whatever the soirée meant to Catullus, he did not allude to it in his book of poems.

The ancient biographer Suetonius, however, considered this an event so momentous that he drew special attention to it in his historical account of Caesar. Suetonius seems to have been heartily impressed by the commander's reaction:

He did not pretend that with his poems about Mamurra he had not put a permanent stain upon him, but on the same day as he apologised, Caesar invited him to dinner, and his friendship with his father continued as it had before. [29]

Acts of clemency were not unusual among the later emperors, who formed the focus of the remainder of Suetonius' book. Whereas the historian Tacitus recorded that Caesar endured the harsh verses of both Furius, Catullus' rival, and Catullus, Suetonius made no reference to Furius' poems. If only because of his father's friendship with Caesar, Catullus' verses were the more shocking. As far as Suetonius was concerned, Catullus' poems had provided Caesar with an opportunity to demonstrate his great benevolence.

But Suetonius might not have known the whole story. While so many of his friends had been won over by Caesar's charms and accomplishments, Catullus had not. His father was a friend of Caesar; his friend Calvus had been reconciled with Caesar; and Cinna was also to be friends with Caesar: when he eventually reached the tribunate, Cinna would even draw up a bill proposing that Caesar should be allowed to marry as many women as he liked 'for the sake of begetting children'.[30] Surrounded by ties to the man whom, as far as anyone reading his poetry could tell, he detested, Catullus was well placed to hatch a plan.

If he could obtain a reaction and public gesture of magnanimity from Caesar for something still cruder than his friend Calvus' Bithynian verses, Catullus would acquire an indelible notoriety of his own. On Caesar's side, if he could be seen to take these verses immediately in his stride, he would appear the bigger man. The risks were high, with Catullus particularly liable to go too far, but both men could benefit from a mutual agreement. It would have been, perhaps, the only thanks Catullus' father was prepared to accept from his hibernal houseguest.

There remained among Catullus' surviving poems an additional threat, tacked on to the end of a series of insults directed at various men, presumably Caesar's subordinates: 'You'll rage again at my innocent iambics, unparalleled commander' (Poem 54). Had Caesar truly found the poems so offensive, he would have done everything he could to ensure that all copies were destroyed before they could be included in Catullus' poetry collection. If some such arrangement did take place between Caesar, Catullus' father, and Catullus, then they deceived not only Suetonius, but millennia of historians in their wake.

A FLOWER ON THE
EDGE OF THE MEADOW

All-powerful Jupiter, I wish the ships of Cecrops

Had not touched the shores of Cnossos in the first place,

That the traitor, bringing a gruesome tribute to

The ungovernable bull, had not tethered his ship in Crete,

That the evil man did not hide his cruel plans

Behind a handsome exterior

And stay here as a guest in our home.

For where can I take myself now?

(Poem 64, lines 171–77)

ALTHOUGH CATULLUS ENJOYED SEX, he believed that certain boundaries needed to be observed. He was liberal with kisses, and his first reaction upon growing aroused in one of his poems was to arrange an imminent meeting with a lover. He found humour in the idea that vigorous intercourse could have a slimming effect upon a man, and joked about the sexual appetites of youth. Through his poems about Caesar and Mamurra, he had learned also how powerfully sex lent itself to invective.

The poems he had gathered for his collection had lately begun to bulge with verses lambasting a certain Gellius, most often for incest. His unfortunate victim, evoked in no fewer than six of his poems, might have been Lucius Gellius Publicola who would one day serve under Mark Antony in the civil war. His relatives were known allies of Clodius, whose disputes with Milo, the young politician who had helped to recall Cicero, were raging at Rome.

While some Romans languished on luxurious beds in smart houses, others visited brothels, known as lupanars *(wolf-dens). Over each door hung a tablet bearing the name of the prostitute and her price. She turned the tablet over when she was* occupata *(busy).*

Catullus had once considered him a friend. Gellius was learned and cultured enough to appreciate the poetry of Callimachus, providing them with much to talk about. So when barbs began to fly between them, Catullus' first thought was to send Gellius some Latin translations he had made of Callimachus' poetry as a gesture of reconciliation. But then, he thought to himself, what was the point? Whatever Gellius had done (in Poem 91 Catullus accused him of seducing one of his lovers), it was enough to make Catullus give up on their relationship altogether.

He might have guessed their friendship would end with Gellius doing something foolish. In his youth, Gellius Publicola had made a name for himself for sexual excess. His father, a former consul, had accused him of plotting parricide and of sleeping with his stepmother.[1] He put his son before a line of senators at a family tribunal. Both the deciding committee and his father acquitted him of both charges, but as far as Catullus was concerned, Gellius had never ceased to be a sexual fiend. He proceeded to paint an extreme caricature of the fellow. His Gellius liked to sleep with his mother, aunt, sister, and other close female relatives, and carried the evidence for this in his physique. He was trim, and his lips were also perpetually stained with the ejaculate of another man, this time no relation:

Something's up. Is the rumour true that

You suck a man's bulging balls?

You bet it is. The ruptured testicles of poor Victor

Proclaim it – and your lips etched in drained semen.

(Poem 80)

Anticipating that his portrait might be incredible, Catullus sought a motive for his former friend's depravity: by seducing his aunt, Gellius had hoped to censor his uncle from disparaging his sexual habits. Roman uncles were famed for their severity, and Gellius' would only bring the incest rumours to light again if he sought to punish him. In Poem 78, Catullus described a 'Gallus' who taught his nephew how to be an adulterer. This was quite some family. Young Gellius, it seemed, seduced his aunt on the advice of another uncle, rendering him as much a victim as a perpetrator of his family's profanity.

In Catullus' poetry, the breakdown of a family unit, such as that of Gellius, acted as a paradigm for the breakdown of the state, a bitter microcosm of a more total destruction.[2] The fractured *mores* and perversions Catullus perceived in Gellius' family added further nuance to the picture of Iron Age Rome he envisaged at the end of his Bedspread Poem:

Father longed for the premature death of his son

So freely he could get purchase on the flower of a new wife,

Mother lay herself down beneath her naïve son,

Wrongful and unafraid of doing sacrilege to her household gods –

(Poem 64)

For Catullus, however, Gellius' behaviour was more than a reflection of the city as it stood; it was an indication of where it was going. For centuries, the western world had associated incest with the decadent East. In late autumn 55 BC, Crassus boarded a galley with a dream of conquering territories still deeper in the East than those to which Pompey and Catullus had travelled.

Caesar had agreed that Crassus and Pompey should proceed to five-year commands following their consulships, and while Pompey was content to conduct his command of Nearer and Further Spain from home through legates, Crassus could not wait to leave Rome. If he needed reminding of how far he had slipped to the background of the political landscape, he had only to read Catullus' poems and their criticism of the 'father- and son-in-law': Crassus was quite absent from his picture. He still had his wealth – on the point of his departure he had an extraordinary 7,100 talents – but was sixty years old and lacked the glory of a foreign victory to rival that which Caesar, Pompey, even Lucullus the fishpond-loving former brother-in-law of Clodia had acquired before him.

Catullus could now see where Crassus' ambitions lay. Although the triumvirs had agreed that their wealthiest member would leave for Syria, this was merely a stepping stone to war against the Parthians, an Iranian people renowned for their cavalry skills and ability to shoot arrows whilst mounted on horseback. Parthia need not have been the extent of Crassus' ambition:

. . . He would consider neither Syria nor even Parthia the

boundary of his noble venture, but showing up the campaigns

of Lucullus against Tigranes and of Pompey against

Mithridates as those of a mere infant, all the way to Bactria

and India and the Outer Sea he soared on hope.[3]

It was the wider map that Catullus appeared to envisage, too, writing of 'furthest India' alongside the extremities of Gaul and Britain, and of Parthian *sagittiferos* (arrow-bearers), a compound that at once conveyed the swift flight of the weapons and the inseparability of each man from them. As Crassus made his way to Syria and looked forward to a year of mustering more troops for his invasions, Catullus brought an element of Parthia back to Rome in his references to the 'arrow-bearing Parthians' and to incestuous Gellius. 'Let a magus be born from Gellius and his mother and their nefarious union and may he learn Persian divination . . .' (Poem 90), he wrote, momentarily reverting to cliché. It was an oblique comment upon Rome's expansion into worlds which were at once unknown and familiar.

Much though Catullus disapproved of the luxury and incest-loving man traditionally associated with the East, he found that he could employ these labels just as conveniently to the man in Rome. On balance, the prospect of Romans visiting remote places like Parthia proved to him more thrilling than threatening. And yet, Catullus would only be able to imagine himself joining Crassus and his men, who included the aspirate-loving Arrius, as they made their way across the '*Hionian*' (Ionian Sea).

In Rome, meanwhile, Catullus found himself in a rather more domestic situation. He had received an invitation to dinner at the house of Publius Sestius, a politician who had been at the fore-front of the battle for Cicero's recall from exile.

Catullus was keen to impress him. Some ten years his senior, Sestius was a former tribune whom the Senate kept faithfully on side. Cicero's enemies had tried to indict him for bribery and violent conduct during his attempt to have the orator recalled, and Cicero had seen him acquitted of the charges. Before dinner, Catullus sat down to read Sestius' oratory, feeling that he ought to be up-to-date on what his host had achieved. Sadly, Catullus could not even feign excitement. In a poem he bemoaned how turgid his speeches were, 'brimming . . . with poison and pestilence', and how 'sumptuous' the dinner he proceeded to feed him (Poem 44).

Decades earlier a 'sumptuary law' had been passed by a tribune named Gaius Antius Restio, in order to try to limit the luxuriousness of dinner parties and thus curtail the use of lavish private gatherings for political ends. As though determined to go one better than his predecessors, who had, under Sulla, passed similar acts with little success, Antius stipulated that magistrates could only dine at the homes of particular people. Flouting this law completely, Catullus' host had served up a meal as purple as his prose. Together, they sent the poet running for the unfetid air of the countryside.

His stomach sick from the rich food, his lungs filled with cold from having read such frigid writing, Catullus retreated to a villa he had purchased just outside Rome, partial as he was to *peregrinatio*, seasonal sojourns.[4] He had no qualms about admitting that his property sat on a fault line between two areas of contrasting stature: glorious Tibur (Tivoli) on the city side, and its less fanciful cousin further out, the Sabine Plain; it only added to his modesty. Those who wished to please him said that his house was Tiburtine; those who did not called it Sabine. There was considerable social cachet to be gained through owning a villa close enough that one could see the city from the porch, but far enough away for it to feel like a retreat.[5]

Being either just inside or very close to Tibur provided Catullus with much the same opportunity to recuperate as Baiae afforded Clodia's set, only without the excessive, manmade luxury. There were fresh pools and springs here, too, both to drink from and in which to soak his restless limbs; and a waterfall, gushing the long descent from a sky-lying river to a wooded ravine below.[6] Its orchards grew white with foam from the flowing streams, for which they expressed their gratitude by putting forth more fruit and olives than a man could shake his felling stick at.[7] In its perfection, it evoked Scheria, the dream-world island of Homer's *Odyssey*, a curiously Golden Age vision of a place that felt too good to be real.

By August 54 BC, Catullus had recovered his strength sufficiently to return to the city and the Forum, where one of the men who had attempted to incriminate the sumptuous Sestius for his support of Cicero was himself now in the dock. Publius Vatinius, scratching the unsightly growths upon his neck, stood there scowling. The triumvirs had as good as coerced him into using the bribery and force, for which he stood accused, to achieve the praetorship the previous year, so fearful had they been that Cato might win the seat, which he had proceeded to do for 54 BC. Anyone who saw Vatinius standing there might have assumed that the triumvirs had abandoned him. Caesar was busily preparing his second invasion of Britain. Crassus was in the East, pursuing glory. Pompey awaited the birth of his first child with Julia.

As it happened, the triumvirs had given some thought to wretched Vatinius, whose downfall before a hostile crowd would have reflected badly upon them. Cicero despised him, but Caesar did not care. Haughtily, he had told Cicero that he must defend the man at his coming trial.

These days, Cicero was waging an ever more intense war with himself. He did not want to be the triumvirs' yes-man, but if he did not court their favour he would be powerless, trapped between them and the stagnant Senate. For the goodness of his soul, he tried to find a balance between moments in the public eye, admiring Caesar's campaigns in Gaul, and private pleasures in books and conversation. He took increasing delight in his son and nephew, and listened to them as they spoke animatedly of petty disputes and goings on. Caesar, who excelled at applying pressure in the kindest of ways, appointed Cicero's brother Quintus as his legate in Gaul.

It might have been in response to Cicero's volte-face that Catullus praised him so sarcastically as 'the very best advocate of all' (Poem 49). He was less interested in what Cicero had to say about Vatinius, however, than he was in the performance of Vatinius' prosecutor – who was none other than the young, increasingly determined, Licinius Calvus.

Although poetry had proven a solid grounding for Calvus' oratory, a previous attempt he had made to prosecute Vatinius had been unsuccessful.[8] Such was the animosity between the two men that Catullus had developed a particular turn of phrase. Upbraiding Calvus one winter for giving him a copy of terrible poetry as a present, he wrote:

If I did not love you more than my own eyes,

Suave, suave Calvus, that gift

Would make me hate you as much as Vatinius hates you.

(Poem 14)

Calvus was determined to win this time. Catullus looked on, full of pride, as his friend stepped forward to make his prosecution speech. Desperate to make his mark, little Calvus puffed out his chest and gave it all he had. He was full of animation and zeal. He had a way of making his words and sentiments appeal to the ears of the jury, who were not always endowed with long concentration spans. Anyone who heard him could tell that he knew what made a good speech.[9] A small voice piped up from somewhere behind Catullus, 'Great gods, he's eloquent for a little man!', and Catullus laughed (Poem 53). Not even Vatinius could fail to be impressed by Calvus' performance. With a wry smile he turned to the jury and asked whether he was to be condemned because his accuser was so eloquent?[10] But as everyone knew, Vatinius had the infinitely more experienced orator speaking in his defence. Although Calvus spoke well, he lacked the genius and gravitas of Cicero, who carried the day.[11] Now free, Vatinius would travel to Gaul to attend Caesar, and support him against Pompey in the civil war. It was not now far off.

The signs of trouble had been there for some time. The daily trials of men such as Sestius and Vatinius and the havoc wreaked by Clodius were but passing distractions from the fragility of the relationship between Caesar and his colleagues in power. Crassus was old, out of the picture, and at risk of falling victim to the scale of his ambitions in the East. Caesar and Pompey had little more than the marriage that tied them, 'father- and son-in-law', until, all of a sudden, they did not. During late summer, while Caesar was invading Britain, some harrowing news broke over Rome and slipped solemnly through its backstreets. Julia, Caesar's daughter, had died in labour. The baby, the first and last she had delivered with Pompey, had not survived long after leaving the womb. Pompey, beleaguered by the heat of a long season, the relentless demands of the poor in a period of grain shortage, gave way to mourning his double loss. Everything was slipping from his fingers.

With Rome as the compass point, a great spool of thread had been uncoiled and tugged steadily over landmasses and seas, up mountains and along river streams, across Asia and Egypt, the Rhine, Alps, both Britain and Parthia, never fraying or becoming so entrenched in dirt that it collapsed, but holding course, back and forth, turning itself into one giant, lopsided web. Catullus mapped each point in Rome's expansion with an explorer's keen eye. A growing empire came at a cost he could not always tolerate, but in the end it proved to be an inspiration:

> Furius and Aurelius, you are my friends.
>
> Should Catullus penetrate furthest India,
>
> Where the shore is pounded by the far-
>
> Resounding wave of Oceanus in the East,
>
> Or reach the Hyrcani and effeminate Arabs,
>
> Or the Sacae or arrow-bearing Parthians,
>
> Or Egypt where waters from the
>
> Seven-mouthed Nile spread their colour.
>
> Or should he step over the high Alps
>
> As he visits the monuments of great Caesar,

The Gallic Rhine, and terrifying

And far-off Britons —

All of which, and whatever else the will

Of the gods may bring, you are ready

To attempt together;

Deliver a few words, unpleasant ones,

To my girl:

May she live and flourish with her lovers,

Three-hundred of whom she holds in a single embrace,

Loving none truly but repeatedly breaking

All their balls;

And may she not expect my love as she did before,

Which through her fault has fallen like a flower

On the edge of a meadow, touched

By a plough passing by.

(Poem 11)

In light of Caesar's British and Crassus' Parthian expeditions — reflecting back, too, on Pompey's happier days and great triumphs against Mithridates in the East — Catullus pictured the intrepid traveller penetrating each country and recounting the peculiar sights of each: the thunder of the waters east of 'furthest India' where Crassus hoped to wander; the Parthians he faced with their bows and arrows; the Sacae, nomadic tribes driven from Parthia to India in recent times; Egypt; Gaul; and to top them all, 'terrifying and far-off Britons', rendered utterly breathlessly in Latin, as though he was walking the whole way to them. As fond as he appeared to have been of his kidney-bean yacht, he had cast seafaring in a negative light in his Bedspread Poem. Perhaps it was no accident that in Poem II he seemed only to be imagining the prospect of travelling the new world, while rooted in Rome. Here he entrusted Furius and Aurelius, his 'friends', now, with his bitter parting valediction to his mistress. He could no longer even bring himself to face her.

This was probably the last Lesbia poem he ever wrote. No trace of optimism remained. As far as he could see, she had become the very symbol of sexual excess, a ball-breaking machine. His Latin graphically conveyed her movement up and down on one lover's straining penis, then another's, then another's *identidem omnium/ilia*, ('repeatedly all of their balls'), each word dripping into another in a welter of vowels as their bodies came together. Then he reached the climax, *rumpens*, she was 'breaking' them all.

It was an unexpectedly personal ending to a worldlier tale of travel and political expansion, because Rome's new horizons had given love new dimensions. There was no longer any point in loving to the ends of the earth when those ends were being navigated and conquered. Two further lovers in Catullus' collection, Septimius and Acme, set their love against the navigated map (Poem 45). Septimius chose to love his darling Acme over 'all the Syrias and Britains', and if he failed in his love he would venture alone to India or Libya to confront a lion face to face.

The temptation of the world could be overcome more easily than the passion against which it was measured. And yet, when it came to *unloving*, the thread could just as easily be wound up again, and love's contours reduced to a small compass in the belief that love was love, wherever its parameters lay. And so Catullus, falling out of love, became a lonely flower not on the edge of the world, but on the edge of an anonymous meadow, wounded for having ever been touched.

Of all his surviving poems, he wrote just this valediction, and that which he translated from Sappho at the beginning of his love affair with Lesbia, in Sapphic stanzas. Neither named Lesbia specifically, preferring to subordinate details to emotions, emotions carried along by the abrupt stop-starts of the Sapphic metre. Sappho's fallen flower represented a girl, downtrodden not in a field by plough but in the mountains by shepherds.[12] Catullus had come full circle. His return to Sappho cemented what had become of the woman he once watched laughing in the presence of another man. She was the same woman, but no longer the same.

Like the maps of Bithynia and the Spanish napkin, the sail-cloth that had drifted his bean ship over the Aegean, the very papyrus that held their stories, Catullus' bedspread was rolled up. The Golden Age and the Heroic, the terrible Iron Age of Rome, the full stretch of lineage, past to present, layered together, in-distinct. Catullus turned the scroll between his fingers, and looked out across the waves of Lake Garda. A tiny *Argo* cut the horizon in two. The breeze, growing stronger, quivered with the rustle of the pruning hook. Catullus listened for the laughter of the water, but could not hear it. He stayed, watching it lick the land like tears, listening still, until the sun set slowly upon him.

EPILOGUE

CATULLUS DIED IN ROME IN 53 BC. He was in his thirtieth year. His poetry had made him a public figure, and at his passing, people took to the streets to mourn.[1] If only he had known as he slipped away, in the grip, perhaps, of some indeterminate ailment – a 'flu, pneumonia, a chill that went too far – that his name would live on for so much more than a hundred years. It would outlive his world itself.

In 53 BC, Crassus followed him to his grave, together with much of the army he had led against the Parthians. Following a disastrous miscalculation of tactics and forces, they suffered a crushing and unforgettable defeat at Carrhae, near the border that divides modern Turkey from Syria. Gone with them were Rome's legionary eagles, the symbols of her power and authority. Crassus never did achieve the triumph he had been seeking ever since he defeated Spartacus in 71 BC.

For a time, Pompey and Caesar remained allies, but with Julia and Crassus gone, it could only be so long that their partnership endured. By the end of the decade, questions were being asked as to when Caesar would give up his command over Gaul. Though he was willing to let go of Transalpine Gaul, he hoped he might retain Cisalpine Gaul – Catullus' Gaul – for rather longer.

The Senate, anxious to see an end to Caesar's protracted power in the north-west, rallied for change. Committed to Caesar's support, Mark Antony, a young tribune renowned for his sexual appetites and physical strength, travelled to assist him. In 49 BC, flagrantly trampling the Senate's authority, Caesar crossed the Rubicon that marked the boundary line between Cisalpine Gaul and Italy, triggering civil war. By 48 BC, Pompey and the Senate had sent a fleet to Pharsalus, the place in Thessaly where in his Bedspread Poem Catullus had envisaged the wedding of Peleus and Thetis taking place. Serving Caesar, Mark Antony outstripped all in his performance. Pompey fled, but it was not long before Caesar was presented with his head.

Gaius Memmius, who had led Catullus' cohort in Bithynia, died in exile after being charged with attempting to bribe his way to a consulship for 53 BC.

Caelius Rufus, Clodia's former lover, was rising successfully up the political ladder when he became one of the many casualties of the civil war. He supported Caesar, but rebelled through frustration at his lack of progress, and fell victim to Caesar's forces.

Catullus' friend Calvus was dead by 47 or 46 BC.[2] Clodia outlived them both. In 45 BC, Cicero was hoping to buy gardens from a certain Clodia, probably Clodia Metelli herself. He believed that she would be unwilling to let them go, she did not need to. After all she had lost, she clung to her wealth.[3]

The dramatic deaths tend to be the ones that survive history. Caesar cemented his claim to Rome through dictatorship in the early 40s BC. Seeing that no good could come of anything any more, Cato committed suicide, slowly as it turned out, by self-disembowelment. On the Ides of March 44 BC, Caesar was assassinated. He was in his fifty-sixth year. A funeral took place. Directly afterwards, men rushed with fire to the homes of his assassins, thirsty for vengeance, but were driven back. During their withdrawal, they happened upon Catullus' old friend and travel companion – Caesar's 'friend' too – the poet and now tribune Gaius Helvius Cinna.[4] On hearing Cinna's name, the group instantly assumed that he was Cornelius Cinna, a man who made a vituperative speech against Caesar just a day earlier. The ensuing scene inspired Shakespeare:

First Citizen: Tear him to pieces; he's a conspirator.

CINNA THE POET: I am Cinna the poet, I am Cinna the poet.

Fourth Citizen: Tear him for his bad verses, tear him for his bad verses.

CINNA THE POET: I am not Cinna the conspirator.

Fourth Citizen: It is no matter, his name's Cinna; pluck but his name out of his heart, and turn him going.

Third Citizen: Tear him, tear him! Come, brands ho! fire-brands: to Brutus', to Cassius'; burn all: some to Decius' house, and some to Casca's; some to Ligarius': away, go!

Exeunt

(Act III, *Julius Caesar*)

The bacchantes in Catullus' Bedspread Poem hurled dismembered limbs in orgiastic frenzy. The brutes who murdered Catullus' dear old friend Cinna put his head on a spear.

Cicero had achieved a semblance of friendship with Caesar in his final years. When he lost his beloved daughter Tullia after complications of childbirth in 45 BC, Caesar wrote him a letter of condolence. In the aftermath of his assassination, however, Cicero supported the 'Liberators', the members of the Senate responsible for Caesar's murder. He made a series of speeches, the *Philippics*, in which he sought to blacken the character of Mark Antony, who had taken up Caesar's mantle. Following the formation of the Second Triumvirate, comprising Julius Caesar's great-nephew and heir, Octavian (the future Emperor Augustus), his supporter Marcus Aemilius Lepidus, and himself, Mark Antony issued instructions for the assassination of Rome's greatest orator. In 43 BC at his villa retreat near Formiae, Cicero was decapitated and his body deprived of the hand with which he had written his offensive words about Antony.[5]

Clodius Pulcher had died nine years earlier. He was travelling on horseback with some friends and a guard of armed slaves along the Appian Way, that great path his ancestor had commissioned all those centuries ago. Near a shrine of the Bona Dea, the godhead he had so heartlessly desecrated in his younger years, he encountered a large gang of men – gladiators, some of them – and in a carriage their commander, Milo. Clodius and Milo had fought over Cicero's return from exile, and recently clashed again as the former sought the position of praetor, the latter a consulship. The election results had not yet been resolved. A scuffle broke out. A spear was hurled. It struck Clodius. Deciding he was better off dead than wounded, Milo saw that he was finished off.[6] A senator recovered his body and had it returned to Rome, where his widow Fulvia grieved and his allies swarmed in anger.[7]

Catullus had been dead for a decade, but his bloodline continued to flow. His family name crops up sporadically over the next century. Suetonius wrote of a Valerius Catullus, 'a young man of consular family' who boasted that he slept with Emperor Caligula and was exhausted by the experience.[8] A certain Lucius Valerius Catullus Messallinus was consul under the later Emperor Domitian. In 105 AD, a young Valerius Catullus Messallinus was helping in the sacrifices of a body of priests known as the Arval Brethren; it was a role reserved for well-born boys.[9] The satirist Juvenal celebrated a Catullus' escape from a shipwreck in his twelfth satire, which dates to around 120 AD. In honour of this Catullus' safe return, he hoped to offer a bull to the gods that was 'fatter than Hispulla . . . one slowed by its sheer weight, not fed on local grasses, but exhibiting in its blood the fertile fields of Clitumnus'.[10]

Catullus' greatest legacy remains his poetry. Its survival is astonishing. Only Poem 62, one of the wedding hymns, lasted the era from Antiquity to the Middle Ages. It came down in a ninth-century AD manuscript, written by a monk with elegant hand-writing. For the rest, one must return to Verona, where Catullus' journey began.

In 49 BC, Caesar had finally been able to grant the people of Verona full Roman citizenship. Architecturally, the city was growing from strength to strength.[11] It was in these wonderfully replenished surroundings, beneath a bushel, that a sole copy of Catullus' poetry emerged just after 1300, only to be promptly lost again.

Snatches of Catullus' lines had been preserved by other ancient authors, odd quotes here and there which helped to corroborate the full manuscript, not as Catullus' own hand (it was a later copy made by someone who collected his poetry), but rather as his own poetic handiwork. In the tenth century, a bishop of Verona stumbled across Catullus' poetry. If he did not know before, then now he did: Latin lends itself formidably well to sexual expression.

The blushing bishop might well have been the individual who resigned the papyrus to the bushel for another three and a half centuries. A mysterious gentleman of Verona carried that manuscript back to that city 'from distant lands'. His identity was concealed in a mysterious note: a man 'upon whom France bestowed a name from the reeds, and who notes the journey of the passing crowd'. Whoever he was, and wherever the lands from which he retrieved them, it was thanks to him that Catullus' poems were preserved, to be released from the jar and restored to the pale and familiar light of northern Italy.[12] The humanists swiftly got to work, poring over the text and scouring it of errors. The original manuscript disappeared, but they made the copies that survived it. Through their scholarship, the first printed edition of Catullus' work was produced in Venice in 1472.

Fifty years later, Alfonso I d'Este, 3rd Duke of Ferrara, in the Po Valley (formerly part of Catullus' Cisalpine Gaul), was looking for art to adorn his home. His secretary, well versed in classical literature, assembled a montage of texts for a scheme for Alfonso's private study, in one wing of his castle. The story from Catullus' Bedspread Poem was among them.[13] Titian was commissioned to paint its scene.

Titian's canvas became Catullus' bedspread turned inside out, and mildly embroidered. The cloth Catullus painted in words became a cloth inspired by words, most of them Catullus' own.

What Titian embroidered on top of Catullus' bedspread was what Renaissance eyes wanted to see: reminiscences of Italy in the skyline; a painted version of a classical sculpture, the *Laocoön*, recently uncovered from Rome's soils; animals which the painting's patron, the duke, kept in his private zoo.

In the centre of the canvas is Bacchus, leaping from a cheetah-drawn chariot, twirling through the air. He has hungry eyes and parted lips, ready for kissing. Naked, almost, he wears about his shoulders a red cape that is velvet and amazingly billowy for its weight, revealing deliciously strong thighs beneath it. He gazes longingly towards King Minos' daughter, Ariadne, as she stands on the shore of Naxos. But her body is turned away from him, her heart fixed anxiously on the waters. With its canvas sails, Theseus' ship is just visible on the horizon. She is still mourning its departure.

APPENDIX

Poem 64
Catullus' Bedspread Poem

They say that pines were born long ago

From the head of Mount Pelion in Thessaly

And swam the sea, its undulating waves

To Phasis, pheasant river, and

The land of Aeetes the king

As young men, plucked from the

Flower of Greek youth in a mission

To steal the golden fleece

Of Colchis

Dared to skim with speeding stern

The salt sea,

Sweeping turquoise waters

With oars upturned like hands.

*

Divine Minerva, her keep a citadel

In the city's heights

Streamlined the flying chariot to the breeze

Herself, weaving, joining the pines together

To form a curving keel.

She, the ship, inured the innocent sea

To the flight of ships.

No sooner had she torn the capricious membrane

With her beak and with a twist of the oar

Turned the waters white with foam

Than from the whitening whirlpool there emerged

The unpainted faces

Of nymphs glistening in brine and gazing

In wonder at so novel a contraption.

On that day and no other men

Watched keen-eyed – they were human –

The naked bodies of nymphs

Rise until their breasts were free of the eddying white.

Then Peleus is said to have burned in love for Thetis.

Then nymph Thetis did not disparage a wedding to a mortal.

Then father Jupiter himself felt that Peleus ought

To be joined to Thetis in matrimony.

*

Heroes, born in the moment most admired

Beyond measure of all Ages, godly race,

Offspring of a noble mother,

Again and again I beseech you.

I shall commemorate you often in my poem,

Especially you, Peleus, stalwart of Thessaly,

Raised to the stars by so prosperous a match. For Jupiter,

Jupiter, father of the gods, gave up his love to you.

Did nymph Thetis bewitch you with her beauty?

Did Tethys truly allow you to wed her grand-daughter

And Ocean, too, her husband

Who envelops the whole world in sea?

Dawn came in a moment many times imagined and

All Thessaly flocked to her home as one.

The palace was filled

With the jubilant crowd who held gifts before their faces

And faces expressing joy.

Cieros was deserted, Phthian Tempe left behind,

The houses of Crannon, the walls of Larisa, empty;

They convened at Pharsalus, to Pharsalus and its homes

They flocked. No one tended the fields. The necks

Of bullocks grew soft through inactivity,

No curved scythe cleansed the soil beneath the vine,

No bull stooped beneath the yoke to cleave the earth,

No hook pruned the shade from the leaves of the trees,

Decay and rust overran the abandoned ploughshares.

But the house receded every which way

In regal opulence, and sparkled and glimmered

With gold and silver.

Ivory glinted off thrones, cups dazzled off tables,

The whole household delighted in the lustre of

Royal treasure.

Observe the couch at the heart of the palace,

A fine seat for a goddess,

Finished with ivory from India

And spread with purple tinged with the rose-pink

Dye of the murex fish.

This bedspread,

Embroidered with the shapes of men

Who lived long ago, unveils the virtues of heroes

Through the miracle of art.

Looking out from it

On the quietly shifting shore of Naxos

Ariadne watches Theseus

Fading with fast fleet and bears at heart

Fears she cannot temper.

Not yet does she believe she is seeing

What she is seeing,

Barely woken from sleep that deceived

To discover she is abandoned

And pitiful and alone on lonely sands.

But the young man is forgetful and fleeing

And pushes the waves away with oars,

Leaving his promises unfulfilled to the tempest that is stirring.

From afar atop the seaweed, with sad little eyes,

The daughter of Minos watches, ah she watches,

Him, like a stone sculpture of a bacchante.

She ebbs on currents swollen with pain,

Losing hold

On the fine band on her fair head

And the cloth that envelops her body in a gentle clinch

And the rounded bra that bounds her milky breasts.

All the coverings which have fallen from her body everywhere

The salt waves make sport of at her feet.

But neither headband nor fluttering veils vexed her

When in the fullness of her heart

She was missing you, Theseus,

With her every thought, in the fullness of her heart

Clinging to you, completely lost.

*

Poor girl, how Venus felled her with never-ending grief,

Sowing thorny worries in her heart

From the moment Theseus determined

A departure from the port of Piraeus on Athens' arced shore

And reached the palace of the unjust king of Crete.

For they say that Athens, plagued by damnation

To pay the penalty for the murder of Androgeos,

Would at one time provide its pick of youths

And glory of maidens as a feast for the Minotaur.

The fledgling city was suffering the consequences

When Theseus chose to yield his own body

For precious Athens so the living dead of Cecrops

Should not be carried to such deaths in Crete.

And so he put his trust in a light ship and gentle breeze

And came before haughty Minos

And his magnificent enclosure.

The moment the virgin princess clapped her

Widening eyes upon him –

Her pure little bed was still protecting her in a soft

And motherly embrace, breathing sweetly

Over her the fragrant breath

Of myrtle such as the River Eurotas puts forth

Or the breeze spring plucks from flowers of many colours –

And averted her hot eyes from him only when
Her whole body had caught the flame of love
And she burned deep inside to the depths of her marrow.

Wretchedly rousing passions in his cruel heart,
Divine Cupid, weaver of joys with worries among men,
And Venus, ruler of the Golgians and leafy Idalium.
On what waves you inflamed the girl, threw her
From her wits, as she sighed for her fair guest
With breath upon breath.
How huge the fears she carried in her wearied heart.
How many times she paled beyond gleaming gold,
When putting his mind to conquering the savage monster
Theseus sought either death or the fruits of glory.
Promising little gifts to the gods that were not unwelcome
But futile nonetheless, she mouthed vows silently.

Like an oak tree or cone-bearing pine with seeping bark
Shaking its branches on the heights of Mount Taurus
Whose twisting trunk a storm uproots in a flash –
And the tree, torn from the roots,
Falls prostrate and far
Breaking whatever lies in its broad path –
So Theseus laid the beast low, conquering its force
While it tossed its horns ineffectually to the empty breeze.

From there and high on glory the stranger retraced his path,

Steering his wandering course with the delicate thread

So the deception of the enclosure should not defeat him

As he departed from meandering turns of the labyrinth.

But come, I digress from my primary song,

Recollecting further how the girl departed

From the face of her father, the embrace of her sister,

And finally her mother, who tried wretchedly

To feel happy for her lost daughter, who put above

Them all her sweet love for Theseus;

Or how she came to the foaming shore of Naxos

By boat; or how her partner abandoned her as she

Was buried in sleep, sailing away,

Forgetful through and through.

They say that, raging in the passion in her heart,

She would release deeply felt and audible words,

Then climbed the steep mountains in sadness

To extend from there her view over the vast swell

Of sea, then sallied forth into the salt waves

Dancing before her and raising her soft clothes

To bare her calves, uttered in sorrow these final complaints,

Preparing cold little sobs on wet lips:

*

'Was it for this I was taken from my father's hearth, traitor,

For you to leave me on an empty shore, traitor, Theseus?

So you leave me, heedless of the gods' authority,

Forgetful, ah. Do you carry home your perjured vows?

Could nothing alter the intention in your cruel mind?

Could there be no mercy to tempt you to take

Pity on me for all your hardness of heart?

These were not the promises you once made

Me in a warming tone, these are not what you bade

My wretchedness to hope for, but a happy marriage,

Longed-for wedding songs, everything

The wandering breezes have scattered vain.

May no woman now believe a man when he makes a promise,

May no woman hope the words of her man are true.

While their minds are desirous, desperate to obtain something,

They are afraid of swearing nothing,

There is nothing they won't promise.

But as soon as the lust in their desirous minds is sated,

They remember none of their words,

Have no fear of perjury.

There's no doubt I seized you as you tossed

Mid death throes, and more than that I elected to lose

My half-brother rather than fail you,

Deceitful man, in your final hour.

For that I am to be torn apart by beasts and given to birds

As prey – and no mound of earth will be piled upon my corpse.

What kind of lioness bore you beneath a lonely rock,

What sea conceived you and spat you out from its foaming waves,

What Syrtis, what fierce Scylla, what monstrous Charybdis,

You, who offer such returns for your sweet life?

If a marriage to me was not in your heart

Because you feared the savage reprimands of your aged father

You might still have led me to your home

To be a slave to you in a joyous labour,

Washing your white feet with pure water,

Spreading your bed with a purple bedspread.

But I have been felled by trouble so why pile

Fruitless complaints on the dumb winds which lack

The feelings to hear

My words and respond in kind?

He is almost mid ocean now,

No human shape is visible on dull seaweed.

So far does cruel fate mock me in my desperate

Times and begrudge even ears to my complaints.

*

All-powerful Jupiter, I wish the ships of Cecrops

Had not touched the shores of Cnossos in the first place,

That the traitor, bringing a gruesome tribute to

The ungovernable bull, had not tethered his ship in Crete,

That the evil man did not hide his cruel plans

Behind a handsome exterior

And stay here as a guest in our home.

For where can I take myself now?

What kind of hope can I cling to? I am lost.

Shall I make for the mountains of Ida?

But the savage sea divides, separates me

From them, swirling far and wide.

Or should I expect my father to help me?

Did I not leave him as I pursued a young man

Spattered with my brother's blood?

Or should I console myself

With the loyalty and love of a husband,

A man who flees, bending heavy oars in the swirling sea?

Worse, I am on a lonely island, a shore with no shelter,

And no way out reveals itself on the circling waves of water.

There is no means of escape, no hope. Everything is silent,

Everything deserted; everything points to death.

*

But my eyes will not fall shut on me in death,

My senses will not leave my wearied body

Until I demand from the gods rich justice for my betrayal

And in my final hour pray for the loyalty of the gods.

So Eumenides, punishers and avengers of the crimes

Of men, your forehead, fringed with snaky hair,

Exposing the anger exhaled from your chest,

Here, come here, hear my complaints,

Which I am forced in my wretched helplessness

To pour from the depths of my marrow, blazing,

Blinded by mindless madness.

As these truths are born from the bottom of my heart

Please do not allow my grief to turn to dust,

But with the kind of heart Theseus had when he left me,

Goddesses, may he destroy himself and his family.'

After she poured these words from her sad breast,

Troubled, demanding punishment for wicked deeds,

The ruler of the gods

Whose authority goes unchallenged

Nodded his agreement,

At the movement of which the

Earth and choppy seas trembled

And the firmament shook its gleaming stars.

*

But as for Theseus, his mind gripped by murky darkness,

He released from his forgetful heart all the instructions

Which hitherto he was guarding permanently in his mind,

Nor raising the sweet signs to his sad father

Did he show that he had seen the port of Athens safely.

For they say that once, when Aegeus entrusted his son

To the winds as he left the goddess' walls in his ship,

He embraced the young man and gave him these instructions:

'My only son, dearer to me than life's length,

Son, whom I am forced to send into an uncertain situation,

Returned to me only recently at the height of my old age,

Since my fate and your determined virtue snatch you

Away from me against my will, though my tired eyes are

Not yet drunk with the dear shape of my son,

I shall not send you rejoicing with a happy heart

Or allow you to carry the signs of good fortune,

But first I shall free my heart of countless laments,

And pour soil over my white hair and defile it with ash,

Then hang dyed sails from my bending mast

So that sails dipped in Iberian rust may proclaim

This grief of mine, this blaze in my head.

But if Minerva of sacred Itonus, who agreed to defend our race

And the seat of Erechtheus, allows you to sprinkle your

Right hand with the blood of the bull,

Then see that these commands endure,

Kept safe in your remembering heart –

May no time erase them.

As soon as your eyes light upon our hills

Drop each black cloth from the yards

And let your twisted ropes hoist white sails

So as soon as possible I may see them and know

True happiness in my heart, as the blessed

Hour brings you back to me.'

These instructions, which until now Theseus was holding

Constantly in his thoughts, seeped away

Like clouds struck by a blast of wind

From the high summit of a snowy mountain.

But his father, as he sought a view from the top of the citadel,

Spilt a flood of tears from his anxious eyes

As soon as he caught sight of the billowing sails,

And threw himself headlong from the top

Of the cliffs

Assuming Theseus lost to cruel fate.

So savage Theseus entered a household

Decked in mourning for his father's death

And caught the same sort of grief

He had imposed on the daughter of Minos
Through the neglectfulness of his heart.

Then she, watching in her sorrow his ship
Disappearing, drifted from one worry
To another in her wounded heart.

But from another part of the cloth
Flew in vigorous Bacchus
With his throng of Satyrs and Silenes from Nysa,
Seeking you, Ariadne, burning in love for you.
His followers were raging all over, out of their wits.
'Euhoe!' bacchantes tossing their heads with cries 'Euhoe!'
One section were shaking sticks with covered tips,
Another were hurling the limbs of a dismembered bullock,
Others were dressing themselves in plaits of snakes,
Others were gathering in worship of sacraments
Concealed in hollow baskets,
Rites which the profane long to hear, but in vain.
Others were patting drums with outstretched palms,
Or causing round cymbal tin to sing and ring,
Many had horns which blew booming booms
And the Phrygian flute shrieked in shrill song.

*

The bedspread, richly embroidered with shapes like these,
Embraced the wedding bed with its own covering.

When the youth of Thessaly had gazed at it eagerly
Enough they began to make way for the blessed gods.
Here, just as the shivering West Wind wakes the curving
Waves in the early morning with its gust across the calm sea,
While Aurora rises towards the course of wandering Sun,
And at first the waves progress slowly, hit by a gentle breeze,
And resonate with a ripple of little laughter,
Then as the wind builds up they grow larger and larger,
And reflect the light as they swim away from purple dawn,
So then in the atrium the guests left the royal palace
On wandering feet and made their own way home.

The first to arrive after they left was Chiron
From the peak of Pelion, carrying woodland gifts:
All the plains bear, all Thessaly
Grows on her high mountains,
All the flowers the life-giving breeze of the
Warm West Wind nourishes near the stream,
He arranged them all in assorted garlands,
Struck by the pleasant scent of which the household smiled.

*

On his heels Penios the river god came from green Tempe,

Tempe, which hanging woods fringe from above,

[*corruption in text*] . . . leaving to celebrate their dancing.

And not without gifts: for he brought tall beeches with

Their roots and straight-trunked laurel sky-reaching

And nodding plane and the pliant sister

Of fire-consumed Phaethon and airy cypress.

He positioned them all around the palace

Intermingled so the hall would grow green

Decked with soft foliage.

Ingenious Prometheus followed behind him,

Wearing faded scars of his former punishment,

Which once he paid, his limbs tied

To a rock by chains

As he hung from a sheer cliff face.

Then the father of the gods arrived with his blessed wife

And children, leaving in the heavens only you

Phoebus Apollo, with your twin

Who tends the mountains of Idrus:

For you and your sister were united in despising Peleus,

And recoiled from lighting wedding flames for Thetis.

*

After the gods moulded their limbs to white seats

At tables laden generously with all sorts of dishes

With bodies trembling in unsteady gait

The Fates began to sing their prophetic song.

A white shawl swamped their trembling body

And covered their ankles with its purple border;

Pink headbands rested upon their white head

And their hands plucked dutifully

At a task that lasts forever.

The left hand was holding a distaff

Wrapped in soft wool. Drawing the threads gently

The right shaped them with upturned fingers,

Twisting them under the thumb and turning

The weighted spindle with smooth handle,

And a tooth was ever plucking to make the weaving

Even, and pieces of wool which obtruded before

From the light threads dangled from their dry withered lips,

And in front of their feet they were guarding

Soft fleeces of shining wool in little twig-lined baskets.

And plucking the fleeces with a voice of precision

They poured forth what was fated in divine song,

Song no age thereafter could allege was false:

*

'Defence of Thessaly, enriching your magnificence with
Virtues great, dearest to Jupiter son of Ops,
Hear what the Sisters reveal to you in happy light,
An accurate oracle: but you, the fates follow,
    Run on, drawing out the weft, run on, spindles.

The Evening Star will come to you
Bringing what grooms long for,
Come will the wife beneath a well-omened star
To pour out her heart to you with love to distraction,
Ready to languish with you in sleep you share,
Spreading her gentle arms beneath your strong neck.
    Run on, drawing out the weft, run on, spindles.

No house has ever sheltered love like this,
No love has joined lovers in such a pact as
Lives in the harmony of Thetis and Peleus.
    Run on, drawing out the weft, run on, spindles.

Achilles will be born to you, a fearless man,
Known to the enemy not by back but by brave chest,
Ever the victor in the cross-country race,
He will outstrip the fire-quick footsteps of swift deer.
    Run on, drawing out the weft, run on, spindles.

*

There's not a hero who will compare with him in battle
When the Trojan plains grow wet with Greek blood
And Agamemnon, third heir of treacherous Pelops,
Besieges and lays waste to the walls of Troy
In protracted war.
   Run on, drawing out the weft, run on, spindles.

Time and again mothers will speak of his unequalled virtues
And distinguished deeds at the funerals of their sons
As they release unwashed hair from their white crowns
And bruise aged breasts with weak hands.
   Run on, drawing out the weft, run on, spindles.

For as a reaper picks thick bundles of corn
Beneath the blazing sun and harvests the blond fields,
So he will lay low the bodies of the Troy-born
With unforgiving iron.
   Run on, drawing out the weft, run on, spindles.

The River Scamander will witness his great virtues
As it flows in profusion into the rapid Hellespont
And its passage grows narrow through the
Slaughtered bodies that mount up and
Warms its deep waters with indiscriminate blood.
   Run on, drawing out the weft, run on, spindles.

*

The final witness will be the booty paid for with death

When a rounded tomb heaped upon

A high rampart receives the white limbs

Of a virgin slain.

   Run on, drawing out the weft, run on, spindles.

For the moment fate surrenders power

To wearied Greeks, releasing Neptune's bonds

On the city of Dardanus,

The high tomb will grow wet with Polyxena's blood,

As like a sacrificial victim falling beneath the ready knife,

She throws down her headless body as her knees give way.

   Run on, drawing out the weft, run on, spindles.

So come, unite the lovers in the love they have longed for,

May the husband welcome his goddess in happy contract

And the bride be given to her eager husband at last.

   Run on, drawing out the weft, run on, spindles.

Returning at the rise of dawn her nurse

Will not be able to encircle her neck with yesterday's ribbon,

Nor her worrying mother, sad for a difficult daughter

Who sleeps alone, lose hope for dear grandchildren.

   Run on, drawing out the weft, run on, spindles.

*

With predictions like these the Fates once sang

From the divinity of their heart a felicitous song for Peleus.

For the sky-lying gods used to visit the unblemished

Homes of heroes in the past in person

And show themselves in the assemblies of men

When piety was yet to be broken.

Calling upon the shining temples

When the annual rites of festival days arrived

The father of the gods would watch one hundred

Bulls fall prostrate in sacrifice.

Often wayfaring Bacchus led from the high summit

Of Parnassus his Euhoe-crying, wild-hair flowing

Bacchantes, when all of Delphi rushed from the city at once

To welcome the god, rejoicing, with smoking altars.

Often in the death-dealing struggle of war Mars

Or Minerva, mistress of rapid Triton

Or Nemesis Ramnusian virgin

Stood beside armed soldiers

And gave the bands their encouragement.

But after the earth was infected with unspeakable crime

And everyone put justice to flight from his grasping mind,

Brother drenched hands in the blood of brother,

Son ceased to grieve for the death of father and mother,

Father longed for the premature death of his son

So freely he could get purchase on the flower of a new wife,

Mother lay herself down beneath her naïve son,

Wrongful and unafraid of doing sacrilege to her household gods –

All things speakable and unspeakable, muddled together in evil fury,

Have turned the just minds of our gods away from us.

So they do not dignify our assemblies with their presence,

Or even bear to touch the clear light of day.

Note on Currency and Measures

In Rome in the late Republic:

I *sesterce* bought two loaves of bread. An adult labourer typically
earned 3 *sesterces* a day

I *quadrans* was a sixteenth of a *sesterce*. It bought entry to the less
exclusive baths

I *talent* was about 25kg weight, perhaps 24,000 *sesterces*

I *Roman foot* was just under 30cm

A *stadium* (pl: *stadia*) was 625 Roman feet, or 187.5 metres

NOTES

Abbreviations used in Notes

AP – *Anthologia Palatina*

HE – Gow, A. S. F., and Page, D. L. (1965), *The Greek Anthology: Hellenistic Epigrams* Vols I–II (Cambridge, Cambridge University Press)

Prologue

1 Jerome wrote that Catullus lived no longer than thirty years. He put his birth at 87 BC, but that would mean that Catullus died before many of the events he described in his poetry even came to pass. Writers in antiquity agreed that he did not live long (for example, see Ovid *Amores* 3.9.62). The latest datable reference in his poetry is at the very end of 54 BC or beginning of 53 BC, and it would appear that he died at a similar time to the philosopher Lucretius, whose death most scholars put at 55 BC (Cornelius Nepos, 'after the death of Lucretius and Catullus . . .'; *Life of Atticus* 12.4; cf. Schwabe (1862) p. 46). I believe that Catullus died in 53 BC, putting his date of birth at circa 82 BC.

2 Ovid *Amores* 2.4.5.

3 Propertius 2.25.4.

4 There is a good discussion of the various meanings of *nugae* in Newman (1990) pp. 30–6. Both Newman (1990) pp. 356–66, and Wiseman (1985) pp. 191–97, consider the possibility that Catullus also wrote mimes. In the first century AD, Juvenal alluded (at *Satire* 8.186) to a play called *Phasma* ('Ghost') by a certain Catullus, probably a later rendition of a drama by the Athenian playwright Menander.

---

5 Catullus revealed in Poem 79 that Lesbia was a pseudonym for one of Clodius Pulcher's sisters. In patrician families, women were called by the family name in the feminine form, and Clodius had three sisters. Scholars have therefore disputed the precise identity of Catullus' 'Lesbia'. Catullus wrote that his Lesbia was still married when he became involved with her, which I believe happened in Rome in or around 61 BC. The youngest Claudia divorced Lucullus, the general, in 66 BC, and the second sister was widowed in 61 BC. There is no record of them remarrying, although they might well have done so. The eldest Clodia was married to a politician called Quintus Caecilius Metellus Celer until 59 BC, and contemporary descriptions of her involvement in the politics of Clodius, and her interests as a poet herself, seem to chime with Catullus' portrait. Clodia Metelli may have only been a half-sister of Clodius Pulcher (Shackleton Bailey, see for example (2000) p. 181), but as the Roman authors did not distinguish her as such, I follow suit and refer to them simply as brother and sister. On the identification of Lesbia with Clodia, see also Apuleius *Apologia* 10.

6 Hesiod incorporates these myths into his *Works and Days* and *Theogony*.

7 Plutarch *Sulla* 2 on his eyes and complexion.

8 Strabo *Geography* 12.3.1.

9 After Sulla, Marcus Aemilius Lepidus, a consul, demanded the restoration of the tribunate. The Senate appointed him governor of Cisalpine Gaul (Plutarch *Pompey* 16.1), and he dispatched one of his ambassadors, Marcus Junius Brutus (it was his son who would one day become the most famous of Julius Caesar's assassins) to raise an army, while he marched on Rome seeking a second consulship. Pompey put down Brutus and his men, besieging him at Modena. Lepidus retired to the countryside and died soon after.

10 Plutarch *Pompey* 13.

11 Lucullus scored some victories across Armenia, for instance, with whose king Mithridates was allied. Cicero *de imperio Gn. Pompei* 5, *Lucullum, magnis rebus gestis ab eo bello discedere.*

12 Kidnap: Suetonius *Caesar* 4. In the wake of the Hannibalic War and Rome's historic victory over Carthage, formerly the superpower of the seas, Rhodes and Delos lacked the naval capacity to keep the rogues at bay, and it was becoming increasingly obvious that it was in the hands of Italy to address the situation.

13 After Mithridates' suicide, Pompey allowed him to be laid to rest in a

grand mausoleum in the city in which he was born, Sinope in Pontus. On Pompey's struggle against Mithridates the account of Dio *Roman History* 36.45–53 (which dates to *c.*200 AD) is particularly engaging.

14 Appian *Mithridatic Wars* 106.

15 A law was eventually passed granting Pompey control over Bithynia, Pontus and Cilicia and the surrounding territory. Power over the lands Mithridates had acquired around Armenia was bestowed upon chieftains. The remaining lands were divided into eleven city states and added to Bithynia. See Strabo *Geography* 12.3.1.

16 Wiseman (1987) p. 331 (and see Asconius *in Pisonem* 2–3) made this point to show that Catullus' father was likely to have been a governor or magistrate. His argument has been accepted by most scholars of Catullus since. Shortly before Catullus was born, Verona became a Roman colony, but acquired merely *ius Latii*, Latin rights, a second-rate citizenship that did not enfranchise its citizens. Eight years before Catullus was born, his people had joined much of Italy in engaging Rome in a Social War ('War of the Allies') to acquire Roman citizenship, aching for inclusivity as well as the tangible benefits, including the vote. Julius Caesar became anxious to give Cisalpine towns citizenship in return for their loyalty, but would only be able to do so in 49 BC.

I: In search of Catullus

1 The friendship of Julius Caesar and Catullus' father is discussed in Suetonius *Caesar* 73.

2 On Brescia's rusticity and frugality see Pliny the Younger *Epistles* 1.14.

3 Verona sat on an old Roman road that passed from Genoa in the west to Aquileia in the east. The region was vulnerable to attack. Twenty years before Catullus was born, a Germanic tribe, the Cimbri, had marched in its thousands through the Brenner Pass and into the nearby Veneto, plundering everything, making it home. Even after the Romans defeated them they remained, rendering the region a desiccated sea of eager colonists.

4 Pliny *Natural History* 3.23.

5 Herodotus (*Histories* 1.93–4) and Catullus were probably right in thinking that the Etruscans originated in ancient Lydia. In 2007, a genetic variant discovered in the DNA extracted from men whose families had lived in a town in Tuscany for at least three generations was found to be common only to native Turks. The closest blood relatives of these modern-day

Etruscans reside in Izmir, the very area the famine-afflicted Lydians were said to have rested before entering Italy over three thousand years ago. The results of this study were revealed in a paper by Professor Alberto Piazza (University of Turin) at a conference of the European Society of Human Genetics in June 2007. The *Guardian* picked up the story (article by John Hooper, 18 June 2007).

6 Catullus wrote of a friend's mother in Poem 9. If neither Catullus nor his brother nor any other sibling lived to have children, then cousins of the same generation did. The family name lived on at Rome and in Cisalpine Gaul (inscription at Brixia *CIL* V 4484).

7 On the possible aims of the Catilinarians, there is an interesting account in Sallust *Catiline* 38.

8 Under a law passed in 122 BC by Gaius Gracchus, the most famous tribune of the age, Roman citizens were entitled to a trial before any decisions were made about death sentences. The fact that much of Gracchus' legislation had been wholly disregarded for the last half century, and that there was a loophole which meant that such rulings could be overturned in extreme circumstances could conveniently be pushed aside. The tribune, Metellus Nepos, not only vetoed Cicero from making his parting address, but also rallied for Pompey to return from the East and use his army to settle the tensions that lingered across Italy in the aftermath of Catiline's conspiracy. Julius Caesar supported this idea. Metellus Nepos also suggested that Pompey might register as a candidate for another consulship the following year. However, Cato the Younger, a staunch optimate, blocked his request for Pompey to stand for a consulship without entering Rome first. Metellus Nepos fell into such a rage that the Senate had to pass an emergency measure to deprive him of his post. Seizing his chance, Cicero delivered a vituperative speech against him for so heartlessly depriving him of the chance to speak on the last day of his consulship. Nepos fled Rome for the East. For supporting his proposals, Caesar was briefly suspended from office. Metellus Celer wrote Cicero a letter expressing his grievance at the contretemps between him and his brother, Metellus Nepos. Cicero wrote back and told him that he had even approached his sister Mucia and wife Clodia in the hope that they would persuade Metellus Nepos to check his hostility towards him, but had not prevailed. See letters Cicero *ad Fam* 5.1; 5.2.

II: The house on the Palatine Hill

1 Buildings obstructing augurs' views – Cicero *de officiis* 3.66.

2 Plutarch *Crassus* 2.

3 Several historians have suggested that Metellus Celer might have offered Catullus introductions at Rome. See, for example, Burl (2010) p. 31.

4 Cicero *ad Atticum* 1.18.

5 Poets would continue to flock to Rome in the next generation. Ovid would come here from Sulmona, to Rome's east, and Virgil would travel from Mantua. Horace would arrive from Apulia, in the heel of Italy, and Martial from Spain.

6 See Pliny *Natural History* 31.41 on salt and its applications to the intellect.

7 Cicero *de Domo* 37 on his own house in the same area.

8 On the early history of the Palatine Hill see Boni (1913) pp. 242–52.

9 Plutarch *Romulus* 20.

10 Plutarch *Lucullus* 33.

11 Plutarch *Lucullus* 39.

12 Cicero bought the house in 62 BC. The property's trees and extravagant columns, which pre-dated Cicero's residency, became notorious, see Valerius Maximus *Facta* 9.1.4; Pliny *Natural History* 17.1–5.

13 This description is based on typical villas in this region: nothing remains of Metellus' property.

14 Wiseman (1985) p. 21 also looks at this temple. The temple's remains survive today near the Theatre of Marcellus on the Campus Martius.

15 Pliny *Natural History* 35.3.

16 On the distant ancestry see Suetonius *Tiberius* 1.1.

17 Diodorus Siculus *Library of History* 20.36.1–2.

18 The change in spelling took place prior to 61 BC, as Cicero's letters referring to her brother 'Clodius' reveal.

19 A few decades earlier, a Latin poet named Valerius Aedituus had written a version of the same poem, but his word order rendered his lines somewhat clumsier than Catullus'. Valerius Aedituus *cit.* Gellius *Attic Nights* 19.9.10. See Courtney (1993) p. 70.

20 Horace would later adapt the same lines to describe his own tears and frozen tongue. Horace *Carmen* 4.1.33–6.

21 See criticism of 'eyes not dark' in Catullus Poem 43; Cicero's references to Clodia's 'oxen eyes' are ubiquitous in his correspondence with Atticus, his equestrian friend.

22 Plutarch *Caesar* 9.4.

23 Based on the account of Juvenal *Satires* 6.314–45.

24 Clodius incited the mutiny when they were quartering at Nisibis (modern south-east Turkey) in winter 68–67 BC. Many were disillusioned with Lucullus' style of leadership. Clodius proceeded to Cilicia, where he was stationed under Marcius Rex, husband of his second sister, and where he was taken prisoner. He was in Gaul in 64 BC.

25 Cicero *de Haruspicum Responso* 44.

26 Tatum (1999) pp. 74–5.

27 Plutarch (*Caesar* 9) was a biographer who believed this.

28 Suetonius *Julius Caesar* 74; Dio *Roman History* 37.45.

29 Cicero *ad Atticum* 2.1; Cicero *ad Fam* 1.9.

30 Seneca *Epistle* 97.

31 Plutarch *Crassus* 7.

32 Suetonius *Caesar* 10.

33 Dio *Roman History* 37.52–3.

34 Suetonius *Caesar* 7.

35 Plutarch *Pompey* 44. Pompey had seen how hostile Cato had been towards his fervent supporter Metellus Nepos, the brother of Metellus Celer, and clearly hoped that a wedding would soften him.

36 Even the historians were willing to record the rumours, see Suetonius *Caesar* 50.

37 Plutarch *Pompey* 45.

38 Plutarch *Pompey* 42.

39 Cloak: Appian *Mithridatic Wars* 117.

40 Diodorus Siculus *Library of History* 5.26.

41 One of the finest wines of the age, Falernian, a glorious, sweet, nectar-coloured liquid from Campania, superior even to Verona's local, was a favourite among the elite. Raetian was not quite as good as Falernian – Virgil *Georgics* 2.95–6.

III: An elegant new little book

1 On the dedication to Cornelius Nepos see Ausonius *Eclogue* I, who discerns irony in Catullus' apparent modesty.

2 A similar phrase is found in an earlier Roman comedy: Plautus *Aulularia* 84.

3 The episode is said to have taken place when Metellus Celer was in Gaul. See Pomponius Mela *de Chorographia* 3.38; Pliny *Natural History* 2.67.

4 Cornelius Nepos *Life of Atticus* 12.4.

5 Pliny *Natural History* 36.42.

6 A remnant of what he did not include in Cornelius' copy read: 'If any of you chance to become readers of my untimely ramblings . . .' (Poem 14b). It was a draft dedication, or the introduction to a different poetry volume entirely.

7 It might have been modelled on Callimachus' request in his *Aetia*, Fr. 7.14.

8 Propertius 2.25; 2.34; Ovid *Amores* 3.9.

9 In Catullus Poem 53 there is a reference to Calvus as *salaputium disertum*, which Seneca the Elder uses as evidence of Calvus' short stature, *erat enim parvolus statura propter quod etiam Catullus in hendecasyllabis vocat illum salaputium disertum* (*Controversiae* 7.4). It is uncertain what *salaputium* means, but from Seneca and Catullus together we can say it has to do with size: Calvus was small.

10 Suetonius *Caesar* 45.

11 Calvus *lo cit.* Servius *ad Verg. Eclogue* 6.47.

12 Gellius *Attic Nights* 19.13.

13 Virgil *Eclogues* 9.35–6. Cinna was slightly older than Catullus and Calvus.

14 Publius Valerius Cato was said to have taught many distinguished poets, but died an old man in poverty. See Suetonius *de grammaticis* 11. One poet claimed that this Valerius Cato was responsible for *establishing* the poets. Catullus did not go so far, but clearly admired his work, which included grammar books and two (now lost) learned poems, *Lydia* ('a book of great consideration to learned people', according to an erotic poet named Ticidas), and *Diana*, of which Cinna said, 'May the Dictynna [Diana] of our Cato survive down the generations.'

15 On the novelty of Catullus' name see Wheeler (1964) p. 108.

16 Plutarch *Cato the Younger* 1.2.

17 Cicero *ad Atticum* 2.1.8.

18 Possibly the lawyer and writer Publius Alfenus Varus, of whom very little is known today, see Neudling (1955) p. 2.

19 Varus and Suffenus were probably one and the same, Nisbet (1995) p. 411.

20 Cicero used these terms after 50 BC, see for example *ad Atticum* 7.2. He also called them *cantores Euphorionis*, 'singers of Euphorion' (*Tusculanae* 3.45 (*c.*45 BC)). The Greek poet Euphorion perpetuated Callimachus' legacy, and Catullus might have been familiar with his hexameter works.

21 These poets included Valerius Aedituus, Quintus Lutatius Catulus, and Laevius. On these poets and the surviving fragments see Courtney (1993). The satirist Gaius Lucilius would also have been an influence.

22 See Trimble (2012) on expurgated commentaries of Catullus.

23 In 1989 the decision to include three of Catullus' more risqué poems on a Latin A-level syllabus inspired a heated media debate. Eventually, the board resolved to keep the poems on the syllabus, but set no questions on them.

24 *Doctus:* Tibullus 3.6.41; Ovid *Amores* 3.9.62 *et ubique*.

25 Catullus was more familiar with the recent history, which had seen Rome inherit the kingdom from the Ptolemies of Egypt, who themselves had assumed rule over the region in the era after Alexander the Great. Embassies and trade had passed between the Ptolemies and Rome for some time.

26 Quintus Lutatius Catulus, for example, adapted Callimachus *Epigram* 41.

27 Callimachus Fragment 398.

28 Cicadas over asses, from the prologue to Callimachus *Aetia* (Fragment 1.29–30).

29 Cicero *Brutus* 171.

30 Holland (1979) pp. 11–13.

IV: Sparrow

1 An erotic poet in Rome named Ticidas was also using a pseudonym, 'Perilla' (—◡◡), for his lover Metella (—◡◡), and later poets would follow suit. Ovid would study Catullus' poems to Lesbia as he went about developing the genre of love elegy. In around 15 BC, he would publish his *Amores*, elegies which drew upon his relationship with his lover 'Corinna', the name of a real Greek female poet.

2 Cicero *Pro Caelio* 27.

3 Stevenson (2005) p. 35 convincingly argued that this poet, Cornificia, wife of Camerius, was part of Catullus' circle. Cornificia was commemorated alongside her brother in a monument inscription (*CIL* 6.1300a) in Rome: CORNIFICIA Q. F. CAMERI Q. CORNIFICIUS Q. F. FRATER PR. AUGUR (Cornificia, daughter of Quintus, wife of Camerius; her brother Praetor and Augur, Quintus Cornificius, son of Quintus). Cornificius found success on the back of political rather than poetical ventures, though in Poem 38 Catullus requested a poem of him 'sadder than the tears of Simonides', a Greek poet who lived a century after Sappho. A surviving fragment of Cornificius' work shows he admired Callimachean brevity: *deducta mihi voce garrienti*, perhaps, 'My voice is reduced to mere chatter' (*cit.* Macrobius *Saturnalia* 6.4.12).

4 I believe that Calvus' Quintilia was synonymous with the 'Quintia' of Catullus Poem 86. Some later authors believed that Calvus was married to Quintilia (cf. Diomedes 376 Keil *Calvus alibi ad uxorem 'prima epistula videtur in via delita'*), but he was more likely to celebrate a lover in verses as he did.

5 On Roman attitudes to disability, see Garland (1995). Many babies with disabilities were 'exposed', that is: left outside to die at birth. Catullus was not blind, but if he had a lazy eye it might have proved of interest to some Romans; Homer was conventionally viewed as blind, and represented as such in sculptures.

6 Cato the Elder *cit.* Aulus Gellius *Attic Nights* 10.23.4; no examples of this law being used survive.

7 Sappho Fragment 1.

8 Meleager *AP* 7.195.

9 Shakespeare *Romeo and Juliet* 2.2.182.

10 Dio *Roman History* 37.49.

11 Cicero *ad Atticum* 1.19.

12 On Lucullus' achievements prior to his replacement by Pompey see Cicero *de imperio Gn. Pompei* especially 20–6.

13 Clodia served as Clodius' go-between as she relayed his conversations to Atticus, Cicero's friend (Cicero *ad Atticum* 2.9), see also Cicero *ad Atticum* 2.14.

14 Over a century later, the biographer Plutarch (*Cicero* 29.3) claimed that Cicero's wife Terentia jealously believed that Clodia Metelli wanted to

marry Cicero. This is almost certainly inaccurate, and even if true says more about Terentia's temperament than Clodia's ambitions.

15 Cicero *ad Atticum* 2.1.

16 Cicero *ad Atticum* 2.1; see also Dio *Roman History* 37.51.

17 Ovid *Amores* 2.12(13).3–4.

18 Virgil *Aeneid* 2.242–43: *quater ipso in limine portae / substitit.*

19 Cicero *ad Atticum* 12.52; 13.7. Cicero wrote a series of letters to his friend Atticus in 45 BC expressing his desire to purchase some gardens. He found himself particularly enamoured of land a Clodia owned near the Tiber. Enquiring about its availability, he happened to mention the divorce between one of the patrician politicians whom Caesar supported, Publius Lentulus Spinther, and a certain Metella. The context of his letter implied that the Metella in question was the daughter of Metellus Celer and his wife Clodia. Metella would have an affair with Publius Cornelius Dolabella, the husband of Cicero's daughter Tullia (see Cicero *ad Atticum* 11.23). The connection between Clodia Metelli, the gardens, Metella and Lentulus Spinther was discussed by Shackleton Bailey (2004) pp. 412–13, citing an earlier scholar, Münzer, and remains convincing. Metella, the daughter of Clodia, may even have been the Metella whom Ticidas, an erotic poet connected to Catullus' set, wrote poems for under the pseudonym 'Perilla'. Little is known of Ticidas, but see Ovid *Tristia* 2.433.

20 Pliny *Natural History* 29.27.

21 Soranus *Gynaecology* 1.20, writing in the first century AD.

22 Soranus *Gynaecology* 1.60–1. See Hopkins (1965) pp. 134–35 on ancient contraception.

V: The rumours of our elders

1 The identification of Catullus' Furius with the poet from Cremona Marcus Furius Bibaculus is likely, especially as Tacitus wrote of both poets in the same line in reference to verses they wrote about Julius Caesar, *carmina Bibaculi et Catulli . . . (Annals* 4.34). Few fragments of Furius Bibaculus' work survive, but Suetonius quoted him in *de grammaticis* 11. Among other surviving fragments of his work is a reference to Memnon, a king of Ethiopia whom Achilles was said to have killed (Horace *Satires* 1.10.36).

2 Theophrastus *Characters* 4; 25. On the concept of 'softness', see Aristotle *Nicomachean Ethics*.

3 Fragment 2, attributed to Catullus, *cit.* Nonius. The line may have been spoken by Priapus, and refer to another activity; there is no certainty as to its reference.

4 So Propertius (2.34.87–8) recalled how the writings of Catullus made Lesbia notorious.

5 Dupont (1992) p. 110.

6 Seneca *Epistle* 97.

7 Polybius *Histories* 6.57.

8 Horace *Satires* 1.1.100–01. It was Clodia's later lover Caelius Rufus who spoke of her frigidity *cit.* Quintilian *Institutio Oratoria* 8.6.53.

9 Lucretius *de Rerum Natura* 4.1274.

10 Martial *Epigram* 11.15.

11 Scholars have observed that Catullus seems to recognise Furius as a critic, for example, Green (1940) p. 353.

12 Gutzwiller (2012) pp. 83–4.

13 Ellis (1889) p. 22.

14 Cf. Kutzko (2006) p. 408.

15 Ovid *Tristia* 2.427–29.

16 Skinner (2003) p. 100.

17 Furius Bibaculus *cit.* Suetonius *de grammaticis* 9 on the learned Lucius Orbilius Pupillus, who lived long but lost his memory.

VI: The power of three

1 Such was the voting system for the consuls. Even in the elections for tribunes, citizens were divided into tribes in order to vote. It was rare that men living outside Rome had a voice in these elections, since they needed to present their votes in Rome in person.

2 Q. Arrius: Cicero *ad Atticum* 1.17; *Brutus* 242–43; *ad Atticum* 2.5. In other letters to Atticus, Cicero mentioned an irritating man called C. Arrius, who was possibly the same character: see Cicero *ad Atticum* 2.14; 2.15 and Ramage (1959) pp. 44–5.

3 Quintilian *Institutio Oratoria* 1.5.19–20.

4 Plutarch *Pompey* 2.

5 Virgil *Aeneid* 6.830.

6   Cicero *Pro Caelio* 24.

7   The identification of Manlius Torquatus is not certain, but many scholars have considered it likely.

8   On Roman marriage, Williams (1958) pp. 16–29 is still a valuable overview.

9   Ovid *Metamorphoses* 3.353, *cit.* Anderson (1997) p. 375.

10 From Callimachus *Epigram* 27.

11 Meleager *Epigram* 5.8.5 *cit.* Gutzwiller (2012) p. 82.

VII: I hate and I love

1   Cicero *Pro Caelio* 7.

2   Cicero *Pro Caelio* 36.

3   Varro *On Agriculture* 2.11.10, *cit.* Zanker (2005), whose chapter on Hadrian's beard is highly informative.

4   Cicero *ad Fam* 8.1.

5   Cicero *Pro Caelio* 30. Unlike Verona, Caelius' Interamnia had Roman citizenship, which made him eligible to join a propraetor's cohort.

6   Archilochus Fragment 23.14–16 (West); Meleager anthology *AP* 12.103. See discussion in Gutzwiller (2012) p. 82.

7   Suetonius *Caesar* 20.

8   Cicero *ad Atticum* 2.7.

9   The historian Beesly (1878) wrote an impassioned chapter on Catiline, whom he rightly viewed as the successor not only of the Gracchi, but of Saturninus, Drusus, Sulpicius, and Cinna, and as someone who assumed the position of figurehead of the popular cause when Pompey was in the East facing Mithridates.

10 Plutarch *Pompey* 46.

11 Cicero *ad Quintum* 1.3.

12 Cicero *ad Atticum* 3.10, sent from Thessalonica.

13 Thomson (1997) p. 297.

14 Caesar *Gallic War*, see especially I.11–30.

VIII: Farewell

1 See, for example, Hesiod *Theogony* 55.

2 Consul 69 BC. Cicero wrote of him as 'Hortalus' in *ad Atticum* 2.25.

3 Ptolemy would have returned sooner, but a tribune at Rome discovered an oracle that warned against the Romans helping him. On the deputation, see Chapter 12.

4 Aelian *Various Histories* 14.43.

5 Callimachus Fragment 110.1.

6 Alexander Pope also wove a reference to Berenice's hair in *The Rape of the Lock*, Canto V.

7 Cicero might have found quite a different parallel here, between Berenice and Clodia, tempted as he was to refer to Clodius as her 'husband' rather than her 'brother' in relation to their alleged incest. Cicero maintained that Clodia had poisoned Metellus Celer. Catullus did not pursue this lead.

8 The identity of the addressees of Poem 68 is one of the most vexed issues in Catullan scholarship. In most manuscripts, Manlius is written 'Mallius'. Were Mallius and Allius one and the same? It is unlikely. Manlius Torquatus had a brother called Aulus, but even then it is stretching it to believe that Catullus' poem is written for two brothers. Poem 68 perhaps contains one poem and one incomplete draft, which were put together by whoever first organised the collection.

9 In the fifth century BC, Sophocles dramatised Ajax' death. Scholars have observed that Catullus' particular reference to the Rhoetean shore might have reflected a poem by Euphorion.

IX: A sea of mackerel

1 Suetonius *Caesar* 23.1.

2 Gaius Memmius also tried to indict Vatinius, the tribune, who had helped Caesar to secure his commands. Cicero *in Vatinium* 14.

3 Plutarch *Lucullus* 37. This took place in 66 BC.

4 Memmius, author of rude verse: Ovid *Tristia* 2.433; Gellius *Attic Nights* 19.9.7.

5 Cicero *Brutus* 247.

6 Cicero *ad Fam* 13.1.

7 Diogenes Laertius *Lives of Eminent Philosophers* 10.16.

8 Some scholars have discerned traces of its language and ideas in Catullus' poetry, including his 'Bedspread Poem'. Jenkyns (1982) pp. 130–32.

9 Pliny the Younger *Epistles* 10.15–17.

10 A dense account of the Thracian origins of Bithynian peoples is given by Strabo *Geography* 12.3.3.

11 In a poem discovered in 2014 and attributed to Sappho. On Charaxus in the trading port of Naucratis, see Herodotus *Histories* 2.135.

12 Strabo *Geography* 12.4.2.

13 Pliny the Younger *Epistles* 10.49.

14 Strabo *Geography* 12.4.7.

15 Suetonius *Caesar* 2.

16 Suetonius *Caesar* 49.

17 Suetonius *Caesar* 2.

18 Caesar claimed paternal descent from Venus, see Suetonius *Caesar* 6; loss of virginity, Suetonius *Caesar* 49, quoting Cicero.

19 Pliny the Younger *Epistles* 10.17. Pliny examined the Bithynians' accounts and realised that great debts were owed to Rome.

20 Pliny the Younger *Epistles* 10.31.

21 The picture of incomplete projects and ill-advised architectural ventures comes from the collected letters of Pliny the Younger to Trajan, *Epistles* Book 10.

22 Half a century later, a certain Lucius Valerius Catullus, a cousin perhaps of the poet, married a Terentia Hispulla, who is likely to have been a relative of this Terentius Hispo. It is not inconceivable that Catullus or his father struck up such a friendship with Terentius Hispo the business-man, that their families were later united in marriage. Wiseman (1987) pp. 336–40 suggests that Catullus might have travelled to Bithynia *as* one of the financial agents, which is a possibility. He uses Hispo as an example of a taxman who might have been in Bithynia at a similar date to Catullus, and connects his family with that of Catullus. Hispo was definitely in Bithynia in 51–50 BC, but might also have been there earlier. The letter can be found in Cicero *ad Fam* 13.65.

23 Oppian *Fishing* 626 *cit.* Bekker-Nielsen (2005) p. 91; translation my own.

24 See King (2004) pp. 13–18 and his discussion of Strabo *Geography* 1.3.6.

25 *Garum* was consumed in Greece since at least the fifth century BC; it is mentioned in Athenaeus 2.67c.

26 Martial *Epigrams* 11.27.

27 Seneca the Younger *Epistle* 95.

28 Pliny *Natural History* 31.44.

29 From the *Geoponika* 20.46.

30 Wiseman (1987) pp. 339–40 identified an amphora from Spain, which carried the name C. Valerius Catullus. It was of the type used to carry *garum* (Dressel type 7–11. *CIL* 15.4756). Wiseman established a connection between the *garum* industry and the Valerii Catulli. On salting fish in this area see Strabo *Geography* 7.6.2; Polybius *Histories* 4.38.

31 On the fish plant at Baelo see Bekker-Nielsen (2005) pp. 52–72.

32 Pliny *Natural History* 9.92.

X: Canvas

1 Isidorus *Origines* 6.12.1. It is unclear whether it was by Aratus, or written in the style of Aratus, who was known for writing poetry on the constellations.

2 In the Suda it says Cinna took Parthenius from Bithynia when Mithridates was defeated, so probably 66 BC, although some scholars argue for 73 BC. On Parthenius, see Lightfoot (1999). On Cinna setting him free: Suda Pi 664.

3 Macrobius *Saturnalia* 5.17.18.

4 On the Greek verbosity of Bithynians see Pliny the Younger *Epistles* 5.20.

5 Erycius *Palatine Anthology* 7.377.

6 Isidorus *Origines* 6.5 with Cicero *de finibus* 3.2.7. The books Lucullus had on Stoicism probably came from the library he acquired from Mithridates.

7 Cinna's 'Zmyrna' required a commentary, see Suetonius *de grammaticis* 18.

8 Fragment of Cinna's *Zmyrna*, *cit.* Servius *ad Verg.* G. 1.288.

9 Sculpture with dedication to Loukios Mustios Herakles, first century BC, from Smyrna; on display in the Museo Maffeiano Lapidario, Verona.

10 Cinna as tribune: Appian *Bellum civile* 2.147; Plutarch *Caesar* 68.

11 Tacitus *Dialogus* 34 notes that Calvus was not much older than twenty-one when he started making impressive legal speeches.

12 Calvus Fragment 16. Propertius 2.34.89–90 mentioned Calvus' singing of the death of Quintilia. See earlier note in Chapter 3 on the possibility that Quintilia was Calvus' wife.

13 Homer *Odyssey* 12.70; Pindar *Pythian* 4; Varro *Argonautica.*

14 Strabo *Geography* 11.2.19; Appian *Mithridatic Wars* 103.

15 For much of its history, the Western world had known no mountain range more remote than the Caucasus. Its remoteness gave rise to stories, see Herodotus *Histories* 1.203 on the Greeks' picture of its villages of primitive, uncouth peasants who painted their bodies and had sex out in the open like wild beasts.

16 Appian *Mithridatic Wars* 103.

17 Apollonius *Argonautica* 3.844–68.

18 In the 1980s adventurer Tim Severin constructed a twenty-oared ship from pine and encountered the same struggles as his crew retraced the journey that Apollonius described. See Severin's book based on the adventure (1985).

19 The lower depths of the Black Sea are so toxic that no one could survive the descent. Not even molluscs can live in such conditions, which is what makes this sea so promising. *Argo* or not, the first ever ship to sail this sea, at least, is almost certainly still down there, lifeless on the seabed. Robert Ballard, the explorer who excavated the *Titanic*, has already lifted a number of ancient wreckages from its beds. But with the remains of every ship – perhaps 50,000 – that ever swam there and sank still resting in the darkness, there is no telling if or when the very oldest ship among them will be found (Dahlby, 2001, and see King, 2004, p. 18).

20 On *currus* for ship see Gaisser (2007) p. 253.

21 In anger at Prometheus giving men fire, the gods were said to have sent diseases and the first woman, Pandora, to earth. This set the path for the times subsequent to the Golden Age. See Servius *ad Verg. E* 6.42; Hesiod *Theogony* 570 and *Works and Days* 70; 100; and 43–8 on the Golden Age type of life that might have persisted had Prometheus not intervened in the divine order.

22 Hesiod *Works and Days* 236–37; Aeschylus *Prometheus Bound* 467–68; Horace *Carmina* 1.3.27–33.

23 Several academics have commented on the Golden Age imagery of 64.38–42; Pasquali (1920, p. 17) may have been the first. As many also comment, the presence of rust on tools undermines the Golden Age

picture, see Bramble (1970, p. 39). Fitzgerald (1995, pp. 148–49) and Konstan (1977, p. 31) are rare in appreciating the importance of the Golden Age to the poem.

24 Heracles released Prometheus in a scene in Aeschylus' *Prometheus Lyomenos*, the third play in his Prometheus trilogy. The play is now lost but for some fragments.

25 Haupt (1875–76) 2.73 seems to have been first to recognise this disparity.

XI: The boxwood *Argo*

1 Herodotus *Histories* 7.30.

2 I follow here Ovid's description of the origins of Cybele's arrival in Rome at *Fasti* 4.179–372.

3 Ovid *Fasti* 4.303.

4 Ovid *Fasti* 4.309–10.

5 It was said that Claudia Quinta was a descendant of Clausus, one of the men who helped Aeneas to found Rome. Cicero spoke of Clodia as a relation of Claudia Quinta.

6 The predecessor was Gaius Papirius Carbo, who was later condemned. There is some suggestion that Memmius was hailed as an *imperator* during his time in Bithynia, meaning that he must have confronted an enemy, but this honour is more likely to have been bestowed upon him for his work in an earlier expedition. See discussion in Brennan (2000) p. 405.

7 Strabo *Geography* 7.3.18.

8 Cinna *cit.* Isidorus 19.4.7.

9 Strabo *Geography* 12.3.10.

10 It was meant to be a river, but as Pliny the Younger observed in a letter to Trajan (*Epistles* 10.99), it had in fact become a sewer.

11 Juvenal *Satires* 15.127–28.

12 Horace *Odes* 3.2.28–9.

13 Svennung explained that it was possible, (1954) pp. 109–24, *cit.* Putnam (1962) p. 10.

14 Alfred, Lord Tennyson *Frater Ave Atque Vale.*

15 Ezra Pound *Cantos* 78.492.

16 See analysis of the so-called 'Grotto of Catullus' in Roffia (2005) p. 41.

17 The location of the finds is beneath Rooms 73, 88, and 111 of the later villa. Account based on information retrieved at the museum at Sirmio and Roffia (2005) pp. 21–2.

18 Some of these objects might have been Augustan, but most can be dated only loosely.

19 Most fragments have been dated to after 20 BC, but some look slightly earlier, encapsulating the so-called Second Style of wall painting, which coincides with Catullus' dates.

20 See Morgan (2010) p. 128.

21 See Beard (2014) pp. 72 and 239n.12, 'Cackles or giggles or ripples?' The Latin poet Laevius used the same verb earlier in the century, but not of water, *cit.* Nonius 209.

22 Cicero *Pro Caelio* 36. In 45 BC Cicero would seek to purchase them. The right bank was predominantly occupied by traders.

23 Like Pompeii, just south along the coast, Baiae sat on Mount Vesuvius' path. The volcanic Phlegraean Fields which run beneath it have puckered the land through seismic shifts up and down, but mainly down: much of ancient Baiae now wallows deep beneath the sea of the Bay of Naples. It was to the surprise of the locals that landslides, triggered by heavy flooding in January 2014, uncovered part of Baiae's ancient walls for the first time in centuries.

24 D'Arms (1970) p. 42.

25 Horace *Epistles* I.83.

26 Seneca the Younger *Epistle* 51.

27 Diodorus Siculus *Library of History* 36.3.

28 Reference to hair oil, Quinn (2000) p. 123.

29 It seems likely that Veranius and Fabullus first made a trip to Spain, from which they brought Catullus back napkins, and later served under Piso in Macedonia.

30 Evoking much the same picture, a eulogy was set up centuries later in Poets' Corner to honour seventeenth-century poet Samuel Butler: 'While Butler, needy wretch!, was yet alive, no generous patron would a dinner give: see him, when starved to death and turned to dust, presented with a monumental bust! . . .'

31 Egnatius might have been an Epicurean poet by that name who, like

Lucretius, wrote a book 'on the nature of things', *de rerum natura*, in several volumes. This Egnatius' work is now fragmentary, but Macrobius preserves some of the fragments at *Saturnalia* 6.5.2; 6.5.12.

32 Pollio was born in 76 BC (cf. Tacitus *Dialogus* 34) and manhood typically began at the age of sixteen. Catullus perhaps refers to him as a 'boy' because of his precocious talent. Pollio wrote *Histories* and was celebrated for both his writing and oratory.

XII: Godly rumbling

1 For this account of the tensions over Cicero's recall see Dio *Roman History* 38.30; 39.6–11.

2 Cicero *Pro Sestio* 77.

3 Dio *Roman History* 39.20; Cicero *de Haruspicum Responso* 9.

4 The Saturnalia had in fact swollen to a week-long festival by the late Republic.

5 It was fortunate for Clodius that Cicero had just recently helped Pompey to take control of Rome's grain supply; the hungry and disaffected were always quickest to riot, so it looked feasible that the upheaval was caused rather by the desperate during the time of a grain shortage.

6 Cicero *de Haruspicum Responso* 24.

7 In 57 BC, the Senate agreed that Rome should help Ptolemy regain his rule, and Ptolemy campaigned for Pompey, with whom he was friendly, to take control of the campaign himself. Then, however, a tribune blocked the measure, citing an oracle that forbade it. Ptolemy waited in Ephesus for a few years until negotiations reopened and he at last regained his throne.

8 Pliny *Natural History* 27.2.

9 Nicholson (1997) pp. 251–61 recognised the connection between 'Rufus', Caelius Rufus, and Bestia, and explained the references in Catullus' poems to the 'bad beast' and goat.

10 As Cicero knew, a certain Publius Asicius had been tried and acquitted for the murder of Dio. He perhaps thought that there was little point in addressing the charge of Caelius' involvement in the deed, although he should have dealt with it more thoroughly than he did.

11 Quintilian *Institutio Oratoria* 8.6.53.

12 Cicero *Pro Caelio* 26.

13 Cicero *Pro Caelio* 8.

14 Ennius *cit.* Cicero *Pro Caelio* 8.

15 Jenkyns (1982) pp. 90–7 argues against the idea that the crimes listed in Poem 64 relate to modern Rome; Konstan (1977) p. 101 takes the opposite view; cf. also Ross (1975) pp. 1–17.

XIII: The Roman stage

1 The mule image comes from Catullus Poem 17, in which he imagines an objectionable man trapped in a mire.

2 See the account in Plutarch *Cato the Younger.*

3 Tacitus *Annals* 14.20. A row of houses near today's Largo Argentina preserves the mighty curve of his auditorium. On the row of houses built on the bow of the former auditorium, a modern theatre even hints knowingly at the once greater existence.

4 Propertius 2.32.11–13; Ovid *Ars Amatoria* 1.67 and 3.387, on *Pompeias umbras*; Martial *Epigrams* 11.47.

5 Cicero helped to purchase land for Caesar's new forum, the Forum Iulium, which was completed by Octavian, the future Emperor Augustus, after Caesar died.

6 The temple was destroyed by fire some decades later, but of the temple that the second emperor, Tiberius, constructed to replace it there remain three Corinthian columns with a small entablature resting on top. There was some history of 'dishonourable people' lurking behind the temple, see Plautus *Curculio* 4.1. On Clodius preventing access to the temple, see Cicero *de Domo Sua* 42. Nine column widths to the right of the temple, keeping the Palatine Hill on one's left, lies the footprint of some ancient shops.

7 Suetonius *Caesar* 53.

8 From the first winter of Caesar's Gallic governorship, when he established private quarters in Cisalpine Gaul, to the winter of 55–54 BC, as he prepared for his second British invasion, there was opportunity to meet Catullus' father. On Caesar's quarters see *Gallic War* 2.1.1; 5.1.2.

9 Blue-skinned Britons: Caesar *Gallic War* 5.14. They probably used woad as a dye, which Vitruvius (7.14) said could be mixed with Selinusian or anularian chalk or clay to produce a deep blue colour. According to Pliny (*Natural History* 35.56), Selinusian was used by women as a cosmetic.

10 Horace *Satires* I.10.36.

11 Cicero *Brutus* 261–62; *et cit.* Suetonius *Caesar* 56.

12 Suetonius *Caesar* 4; Plutarch *Caesar* 3.

13 Suetonius *Caesar* 56.

14 Some scholars believe Caesar's commentaries on the Gallic War were circulated as each book was completed; others suggest it was written in around 52 BC. I think it is likely Caesar would have published at least dispatches from it as the wars were still waging, to enhance the picture of his mounting glory.

15 Pliny *Natural History* 36.7.

16 Giglioli, 393 and Muenzer, col 966.48–50 *cit.* McDermott (1983) p. 295.

17 'Ammia', a form perhaps of 'Ameana', is a name found in several inscriptions found at Rome belonging to slaves or freedwomen, *CIL* 1239, 1330, 1398 *cit.* Neudling (1955) p. 3.

18 Suetonius *Caesar* 51.

19 Suetonius *Caesar* 47.

20 Suetonius *Caesar* 54.

21 Calvus Fragment I, the line probably describes Quintus Curius, a senator, who was a well-known gambler.

22 Civilised: Caesar *Gallic War* 5.14.

23 Caesar *Gallic War* 4.38.

24 Horace *Satires* 2.5.40; I.10.36–7. See commentary by Gowers (2012) pp. 323–24. Courtney (1993) p. 200, notes that Catullus 11 could be taken as a sarcastic reference to Furius Bibaculus' *Bellum Gallicum*.

25 Caesar *Gallic War* 4.17–19, summer 55 BC.

26 As Pliny the Elder observed, *Natural History* 36.7.

27 Suetonius emphasises Caesar's role in offering forgiveness to those who offended him, whereas Tacitus said that Caesar put up with and let be Catullus' poems and those of Furius Bibaculus too.

28 Suetonius *Caesar* 49.

29 Suetonius *Caesar* 73.

30 Suetonius *Caesar* 52.

XIV: A flower on the edge of the meadow

1 The stepmother might have been the Palla whom Caelius Rufus had been accused of stealing property from during his trial in 56 BC.

2 More than one reader of Catullus' poetry has discerned in his grief over Lesbia, for example, a deeper comment on contemporary politics and life, see Ross (1975) pp. 1–17.

3 Plutarch *Crassus* 16.2. Bactria lay in what is now Afghanistan, the Outer Sea was the Atlantic Ocean.

4 Cicero *ad Atticum* 16.3 uses the term.

5 Strabo *Geography* 5.3.11 says Tibur was visible from Rome.

6 Strabo *Geography* 5.3.11.

7 Streams: Horace *Odes* 1.7.

8 Calvus' legal experience included a successful defence of Gaius Cato, a tribune of 56 BC, who delayed the elections for the following year, and therefore contributed to the fact that seats would be empty at the start of 55 BC. Asinius Pollio, the brother of the man Catullus chastised for stealing his napkins, had been the prosecutor.

9 So Tacitus *Dialogus* 21 praised Calvus' 'second speech' against Vatinius, which was probably the speech before this accusation, made in 56 BC.

10 Seneca *Controversiae* 7.4.6.

11 Tacitus *Dialogus* 21 on lack of *ingenium* in general, not by comparison with Cicero. Tacitus nonetheless praised this speech above most of Calvus' other speeches, of which he counted twenty-one booksful.

12 Sappho Fragment 105c.

Epilogue

1 The note about public mourning comes from a short biographical passage included in the first and second printed editions of Catullus' poems, by Gerolamo Squarzafico in 1472 and 1475. It is believed that he may have taken his information from a now lost biography by Suetonius. See Gaisser (1993) pp. 25–6.

2 Cicero refers to him in the past tense in *Brutus* 283, which dates to this time.

3 Cicero *ad Atticum* 12.42.

4 I follow here the version of events given by Suetonius *Caesar* 85. Very

similar accounts are given by Valerius Maximus *Facta* 9.9.1; Appian *Civil Wars* 2.147; Plutarch *Caesar* 68; Plutarch *Brutus* 20; Dio *History* 44.50. For the identification of this Cinna with the poet see Wiseman (1974) pp. 44–6.

5 Plutarch *Cicero* 48.4.

6 Asconius *Commentaries on Cicero* 30–1.

7 After Clodius' death, Fulvia remarried twice, the second time to Mark Antony.

8 Suetonius *Caligula* 36.1.

9 Wiseman (1987) pp. 348, 361–62 discusses each of these references.

10 Juvenal *Satires* 12.1–82. The possibility of a connection between the family of Catullus and the Bithynian tax collector Terentius Hispo, of whom Hispulla might have been a relation, has been raised by Wiseman (1987) pp. 338–40.

11 One has to look hard to find Catullus there today. Two magnificent ancient gates mark the ends of the city, like screens from a forgotten stage set. Catullus might have seen their foundations laid, but did not live long enough to appreciate their full majesty. Verona's mighty amphitheatre anticipated Rome's Colosseum by an impressive stretch of six emperors, but was only begun perhaps a hundred years after Catullus' death. The Ponte Pietra, Verona's oldest surviving bridge, is a more promising spot, carrying strollers over the fast-flowing Adige river to Verona's luscious hills. Any buildings Catullus found on their incline, however, were cleared a short time after he lived to make way for a Roman theatre. The forum that lies beneath the market square, Piazza delle Erbe, was opened shortly after he died. The original gates, Porta Borsari and Porta Leoni, were built in the late Republic, when a 'new' Roman town was built in Verona, after 49 BC. The forum and Capitolium (at Corte Sgarzerie) date to this time. The construction of the Roman theatre the other side of the river eliminated any traces of an earlier Roman town there (with thanks to Riccardo Bertocchi, art historian, and Simon Thompson, archaeologist, of Verona).

While on frantic days, Catullus might well have imagined how wonderful it would be to fly like Mercury on winged heels, today he has his own airport: Valerio Catullo. A smart residential terrace called Via Valerio Catullo branches off the old Roman road of Verona's main thoroughfare, as if braced for the day Catullus comes back. One suspects that he would have felt decidedly more at home at the House of Juliet. The medieval courtyard here has become less suited to a Capulet than to someone who could have found beauty in the messages which litter it like graffiti on a brothel door. For decades lovers have pinned letters and poems and tear-drenched gauze to walls, dedications to make love flourish or broken hearts mend. One woman curses her husband for visiting a stranger's bed. In the same breath, she begs him to come back to her. Another, French, celebrates her recent engagement and prays for a long life of love. Not all the messages are so sentimental. Someone has requested in hasty hand a 'quickie' at the Arco dei Gavi.

12 The lines describing the mysterious gentleman were part of an epigram written by Benvenuto Campesani of Vicenza to celebrate the rediscovery of Catullus' work.

13 It was recognised as early as the late sixteenth century that a section of Catullus 64 inspired Titian's *Bacchus and Ariadne*. Titian and Mario Equicola, the secretary who compiled the programme for the artistic scheme of Alfonso's *camerino*, may have consulted Battista Guarino's edition of Catullus' text, which included a commentary, and the translation of Dolce. On the versions of text available to them see Holberton (1986) pp. 344–50. They combined Catullus' version of the Ariadne myth with that provided in Ovid *Ars Amatoria* 1.529–62. On the influence of Ovid on the painting, see Thompson (1956) pp. 259–64.

SELECT BIBLIOGRAPHY

Anderson, W. S., *Ovid's Metamorphoses, Books 1–5* (Norman, University of Oklahoma Press, 1997)

Beard, M., *Laughter in Ancient Rome* (Berkeley; London, University of California Press, 2014)

Beesly, E. S., *Catiline, Clodius, and Tiberius* (London, Chapman and Hall, 1878)

Bekker-Nielsen, T. (ed.), *Ancient Fishing and Fish Processing in the Black Sea Region* (Aarhus, Aarhus University Press, 2005)

Boni, C., 'Recent discoveries on the Palatine Hill, Rome', *Journal of Roman Studies* Vol. 3, No. 1, 1913, pp. 243–52

Bramble, J. C., 'Structure and Ambiguity in Catullus LXIV', *Proceedings of the Cambridge Philological Society* No. 196.16, 1970, pp. 22–41

Brennan, T. C., *The Praetorship in the Roman Republic* Vols I and II (Oxford, Oxford University Press, 2000)

Burl, A., *Catullus, A Poet in the Rome of Julius Caesar* (Gloucestershire, Amberley, 2010)

Courtney, E. (ed.), *The Fragmentary Latin Poets* (Oxford; New York, Oxford University Press, 1993)

Crowther, N. B., 'Valerius Cato, Furius Bibaculus, and Ticidas', *Classical Philology* Vol. 66, No. 2, 1971, pp. 108–09

Dahlby, T., 'Deep Black Sea', *National Geographic*, May 2001

D'Arms, J., *Romans on the Bay of Naples* (Cambridge, MA, Harvard University Press, 1970)

Dupont, F., *Daily Life in Ancient Rome*, translated by Christopher Woodall (Oxford, Blackwell, 1992)

Du Quesnay, I., and Woodman, T. (eds), *Catullus: poems, books, readers* (Cambridge, Cambridge University Press, 2012), especially K. Gutzwiller, 'Catullus and the Garland of Meleager', pp. 79–111

Ellis, R., *A Commentary on Catullus* (Oxford, Clarendon Press, 1889)

Fitzgerald, W., *Catullan Provocations* (Berkeley; London, University of California Press, 1995)

Gaisser, J. H., *Catullus and his Renaissance Readers* (Oxford, Clarendon Press, 1993), especially 'Threads in the Labyrinth: Competing Views and Voices in Catullus 64', pp. 217–58

——(ed.), *Catullus* (Oxford, Oxford Classical Press, 2007)

Garland, R., *The Eye of the Beholder: Deformity and Disability in the Graeco-Roman World* (London, Duckworth, 1995)

Gow, A. S. F., and Page, D. L., *The Greek Anthology: Hellenistic Epigrams* Vols I–II (Cambridge, Cambridge University Press, 1965)

Gowers, E., *Horace Satires Book I* (Cambridge, Cambridge University Press, 2012)

Green, E. H., 'Furius Bibaculus', *The Classical Journal* Vol. 35, No. 6, 1940, pp. 348–56

Harrison, S. J., and Stray, C. (eds), *Expurgating the Classics* (London, Bloomsbury Academic, 2012), especially G. Trimble, 'Catullus and "Comment in English": the tradition of the expurgated commentary before Fordyce', pp. 143–62

Haupt, M., *Opuscula* II (Leipzig, Salomen Hirzelli, 1875–76)

Heidel, W. A., 'Catullus and Furius Bibaculus', *The Classical Review* Vol. 15, No. 4, 1901, pp. 215–17

Holberton, P., 'Battista Guarino's Catullus and Titian's "Bacchus and Ariadne"', *The Burlington Magazine* Vol. 128, No. 998, 1986, pp. 344, 347–50

Holland, L. A., *Lucretius and the Transpadanes* (Princeton; Guildford, Princeton University Press, 1979)

Hooper, J., 'The enigma of Italy's ancient Etruscans is finally unravelled', *Guardian*, 18 June 2007

Hopkins, K., 'Contraception in the Roman Empire', *Comparative Studies in Society and History* Vol. 8, No. 1, 1965, pp. 124–51

Jenkyns, R., *Three Classical Poets* (London, Duckworth, 1982)

King, C., *The Black Sea: a history* (Oxford, Oxford University Press, 2004)

Konstan, D., *Catullus's Indictment of Rome, The Meaning of Catullus 64* (Amsterdam, Hakkert, A.M., 1977)

Kutzko, D., 'Lesbia in Catullus 35', *Classical Philology* Vol. 101, No. 4, October 2006, pp. 405–10

Lightfoot, J. L., *Parthenius of Nicaea* (Oxford, Clarendon Press, 1999)

McDermott, W. C., 'Mamurra, "Eques Formianus"', *Rheinisches Museum für Philologie*, Neue Folge, 126. Bd. H. 3/4, 1983, pp. 292–307

Morgan, L., *Musa Pedestris* (Oxford, Oxford University Press, 2010)

Neudling, C. L., *A Prosopography to Catullus* (Oxford, imprint of thesis, 1955)

Newman, J. K., *Roman Catullus and the modification of the Alexandrian Sensibility* (Hildesheim, Weidmann, 1990)

Nicholson, J., 'Goats and Gout in Catullus 71', *The Classical World* Vol. 90, No. 4, 1997, pp. 251–61

Nisbet, R. G. M., and Harrison, S. (eds), *Collected Papers on Latin Literature* (Oxford, Clarendon Press, 1995), especially R. G. M. Nisbet, 'The Survivors: Old-Style Literary Men in the Triumviral Period', pp. 390–413

Pasquali, G., 'Il carme 64 di Catullo', *Studi Italiani di Filologica Classica* I, 1920, pp. 1–23

Putnam, M. C. J., 'Catullus's Journey (Carm. 4)', *Classical Philology* Vol. 57, No. 1, 1962, pp. 10–19

Quinn, K., *Catullus, The Poems* (London, Bristol Classical Press, 2000)

Ramage, E. S., 'Note on Catullus's Arrius', *Classical Philology* Vol. 54, No. 2, 1959, pp. 44–5

Roffia, E., '*Le grotte di Catullo*' a Sirmione (Milan, ET, 2005)

Ross, D. O., *Backgrounds to Augustan Poetry* (Cambridge, Cambridge University Press, 1975)

Schwabe, L., *G. Valeri Catulli liber* Vol. I (Gissae, I. Ricker, 1872)

Severin, T., *The Jason Voyage* (London, Hutchinson, 1985)

Shackleton Bailey, D. R., *Cicero: Select letters* (Cambridge, Cambridge University Press, 2000)

——*Cicero, Letters to Atticus: Vol. 5* (Cambridge, Cambridge University Press, 2004)

Skinner, M. B., *Catullus in Verona* (Columbus, Ohio State University Press, 2003)

Stevenson, J., *Women Latin Poets* (Oxford, Oxford University Press, 2005)

Svennung, J., 'Phaselus ille. Zum 4. Gedicht Catulls' in *Opuscula Romana* Vol. I, C. W. K. Gleerup, Lund, 1954, pp. 109–24

Tatum, W. J., *The Patrician Tribune, Publius Clodius Pulcher* (Chapel Hill; London, University of North Carolina Press, 1999)

Thompson, G. H., 'The Literary Sources of Titian's *Bacchus and Ariadne*', *Classical Journal* Vol. 51, No. 6, 1956, pp. 259–64

Thomson, D. F. S., *Catullus, edited with a textual and interpretative commentary* (Toronto; Buffalo; London, University of Toronto Press Inc., 1997)

Wheeler, A. L., *Catullus and the traditions of ancient poetry* (Berkeley, University of California Press, 1964)

Williams, G., 'Some Aspects of Roman Marriage Ceremonies and Ideals', *Journal of Roman Studies* Vol. 48, No. 1/2, 1958, pp. 16–29

Wiseman, T. P., *Cinna the Poet and other Roman Essays* (New York, Leicester University Press, 1974)

——*Catullus and his world: a reappraisal* (Cambridge, Cambridge University Press, 1985)

——*Roman Studies, Literary and Historical* (Liverpool; New Hampshire, Francis Cairns, 1987)

Zanker, P., *The Mask of Socrates*, translated by Alan Shapiro (Berkeley; Oxford, University of California Press, 1995)

LIST OF
ILLUSTRATIONS

third century AD (Photo by DEA PICTURE LIBRARY/De Agostini/Getty Images)

p. 6: Theseus Liberator, Herculaneum, first century AD (© De Agostini Picture Library/G. Nimatallah/Bridgeman Images); Attis and Cybele relief sculpture, Asia Minor, second century BC (Photo by Leemage/Universal Images Group/Getty Images)

p. 7: *Bacchus and Ariadne* by Titian, 1522–23 (Courtesy Google Cultural Institute); *Prometheus Bound* by Rubens, 1611–18 (Courtesy Google Cultural Institute)

p. 8: *The Bay of Baiae with Apollo and Sibyl* by J. M. W. Turner, 1823 (Photo by Art Media/Print Collector/Getty Images); Sirmione viewed from Lake Garda (© Daisy Dunn)

ACKNOWLEDGEMENTS

From the beginning I was determined that this would be a book about Catullus, not me. In my dogged, sometimes lonely pursuit of the man, however, I found myself carried forwards by conversations in which I could enthuse about the timelessness of his words.

Who hasn't fallen in love with the wrong person, or believed that a lover's words ought to be written on the wind and running water? With a few slippery exceptions, Catullus had the support of his friends to fall back on. It is friends – and family – whom I must also thank for sustaining me through what has undoubtedly been a deeply passionate affair with Catullus.

My agent, Georgina Capel, has been full of excitement since day one, and I thank her for her enthusiasm and enduring support. Philippa Brewster, Rachel Conway, Valeria Huerta and Romily Withington of the same agency have been immensely helpful in bringing this book to fruition.

My editor, Arabella Pike, took me on as a first-time author and strove to get the very best out of me. I am grateful for all she has done. Kate Johnson was a particularly sensitive copy editor. At HarperCollins I also thank Katherine Josselyn, Kate Tolley and Joseph Zigmond, and in the US, my editor Terry Karten and Jillian Verrillo.

Professor Paul Cartledge and Professor Greg Woolf were kind enough to read my manuscript and offer extremely incisive comments upon it. I am so very grateful to both for their support, and to Dr Matthew Robinson for his earlier guidance.

Thanks also to Professor William Fitzgerald and Professor Peter Wiseman for illuminating conversations about our favourite poet. Their scholarship was a source of inspiration to me, and I acknowledge it with gratitude in my Notes and Bibliography.

Dr Claire Jamset cast her eagle-eye over my translations of the poems from Latin, while Hugo Williams gave his unparalleled critique upon them as a poet. I was fortunate to have such sensitive eyes.

In Verona, Riccardo Bertocchi was a diligent and dedicated guide. My thanks to Ellida Minelli for putting us in touch. Thanks to Simon Thompson for discussing with me the ancient archaeology during a trip to Corte Sgarzerie, and to Alessandro Scafi for his hospitality in Rome.

James Cullen, Lucy Purcell and Gary Sanders were the best of companions in Verona and Sirmione. They may never forget 'the Roman inscription museum' or my enthusiasm for potsherds on a scorching hot day.

Huge thanks to David Rhodes for his vigilance for all things Catullan; to Walter Donohue for his suggestions on my introduction; to Aaron Jaffa and Sam Willis for answering my questions on naval matters; to Anthony Crutch, Saul David, Richard Foreman, Tom Hopkins, Dan Jones and Harry Mount.

Above all I dedicate this book to my family: my loving grandparents, Don and Wendy, my immensely supportive and inspirational parents, Jeremy and Amanda, and my generous sister, Alice. This book would not have been possible without their love, guidance and patience.

INDEX

supports Caesar in his bid for consulship 93
underestimates Clodius Pulcher 190
Cremona 74
Crete 134–5, 171
Cybele 170–1, 194
Cyclades 287
Cyprus 115, 148, 204
Cyrene 53, 68, 75, 125
Cytoris 176

Dacan people 97
Daedalus 135
Darius III 176
De Rerum Natura (Memmius) 133, 134
Delos 135, 177, 272
Diana (Publius Valerius Cato) 278
Dido 161
Dio 198, 273, 289
disabilities 60, 279
Dolabella, Publius Cornelius 280
Domitian, Emperor 241
Drusus, Saturninus 282
Dyrrachium (Durrës in Albania) 117

Egnatius 186, 195, 207, 288–9
Egypt 124, 233, 234, 278
Ennius 50, 155, 163, 199
Ephesus 135
Epicurus 133
Equicola, Mario 294
Ethiopia 281
Etruscans 17, 18, 181, 273–4
Euphorion 278, 284

Fabullus 185, 186, 187, 288
Falernian wine 40, 276
Flavius 81–2
Fordyce, C.J. 51
Formiae 212, 215, 240
France 3, 117, 242
Fulvia (wife of Clodius Pulcher) 112, 240, 293
Furius *see* Bibaculus, Marcus Furius
Further Spain 36–7, 89, 143, 227

Gabinius, Aulus 114
Gallic War 17, 211, 216, 217–18, 291
Gallic War (Caesar) 211, 216
Ganymede 139
garum (fish sauce) 142–3, 285
Gaul, Gauls 17, 34, 43, 47, 132, 214, 217, 228, 231, 234
see also Cisalpine Gaul; Transalpine Gaul

Gellius *see* Publicola, Lucius Gellius
Geneva 117
Genoa 273
Georgia 9, 12, 273
Germanic tribes 117, 217
Gracchus, Gaius 114–15, 274
Gracchus, Tiberius 114
Greece, Greeks 4, 75, 78–9, 132
Greek poets 53, 109, 146
Guarino, Battista 294

Hannibal 170, 171, 272
Hecale (Callimachus) 54
Hellespont 136, 142, 164
Helvetii 117
Heracleia 9
Heracles 177, 287
Herakles, Leukios Mustios 285
Herodotus 273, 286
Hesiod 157, 272, 286
Hispo, Publius Terentius 140, 284
Hispulla 241, 294
Hispulla, Terentia 284
Histories (Pollio) 289
Homer 3, 50, 99, 129, 138, 146, 150, 164, 230, 279
Horace 5, 156, 183, 187, 211, 275
Hortalus, Quintus Hortensius 123–4, 125

Iberia 273
Iliad (Homer) 129, 146
Illyricum 97, 132
In Praise of Baldness (Synesius of Cyrene) 46
In Praise of Hair (Dio Chrysostom) 46
India 228, 234
Io 149
Iolcus (Volos) 151
Ionian Sea 228
Ipsitilla 69
Isis 177
Italy, Italians 3, 141, 238
Izmir (Smyrna) 170, 274, 286

Jason and the Argonauts 4, 8, 12, 53, 151–65, 200
Judaea 273
Julia (daughter of Caesar) 94, 230, 232–3
Jupiter 134, 152, 155, 157–8, 205
Juvenal 6, 241, 271, 293
Juventius 85, 86–7

Kent 216